Beginning ethnic
American literatures

Beginnings
Series editors: Peter Barry and Helen Carr

'Beginnings' is a series of books designed to give practical help to students beginning to tackle recent developments in English, Literary Studies and Cultural Studies. The books in the series:

- demonstrate and encourage a questioning engagement with the new;
- give essential information about the context and history of each topic covered;
- show how to develop a practice which is up-to-date and informed by theory.

Each book focuses uncompromisingly upon the needs of its readers, who have the right to expect lucidity and clarity to be the distinctive feature of a book which includes the word 'beginning' in its title.

Each aims to lay a firm foundation of well understood initial principles as a basis for further study and is committed to explaining new aspects of the discipline without over-simplification, but in a manner appropriate to the needs of beginners.

Each book, finally, aims to be both an introduction and a contribution to the topic area it discusses.

Also in the series

Beginning theory
Peter Barry

Beginning postcolonialism
John McLeod

Beginning postmodernism
Tim Woods

Beginning ethnic American literatures

Helena Grice, Candida Hepworth
Maria Lauret and Martin Padget

Manchester University Press
Manchester and New York

Published by Manchester University Press
Oxford Road, Manchester M13 9NR, UK
and Room 400, 175 Fifth Avenue, New York, NY 10010, USA
www.manchesteruniversitypress.co.uk

Distributed exclusively in the USA by
Palgrave, 175 Fifth Avenue, New York NY 10010, USA

Distributed exclusively in Canada by
UBC Press, University of British Columbia, 2029 West Mall,
Vancouver, BC, Canada V6T 1Z2

British Library Cataloguing-in-Publication Data
A catalogue record for this book is available from the British Library

Library of Congress Cataloging-in-Publication Data
A catalog record for this book is available from the Library of Congress

ISBN 0 7190 5763 9 paperback

First edition published 2001 by Manchester University Press

First digital, on-demand edition produced by Lightning Source 2006

Contents

Acknowledgements   *page* vii

1 **Introduction**   *Maria Lauret*   1

2 **Native American fiction**   *Martin Padget*   10
   Overview and antecedents: the evolution of Native
        American fiction   10
   Native American fiction and recent literary theory   21
   Case studies: three important works of Native
        American fiction   25
   Investigating further   59
   Annotated short bibliography   60

3 **African American fiction**   *Maria Lauret*   64
   Overview and antecedents: the evolution of
        African American fiction   64
   African American fiction and recent literary theory   85
   Case studies: three important works of African
        American fiction   99
   Investigating further   125
   Annotated short bibliography   128

4 Asian American fiction   *Helena Grice*   133
Overview and antecedents: the evolution of
  Asian American fiction   133
Asian American fiction and recent literary theory   149
Case studies: three important works of Asian
  American fiction   157
Investigating further   184
Annotated short bibliography   185

5 Chicano/a fiction   *Candida Hepworth*   189
Overview and antecedents: the evolution of
  Chicano/a fiction   189
Chicano/a literature and recent literary theory   203
Case studies: three important works of
  Chicano/a fiction   212
Investigating further   237
Annotated short bibliography   239

Index   245

Acknowledgements

Helena Grice wishes to thank Sau-ling Wong and Amy Ling for inspiration, and Tim Woods for support.

Candida Hepworth is greatly in debt to friends and colleagues for their unwavering support. Mike, Bev, Alan, Pete, Martin and Helena – to you, especially, many thanks.

Maria Lauret wishes to thank Maria Balshaw, Christa Schwarz and Simon Booy whose work (as yet unpublished) has informed her own.

Martin Padget is grateful to the British Academy and the Newberry Library in Chicago for funding a resident fellowship to conduct research at the Newberry and participate in activities hosted by the D'Arcy McNickle Center for the History of the American Indian. He also thanks Sara for her support and bonhomie.

Introduction

Maria Lauret

> When African Americans, Native Americans, Hispanic Americans, and Asian Americans write, they're not just engaging in a parlor exercise – they are writing for their lives ... lives that are our national heritage. And once these voices have been heard, there is no turning back. (Ishmael Reed, Foreword to *Hispanic American Literature: a Brief Anthology and Introduction*, HarperCollins, 1995, p. xi)

Readers who come to study ethnic American fictions are rarely absolute beginners. *Tracks* or *The Woman Warrior, The House on Mango Street* or – perhaps above all – *Beloved* have often already been read and enjoyed before students encounter them on an academic syllabus. Because so many so-called ordinary readers have been fascinated by so-called ethnic writers' storytelling and by their distinctive ways of envisioning the world, beginning the study of ethnic American fictions is usually motivated by enthusiasm: choice rather than academic chore or bore. Coming from outside or from inside African American, Chicano/a, Native American or Asian American culture, readers rejoice in a sense of recognition or are intrigued by the difference that ethnic literature presents them with. In either case, they tend to find something of themselves articulated in it, something new and exciting that the dominant culture does not have access to. But this is only one side of the story. For the student of ethnic fiction who is prepared to analyse and interrogate his or her initial enthusiasm, there is another, more troubling side too: cultural difference can also be baffling, frustrating or alienating, whereas an attachment to literature based on identification and familiarity often obscures the aesthetic dimension of the writing. Familiarity with African American fiction, furthermore, does not necessarily carry over into informed readings of Asian American or Chicano/a literature. Both sets of responses therefore, whether they come from inside or from outside the culture in question, can prevent us from reading creatively and critically. There is, as Ishmael Reed asserts in the epigraph to this introduction, more at stake in the writing and reading of ethnic American fictions than mere exotic interest or the pleasure of self-expression and mirroring: we are, as outsiders, confronted with our own ignorance and preconceptions, or as cultural insiders with a representation of an 'us' that can appear homogenised, stereotyped or simply wrong.

Four authors writing about different literatures to a common brief is an unusual format for an academic textbook, particularly so since all four are cultural outsiders with both a specific and a more general interest in ethnic writing. Yet the reason why this book is organised as it is has everything to do with the mixture of fascination and bafflement, recognition and anxiety that tends to characterise non-professional readers' responses to Chicano/a and Native, Asian and African American fiction. *Beginning ethnic American literatures* wants to help ease the passage from first, enthusiastic but also relatively unreflexive encounters to a more informed critical approach that enables readers to study this writing on its own terms and in the context of its own distinctive histories and cultural situations. It also wants to keep a balance between such specificity on one hand, and the sense that ethnic writers are engaged in a common project on the other; a project which consists in rather more than the label of ethnicity pure and simple would suggest.

That label in itself is notoriously problematic. As the extensive literature on the theory of ethnicity proves, the concept is hard to define and ethnic cultural practices are, if anything, even more elusive because constantly in flux. The German sociologist Max Weber, however, provided a working definition as early as 1922 which is still useful. In 'What is an Ethnic Group?' Weber wrote:

> We shall call 'ethnic groups' those human groups that entertain a *subjective belief* in their common descent because of similarities of physi-

cal type or of customs or both, or because of memories of colonization or migration ... *it does not matter whether or not an objective blood relationship exists.* [my emphasis] ('What is an Ethnic Group?', in Montserrat Guibernau and John Rex, eds, *The Ethnicity Reader: Nationalism, Multiculturalism and Migration*, Polity Press, 1997, p. 18)

What is worth highlighting here is the subjective nature of belonging to an ethnic group; in this sense ethnicity is less a matter of identity than of identi*fication* with others who are perceived to share the same plight. This plight is often articulated in political terms, as Weber and other theorists since have also pointed out, when they thought of ethnic groups as interest groups rather than communities of people bound by blood or common ancestry. If, so far, we have implicitly defined 'ethnic fiction' as the literature of cultural difference, then it should be clear from Weber's observations that this difference is neither objective and absolute nor static and fixed in the past. In more recent work on the theory of ethnicity the constructedness of ethnic cultural difference and its dynamic, ever-changing nature have been strongly emphasised, especially so in Werner Sollors's studies *Beyond Ethnicity* (1986) and *The Invention of Ethnicity* (1989). In the latter, Sollors gives an instructive example of how ethnicity is continually re-invented under different historical and political circumstances. Citing the Chinese immigrant Lee Chew, Sollors writes:

> It is not any a priori *cultural difference* that makes ethnicity. 'The Chinese laundryman does not learn his trade in China; there are no laundries in China' ... One can hardly explain the prevalence of Chinese-American laundries by going back to Chinese history proper. ('Introduction' to *The Invention of Ethnicity*, Werner Sollors, ed., Oxford University Press, 1989, p. xvi)

This emphasis on invention, or on ethnicity as a 'collective fiction', has gained great currency in recent years, not least because it would seem to enable a move beyond cultural difference to what Sollors and others call a 'post-ethnic society' in which ethnic tensions and conflicts would presumably dissolve. Yet although it is helpful to be aware of the changing contents of cultural difference as ethnic groups respond to and seek to shape new historical and political conditions, there is a danger that too great a stress on ethnicity as a

'collective fiction' obscures its political dimensions. Ethnic identification, whether in Weber's or in Sollors's sense, does not happen in
a vacuum, after all. It tends to come about through the experience of
marginality (economic and political, as well as cultural) – which is
why dominant groups usually do not conceive of themselves in
ethnic terms at all. Kathleen Neils Conzen *et al.* voice such a critique of Sollors's approach when they explain:

> In our view, ethnicity is not a 'collective fiction', but rather a process
> of construction or invention which incorporates, adapts, and amplifies
> preexisting communal solidarities, cultural attributes, and historical
> memories. That is, it is grounded in real life context and social expe-
> rience. ('The Invention of Ethnicity in the United States', in *Major
> Problems in American Immigration and Ethnic History*, Jon Gjerde, ed.,
> Houghton Mifflin, 1998, p. 23)

This is our view too, and it is the reason why in this book we focus
less on the 'inventedness' of contemporary Native American, Chi-
cano/a, Asian American and African American ethnicities than on
their groundedness in particular cultural and historical experiences –
however 'constructed' those experiences, like all experiences, may be.
    Which leads us to another problem in the definition of ethnicity:
that of its relation to race. In the past, this relation was often seen as
one of social and cultural specificity (ethnicity) versus biological/
physiological specificity (race). But since biological/physiological
categories such as race have been comprehensively deconstructed to
reveal their ideological biases (biology/physiology only gains meaning through language and society, and that meaning is therefore a
matter of social construction and not of nature) 'race', like ethnicity,
has also come to be defined in social and political terms. The widespread phenomenon of miscegenation, furthermore, has discredited
any belief in the validity of racial categorisation on the grounds of
distinctiveness or purity. In the cultural sphere (because of migration and assimilation) the same could be said of ethnicity as well: it
never exists in its 'pure' form, because it is always already shaped by
the cultural forces surrounding it. So where does this leave us when
beginning 'ethnic' American fictions?
    Although so far we have been using the phrase 'ethnic fiction' as
a convenient – and currently fashionable – shorthand, many of the

fictions discussed in the chapters which follow are concerned with race as well as ethnicity. This is not because they are the same thing, however, and it is important to make a distinction between them at this point. Howard Winant and Michael Omi's concept of racial formation explains that distinction: whereas they see ethnicity as 'a matter of cultural attributes' shared by a particular group, they 'define *racial formation* as the sociohistorical process by which racial categories are created, inhabited, transformed, and destroyed'. (Omi and Winant, *Racial Formation in the United States from the 1960s to the 1990s*, Routledge 1994, pp. 55-6). Racial formation thus incorporates ethnicities but reaches beyond the cultural into the historical and – most of all – structural, material and institutional operations of categorisation. If we use this concept, then it becomes clear that writing by African Americans, Asian Americans, Chicano/a and Native Americans, whilst emanating from the cultural domain of ethnicity as defined by those groups themselves, also charts and contests the histories of their categorisation *by others* through the processes of racial formation that Omi and Winant identify. In addition, the concept of racial formation enables us to articulate in theoretical terms what the experience of reading ethnic fiction is like: an education, not simply in cultural diversity, but also and more so in the structural and entrenched features of racial oppression.

To begin ethnic American fictions, then, is no parlour game: it involves, first of all, a recognition of the fact that the writers discussed in the pages which follow are indeed writing for their lives, that those lives are American lives, and that listening to and hearing what these voices have to say means that our idea of what American literature is, or can be, will never be the same again. 'America is its Native-American tradition, its Afro-American tradition, its Euro-American tradition, its Asian-American tradition, and its Hispanic-American tradition', Bob Callahan says in his contribution to the debate 'Is Ethnicity Obsolete?' (in *The Invention of Ethnicity*, p. 231). Each tradition that Callahan identifies obviously harbours many different ethnicities within it, but it is because the 'Euro-American' part has hitherto overwhelmingly dominated the definition of American literature that we have chosen, in this book, to focus on the other major four which are less familiar yet equally worthy of study. Such study is aided by the fact that Native African,

Asian American and Chicano/a fictions, at least, are now increasingly being taught in universities and schools, that they are available in affordable paperback editions and surrounded by a 'critical mass' of secondary literature to enhance analysis and debate. Each of the chapters which follow therefore begins with a historical overview and a discussion of criticism and theory on the literature in question, followed by three short essays on key novels. Each chapter also includes suggestions for further study and an annotated bibliography of primary and secondary works.

We have decided on this format because, as mentioned above, in reading ethnic American fictions the stakes are high and the risks of incomprehension, misappropriation into familiar patterns of thought, or simply confrontation with our own ignorance or prejudice are considerable. To get beyond the initial fascination to something approaching understanding, we have to know a lot more, and different things, than our education in mainstream, canonical literature has equipped us for. It involves gaining a knowledge of histories, critical reception, politics, literary traditions and cultural heritages which are not just unfamiliar to most readers in English or American Studies, but which transform our very understanding of what those disciplines mean and how they are constituted in the first place. It also involves, necessarily, a transformation of ourselves as readers and as people in the world beyond the classroom or lecture hall. In courses on American ethnic literature which jump from one best-selling (*The Woman Warrior*) to another 'Pulitzer Prize-winning novel of a proud stranger in his native land' (*House Made of Dawn*), a dazzling array of cultural identities is presented which challenge the student (and tutor) to keep in view both – or rather, all four – sides of the question: specific histories and contexts, but also differences within each ethnic culture; recurrent themes and common representational strategies between ethnic writings, as well as differential relations to the dominant culture of 'mainstream' American writing and society. Needless to say, to take all this on board is a tall order, especially so since few teachers of cross-cultural ethnic writing will have the wherewithal to keep up with the latest research and creative writing in what is a burgeoning and ever-expanding field. The following chapters set out culturally specific histories and traditions in some detail, but it may nevertheless be helpful here to sketch in some of the common traits that make the cross-hatched study of American ethnic fiction – whether it is confined to best-sellers or not – so fruitful and rewarding.

What stands out first of all is the historical 'burden of representation' which ethnic writers have to deal with. Whether this burden is placed upon them by readers and critics or whether they willingly take it on, ethnic writers are often engaged in contestations of a dominant historical record which has demeaned or vilified their culture and their people. History has made them invisible, or visible only through the eyes of conquerors, slaveholders, Eurocentric rationalists or monolingual anthropologists. African American, Native American, Chicano/a and Asian American literature usually begins with writing against history, and against the racism and ethnocentrism which characterises it. What is striking, but perhaps not all that surprising, is that this writing against history is often done in autobiographical forms. The slave narratives of the nineteenth century, Carlos Bulosan's *America is in the Heart* and Gloria Anzaldúa's *Borderlands/La Frontera* all insist on the importance of their historical experience and feel the burden of representation upon them.

In the early days of ethnic writing this attempt to set the record straight often meant that novelists, autobiographers and poets tended to function as 'ambassadors to white society', as Helena Grice puts it. Since the social movements of the 1960s and 1970s created a new and more militant discourse of self-representation and autonomy however, ethnic writing has become less a literature of assimilation or protest than one of cultural affirmation. In broad terms, this drive towards affirmation is characterised by a search for identity which is positive and/or confrontational rather than tragic and victimised, as it had often been before. Movements spawned by Chicano/a agricultural workers in California, Asian American students on the Berkeley campus, Civil Rights workers, Black Nationalists and Native American activists all recognised the importance of culture in social change, of which literature was and remains an integral part. But this does not mean that the literature itself merely functions in the service of a particular political programme; the aesthetic features of ethnic writing usually spark the beginning of the reader's first interest and an insight into the politics of representation comes later. Nor is the question of cultural politics in any sense clear-cut. As the writers of subsequent chapters in this book indicate, the first problem to be faced in the definition of Asian, African, Native American or Chicano/a literature is that of classification: who counts as belonging to this or that group, what are the problems with the catch-all terminology of 'Asian American' or 'Native American', who is 'authentic' and who is merely jumping on a bandwagon, and what characteristics does the writing have to have in order to qualify as 'ethnically distinct' – not to mention accurate? Add to this the ways in which gender, class and sexual orientation frequently cut across ethnic identities and the illusion of unified and homogeneous cultural representation is shattered pretty comprehensively.

Once this is understood, it also becomes clear why ethnic fiction is hardly ever about African American, Native American, Chicano/a or Asian American culture per se, but about the hybridity that is inscribed in their very designation. What Martin Padget calls 'the bicultural situation' that ethnic American writers find themselves in, is strikingly often dramatised in their fiction by protagonists who are of mixed ancestry and who thus literally embody that hybridity in themselves. Another feature which is common to ethnic writing is that of mixed genres and forms: frequently autobiography functions as theory, prose is shot through with poetry and song, narrative is also (counter-)historiography. Linguistic mixtures occur too, most obviously in the bilingual texts of Chicano/a writers, but also when African American writers make use of the black vernacular as a 'native tongue', or when Asian Americans and Native Americans intersperse their English with words and phrases from their first language. This mixture of languages and forms extends, of course, to cultural themes and tropes as well, and to readerships which are differentially positioned. There are different messages for different readers, in-jokes to be 'got' or not, and stylistic features which can be taken as innovative or recognised as conventional, according to the reader's familiarity with the cultural tradition in question. Any beginner in American ethnic fiction will also know that folklore, myth and narratives originating in a community's oral tradition figure prominently in ethnic writing as a means of educating the reader and of preserving cultural heritage. What the status of orality is in different cultures, and whether or how it is transcribable into print, are vexed questions which continue to be debated by writers and critics alike. Yet the attempt to validate marginalised oral traditions through hybrid novelistic forms is a recognisable feature of much ethnic writing. Unsurprisingly, it is usually allied with the construction of alternative histories and the preservation of memory in order to counter the damaging effects of 'Anglo cultural imperialism', as Candida Hepworth puts it.

Ethnic American fictions of the kind discussed in subsequent chapters are, then, however culturally distinct, held together by common themes and by modes of representation which highlight the tensions inherent in American national identity. The dominant notion of 'Americanness', after all, is predicated on the idea that 'America is a nation of immigrants'; that is, not one of ex-slaves, not of Native inhabitants, not of the conquered peoples of the Southwest, and not of migrant workers who could be put in internment camps at times of international crisis – whether they were citizens or not. Ethnic writers address the question of belonging to this nation which has sought to exclude them, which is not the same as to say that they long to belong, but rather that they long to transform, from within, the very idea of what America is, was, or will be. Critics of African American, Native, Asian American and Chicano/a writing repeat this common theme in the terms of post-structuralist, postmodernist and post-colonial theories which are also interested in centres and margins, diversity and difference, nation and narration. Ethnic writers themselves, moreover, are not infrequently academics and critics as well, and if in the past theory was indebted to fiction, the reverse is now also true: contemporary ethnic fiction is often informed by theory, or in dialogue with it. Because Toni Morrison's work is a prime example of such dialogism, it is perhaps fitting to close with a statement of hers: 'definitions belong to the definers, not the defined'. As will be apparent in the chapters to follow, ethnic American fictions turn this proposition upside down: the defined are doing the defining, and definers of old had better take note.

2
Native American fiction

Martin Padget

Overview and antecedents: the evolution of Native American fiction

'You meet Indians everywhere'. So declares Simon Ortiz with an exuberant sense of humour that characterises much of his poetry in the collection, *Going for the Rain*, which records the age-old process of journeying beyond one's immediate community and culture to discover oneself in relation to the external world. The journey out comes full circle with the poet-narrator's return to his home in Acoma, New Mexico. His travels throughout the United States help establish a vibrant sense of kinship with fellow Indians and provide a historical understanding of the lingering presence of Indian spirits in locations across the country. Published in 1974 at the height of civil rights activism by Native Americans, *Going for the Rain* conveys an enthusiastic sense of cultural continuity tempered by caution. In the final two stanzas of 'The Significance of a Veteran's Day', the Acomas' profound sense of history and spirituality is juxtaposed with the legacy of Spanish and American colonisation:

> And then later on in the ancient and deep story
> of all our nights, we contemplated,
> contemplated not the completion of our age,
> but the continuance of the universe,
> the traveling, not the progress,
> but the humility of our being here.

Caught now, in the midst of wars
against foreign disease, missionaries,
canned food, Dick & Jane textbooks, IBM cards,
Western philosophies, General Electric,
I am talking about how we have been able
to survive insignificance. (Simon Ortiz, *Woven Stone*, University of
Arizona Press, 1992, p. 108)

Despite the focus on fiction in the ensuing discussion of Native
American literature, I begin by quoting Ortiz's poetry because it
encapsulates the foremost concerns of many contemporary Indian
writers. The term 'veteran' calls to mind the experiences of Indians
who fought for the United States in World War II, Korea and Vietnam, while the phrase 'I am a veteran of at least 30,000 years' from
an earlier stanza conveys the Acomas' great longevity. The narrator
articulates the connection between the people and the land through
writing which derives from and continues the oral tradition. The
word 'insignificance', though, refers to the ways in which Acomas,
and Indians throughout the United States, have grown socially, economically and politically marginalised in modern American society.
Only too aware of how his people have become 'caught' between
competing world-views and socio-economic orders, the narrator
contrasts the symbiotic relationship between land and cultural identity in Acoma society with Western culture's faith in the ideal of
progress, technological development and, in the eyes of the narrator,
superfluous production and consumption of modern commodity
goods. Although the narrator points to the processes which have
rendered Indians 'insignificant' in a mass consumer society, the
poem also imparts a history of endurance and continuance through
which Indians have outlasted the impact of epidemic diseases,
colonisation and assimilation campaigns, and characterises a present
in which they continue to negotiate government bureaucracy, formal
education, and the ideology and products of corporate America. In
the introduction to the omnibus collection of poetry in which *Going
for the Rain* is featured, Ortiz explains that contemporary Native
Americans must work against the 'feeling of no self-esteem, insignificance, powerlessness, and of being at the mercy of powers beyond
[their] control' by striving for a holistic consciousnesss which is
rooted in language – 'not necessarily only native languages but the

consciousness of our true selves at the core of whatever language we use, including English' – and through acting responsibly within the community and towards tribal lands (*Woven Stone*, p. 27).

Having introduced the work of one contemporary Indian writer, we should consider several issues that have surfaced already in this discussion of Native American literature. Indeed the very term 'Native American literature' is somewhat problematic and in using it we are confronted with a series of questions. Who are 'Native Americans' and for what reasons are they distinguished from other Americans? What sorts of 'literature' have they produced? Is there a collective body of Native American literature? Does this literature exhibit common characteristics with writing by non-Indians? What is the relationship between Native American literature and canonical American literature?

The term 'Native American', which I shall use interchangeably with 'Indian', refers to people of indigenous ancestry in the forty-eight contiguous states, Alaska and Hawai'i. Christopher Columbus, convinced that he had sailed from Europe to Asia, used the term *Indios* (Spanish for Indians) to describe the indigenous Arawaks he encountered on making landfall in the Bahamas on 12 October 1492 (Jack Utter, *American Indians: Answers to Today's Questions*, National Woodland Publishing Company, 1993, p. 2). 'Indian', then, is a concept created by colonising Europeans to describe Native Americans who had no equivalent understanding of a shared identity with fellow inhabitants of South and North America and who instead regarded themselves as distinct peoples. As usage of the term became widespread among European powers competing for domination of the Americas, 'Indian' lent a false sense of unity to Native peoples and masked the tremendous diversity of tribes whose subsistence patterns, social organisation, language and culture differed in both profound and subtle ways. The term was also used pejoratively – along with words such as savage, heathen, barbarian and redskin – to express what colonising Europeans and later Americans considered essential racial and cultural differences between themselves and Native Americans. Today, however, at a time when a large proportion of Native Americans in the United States identify themselves as 'Indians', the term provides largely positive connotations and expresses a sense of shared identity among Native people that transcends tribal boundaries.

The National Census of 1990 reported 1,959,234 Indians living in a total population of over 248 million Americans (Utter, p. 17). This figure is almost a four-fold increase on the number of 523,591 Indians reported in the 1960 census, which in turns builds on the population nadir of around 250,000 in 1900. The huge rise in the Indian population is due not only to a consistently high birth rate among Indians but also to the greatly increased number of people who claim Indian ancestry. Russell Thornton, an expert on demography, speculates that '[t]he political mobilization of American Indians in the 1960s and 1970s, along with other ethnic-pride movements, may have lifted some of the stigma attached to an American Indian racial identity'. Thornton continues: 'This would be especially true for persons of mixed ancestry who formerly had declined to disclose their American Indian background. Conversely, persons with minimal American Indian background may have identified as American Indian out of a desire to affirm a "romanticized" notion of being American Indian' ('Population', *Encyclopedia of North American Indians*, ed. Frederick Hoxie, Houghton Mifflin, 1997, p. 501). Thornton's comments in tandem with the population statistics suggest that from the early decades of the twentieth century on there has been an ongoing process of revitalisation within Native American communities across the United States. During the same time, Native American authors and poets have played a key role in dramatising and defining what it means to be an Indian in the United States. Shortly I will say more about how literary works by writers such as N. Scott Momaday, James Welch, Leslie Marmon Silko, Gerald Vizenor and Louise Erdrich have come to form a recognisable and coherent body of contemporary Native American literature, but first we need to clarify the ways in which Indians constitute a distinct community within the United States.

The ancestors of today's Indians are believed by many archaeologists to have migrated to North America from Asia between 15,000 and 35,000 years ago, although some archaeologists contend people started migrating thousands of years earlier. Jack Utter notes that the majority of scientists who have studied the subject think people travelled from Siberia to Alaska by way of a massive land bridge across the Bering Strait created during the last ice age (*American Indians*, pp. 4–6). Common to many Indian myths of origin are stories of migration narrating the journey of a people to their particular homeland, and such stories remain a fundamental part of how tribes define themselves as distinct collectivities. But a number of Indians call into question the Bering Strait theory, especially when their own tribal traditions provide alternative stories of how they came to live in a certain place. For instance, Vine Deloria Jr., a prolific essayist, professor of Native American legal studies and Indian rights activist, has lampooned the Bering Strait theory by suggesting the peopling of Asia and Europe started when people left the Americas rather than vice versa. Author and literary critic Gerald Vizenor, who time and again strives to undermine the epistemological basis on which Euro–Americans gather 'scientific' information about Native American cultures, argues that all written discourses which feature Indians, including those written by Indians themselves, are subject to a colonialist bias. Thus he remains sceptical about claims to truth about the pre-Columbian past that are forwarded under the sign of Western empiricism. Basil Johnson, discussing the cosmology of the Ojibwa or Anishinaubeuk, reports that according to oral tradition 'their people were born on this continent while it was still in its infancy', which puts tribal narrative at odds with those who support the Bering Strait theory. Johnson contends: 'The theory that the North American Indians originally came from Asia is at odds with more recent scholarly studies and discoveries that have suggested that humans have inhabited this continent far longer than was first believed, from as long as 250,000 years ago' (Basil Johnson, *The Manitous: The Spiritual World of the Ojibway*, HarperCollins, 1995, p. xvi). Rex Lee Jim, however, reckons that 'close analysis of the different prehistoric worlds in Navajo oral tradition reveals details that give merit to the Bering Strait migration theory' ('Navajo', *Encyclopedia of North American Indians*, p. 422).

Debates over the validity of the Bering Strait theory notwithstanding, today's Indians constitute a unique population within the United States because they are descended from the Native peoples who lived in North America at the time of European colonisation. Between the sixteenth and nineteenth centuries, European countries competed first with one another and then with Americans for possession of North America. Both Europeans and Americans used a legalistic device, popularly known as the doctrine of discovery, to justify their claim of title to land in North America. As Jack Utter explains, after gaining independence from Britain the US government interpreted the doctrine to justify its right to buy and sell Indian lands, even though Indians may not have wished to relinquish their claims to the land. The Supreme Court came to this conclusion in the case of *Johnson v. McIntosh* (1823). The following passage from this ruling conveys the Supreme Court's belief that Americans had inherited from European nations, and particularly Britain, the right to claim all land they considered a part of the young republic:

> The United States ... have unequivocally acceded to that great and broad rule by which its civilized inhabitants now hold this country. They hold, and assert in themselves, the title by which it was acquired. They maintain, as all others have maintained, that discovery gave an exclusive right to extinguish the Indian title of occupancy, either by purchase or by conquest; and gave also a right to such a degree of sovereignty [over Indians and their land], as the circumstances of the people [of the US] would allow them to exercise. (Utter, *American Indians*, p. 8)

This passage helps us understand both the rhetorical standing on which American claims to title of the land were based and the obligations the United States assumed when exercising its sovereignty over Native Americans. Between the late eighteenth and late nineteenth centuries, as the United States added to its land mass by claiming Indian lands through treaties and warfare, so Indian–white relations moved through a series of changes. Outlining the stages by which government officials assumed a paternalistic relationship with their Indian 'wards' and made Indians increasingly dependent on government agents for their welfare, Francis Paul Prucha, an expert on the development of federal Indian policy, notes that 'Indian dependency increased as the traditional means of survival were weakened and destroyed' (*The Indians in American Society*, University of California Press, 1985, p. 41). By the late nineteenth century, it was government policy to assimilate Indians into mainstream American society. Attempts were made to school Indians into white ways through promoting agriculture on reservations, converting them to Christianity, and removing children from their home com-

munities to be educated in boarding schools. The key legislative act
was the General Allotment Act of 1887, which transformed reservation land from a communal resource to private allotments. (I discuss
the Act in more detail in the case study of Louise Erdrich's novel
Tracks.) Prucha labels the thinking behind such plans 'ethnocentric
paternalism' and concludes that measures which sought to undermine older patterns of culture among Indians largely failed precisely
because Indians maintained a strong sense of the differences
between their way of life and the values and practices of Euro–American society: 'Most of the programs did not work with the Indians
because the Indians received them with a heritage and cultural outlook that negated or destroyed the well–intentioned plans. A communal rather than an individualistic spirit, an emphasis on sharing
rather than on accumulating, a relation with nature that did not
accord with rapid exploitation of resources for profit – these traits
meant that the seeds of the civilization programs frequently fell on
barren ground' (p. 53).

   The traits Prucha outlines here are similar to the values espoused
by Simon Ortiz in both his poetry and the passage I quoted from the
introduction to *Woven Stone*. That contemporary Native American
writers such as Ortiz can claim such a vibrant sense of the 'continuance' of Indian communities is testimony to the tenacity and dignity
with which Indians have strived to remain true to their own tribal
and pan-Indian identities. Continuance is also due to significant
changes in federal Indian policy during the twentieth century. After
the Merriam Report of 1928 concluded that the General Allotment
Act and the assimilation campaign of the late nineteenth and early
twentieth century were in key respects responsible for the grave
poverty of many Indians, there was a new impetus for reform in the
administration of Indian affairs. John Collier, the new Commis-
sioner of Indian Affairs, was instrumental in creating the Indian
Reorganization Act of 1934 which provided new forms of funding
for agriculture, better educational resources and expert advice on
improving tribal economies. Most significantly, the Act provided for
tribal government and thus a certain degree of self-determination
for Indian communities across the United States. Federal Indian
policy, however, changed for the worse after World War II – a conflict in which 25,000 Native Americans served. In 1953 the policy of

termination was voted into law and the Bureau of Indian Affairs began a new campaign of assimilation whereby the special 'trust' status of certain Indian tribes was cancelled and individuals were encouraged to leave reservations for new economic opportunities in cities. It is through this programme of relocation that Abel, the protagonist of N. Scott Momaday's novel *House Made of Dawn*, is sent to Los Angeles in the early 1950s. Donald L. Fixico states of relocation: 'Though many Indians migrated to cities successfully the program was a disaster. After a period of subsidized "adjustment", Indian recruits were abandoned. Poverty and homelessness quickly produced frustration and anger, and these, in turn, produced additional problems: alcoholism, joblessness, and poverty' ('Indian-White Relations in the United States, 1900 to the Present', *Encyclopedia of North American Indians*, p. 294). The policy of termination was revoked in the 1960s, a decade in which Indian activists took a far more pronounced role in campaigning on a national scale for the improved civil rights of Native Americans. Radical political action continued well into the 1970s and echoed the militancy of Black Nationalists in the African American community. Over the past three decades, the provision for self-determination within tribal communities means that Indian leaders, in Fixico's view, 'shoulder enormous responsibilities that include the protection of hunting and fishing rights, water rights, religious traditions, and cultural heritage'. In addition, Fixico notes: 'modern tribal governments struggle to develop successful gaming operations, profitable industrial factories, and effective educational and social-welfare programs' (p. 294).

Turning our attention again to the topic of Native American literature, it is important to note that writers such as N. Scott Momaday, Leslie Marmon Silko, Gerald Vizenor, Simon Ortiz and James Welch came into prominence in the late 1960s and early 1970s in the midst of radical activism and changing attitudes within a large part of the American population toward Native Americans. These writers took a crucial role in reassessing what it meant to be an Indian in contemporary American society. In so doing they frequently referred to traditional aspects of Indian cultures, especially the oral tradition. Since the oral tradition forms such a central part of how Indians, as tribal communities and as individuals, understand them-

selves, we need to establish what it is and how it functions. Historically Indian literatures were predominantly oral – spoken and sung
– and aural – to be listened to in a communal context. Stories, songs,
prayers and chants were all articulated through memory. Many stories and songs were only performed in situations that held a specific
meaning, and it was necessary for individuals to become specially
trained in the knowledge and protocol required of the performer.
For example, the Navajo Night Chant – a healing ceremony of the
southwestern Navajo tribe which is featured in Momaday's *House
Made of Dawn* – contains around four hundred songs and takes nine
days to complete. Much oral storytelling conveys a religious sensibility that stresses ideals of reciprocity, wholeness and beauty and so
expresses a deep sense of attachment between a people and the land
they inhabit. A. LaVonne Brown Ruoff explains the particular ways
in which Native Americans regard language as having a creative
function: 'American Indians hold thought and word in great reverence because of their symbolic power to alter the universe for good
and evil. The power of thought and word enables native people to
achieve harmony with the physical and spiritual universe: to bring
rain, enrich the harvest, provide good hunting, heal physical and
mental sickness, maintain good relations within the group, bring
victory against an enemy, win a loved one, or ward off evil spirits'
(*American Indian Literatures: An Introduction, Bibliographic Review,
and Selected Bibliography*, Modern Language Association, 1990,
p. 7). In large measure Indian tribes understand themselves through
stories passed on through an oral tradition that, for N. Scott Momaday, has always been one generation from extinction. Although Indians have become increasingly familiar with Western forms of written
expression, the oral tradition continues to be a vital part of contemporary Indian communities. Simon Ortiz explains that in his experience the oral tradition is much more than the 'stories, songs,
meditations, ceremonies, ritual, philosophies, and clan and tribal
histories passed from older generations to the next'. For Ortiz the
oral tradition is more fully inclusive and consists of 'the actions,
behavior, relationships, practices throughout the whole social, economic, and spiritual life process of people' (*Woven Stone*, p. 7). As
we shall see in the novels by N. Scott Momaday, Louise Erdrich and
Sherman Alexie, contemporary writers interweave elements of the

oral tradition, in both the narrower and larger senses that are suggested by Ortiz. In the ensuing discussion of Native American literature and critical theory, I will assess the ways in which critics have characterised the relationship between the oral literature and the form of the novel. Louis Owens, for example, contends: 'Native American writing represents an attempt to recover identity and authenticity by invoking and incorporating the world found within the oral tradition – the reality of myth and ceremony – an authorless "original" literature' (*Other Destinies: Understanding the American Indian Novel*, University of Oklahoma Press, 1994, p. 11). But before turning our attention to either recent literary theory or to particular novels, we need to consider literature by Indians that was published before World War II.

Although contemporary Native American fiction arises out of diverse literary and cultural influences, Indian writing since the late eighteenth century has represented an attempt on the part of Indians to come to terms with a bicultural situation. The first published writing by Native Americans came in the form of sermons and autobiographies of the eighteenth and nineteenth centuries, although government officials and ethnologists also published translated versions of Native American oratory and oral literature. Samson Occom, a Mohegan who had converted to the Methodist Church, is widely thought to be the first Indian to have published a text in English. His *Sermon Preached at the Execution of Moses Paul, an Indian*, was published in 1772 and widely read by non-Indians. Over the next two centuries hundreds of Indian autobiographies were published, and they continue to be published to the present day. The first autobiography, entitled *A Son of the Forest* (1833), was written by William Apes, a Pequot Indian. Similar to Occom, he had converted to Methodism and become a minister four years before the book was published. Usually autobiographies published between the antebellum period and the early twentieth century were composed collaboratively by Indian narrators and white writers or editors. Ruoff points out that from the early nineteenth century on, such narratives 'incorporat[ed] elements of oral storytelling and personal statement as well as well as written autobiography', adding that when 'Indians became educated in the white man's language and literature, they began to write autobiographies that frequently

combined oral history, myths and tales, and personal experience'
(*American Indian Literatures*, p. 53). Sermons preached by Indians
converted to Christianity, autobiographies written collaboratively
with Euro-American authors, and fiction created by American Indians who had been schooled in Euro-American forms of literary representation all suggest the necessity for Native Americans of
articulating their written voices through generic forms deriving
from outside 'traditional' cultures. Yet the fact that Indians incorporated aspects of oral expression, such as creation myths, traditional narratives and songs, into those earlier forms of written
representation demonstrates that from the outset Native Americans
adapted these forms to their own purposes.

   The first novel published by a Native American author was John
Rollin Ridge's *The Life and Adventures of Joaquín Murieta, the Celebrated California Bandit* (1854), a sensationalist fiction dramatising
the violent actions of a 'real life' Mexican bandit who raided the California gold fields in the early 1850s. While the authorship of
another nineteenth-century novel, Simon Pokagon's *O-gî-mäw-kwe
Mit-i-gwä-kî: Queen of the Woods* (1899), is disputed, the first flourishing of Native American fiction occurred during the 1920s and
1930s, when short fiction and novels were published (in chronological order of authors' first fictional works) by Zitkala Ša, John Milton
Oskison, Mourning Dove (or Humishima), John Joseph Mathews
and D'Arcy McNickle. Common to these works are debates over
individual and tribal identity in the face of land loss and white acculturation efforts, concern for the mixed-ancestry Indian caught
between Native American and white cultures, and representation of
the struggle of Native peoples to reconcile tribal traditions with the
economic, social and intellectual forces of American modernity. The
picture of Archilde, the young male protagonist of McNickle's *The
Surrounded* (1936), being shackled and led away by white law officers
concludes the novel with an image of resistance and criminalisation
that is echoed in other works of Native American fiction at that time.
The second flourishing of Native American fiction occurred in the
late 1960s and 1970s when the authors N. Scott Momaday, James
Welch, Leslie Marmon Silko and Gerald Vizenor were first published. During the 1980s and 1990s, these major writers have been
joined by Sherman Alexie, Paula Gunn Allen, Louise Erdrich,

Linda Hogan, Thomas King, Louis Owens, Susan Power and Anna Lee Waters. While much of this writing echoes themes articulated in fiction of the 1920s and 1930s – especially the images of individual alienation featured in the earlier works of Momaday, Welch and Silko – it constitutes a diverse body of work that displays commonalities with the literature of fellow ethnic American writers. Writers such as Vizenor and King have also created elaborate pastiches which blend aspects of traditional oral narratives, particularly the figures of tricksters and shamans, with the linguistic play characteristic of much postmodern fiction. Such writing challenges ongoing stereotypes in which 'authentic' Native American identity is associated with a mythological past free of corrupting Euro-American influence.

Native American fiction and recent literary theory

Writing in 1979, Michael Dorris commented that he did not think a body of literature existed that could be justifiably labelled 'Native American literature'. Dorris stated that if such a body of work should come to exist, it would have to demonstrate 'a shared consciousness, an inherently identifiable world-view' (quoted in Owens, *Other Destinies*, p. 20). A decade later, Louis Owens reflected on Dorris's cautious words and concluded that just such a recognisable and coherent literature did now exist, principally in 'novels written by Native Americans about the Native American experience' (p. 20). He reasoned: 'in spite of the fact that Indian authors write from very diverse tribal and cultural backgrounds, there is to a remarkable degree a shared consciousness and worldview defined primarily by a quest for identity: What does it mean to be "Indian" – or mixed-blood – in contemporary America?' (p. 20).

I have quoted Dorris and Owens to make the apparently paradoxical observation that 'Native American literature' is a relatively recent phenomenon. As we move into the new millennium, it appears an increasing amount of Native American fiction, poetry and autobiography is being published and that contemporary Indian writers are now taught more widely than ever in higher education courses. This situation contrasts with the dearth of literature published in the twenty or so years after World War II. Indeed N. Scott

Momaday, whose novel *House Made of Dawn* won the Pulitzer Prize for fiction in 1969 and is often credited with beginning a 'Native American Renaissance' in literature, has commented that at the time of writing his novel he did not know any other works of Native American fiction existed. Momaday was happily proved wrong, and it is partly due to the success of *House Made of Dawn* that novels and short fiction by Zitkala Ša, John Milton Oskison, Mourning Dove, John Joseph Mathews and D'Arcy McNickle have been reprinted and re-evaluated by literary critics over the past two decades. But despite the fact that the critical and popular success of *House Made of Dawn* helped inspire a new generation of Indian writers to write, we still may ask why it has taken so long for a recognisable body of Native American literature to emerge.

To answer this question we must first identify the sort of literature that both Owens and this section of *Beginning Ethnic American Literatures* deal with, namely Native American fiction. In the introduction to *Other Destinies*, the first critical study of Native American novels, Owens differentiates between Indian poets who 'may imagine themselves part of ancient oral tradition of singers or storytellers' and the Indian novelist who 'works in a medium for which no close Indian prototype exists' (p. 10). Although some critics would dispute this distinction between poets and fiction writers, it is important to note that Owens does not think the novelist becomes estranged from the traditional forms of oral storytelling. Rather the novelist takes the opportunity to meld elements of the oral tradition with 'Western' forms of narrative to produce the syncretic or hybridised form of the Native American novel. Owens characterises such fiction as 'an attempt to recover identity and authenticity by invoking and incorporating the world found within the oral tradition – the reality of myth and ceremony – an authorless "original" literature' (p. 11). Simultaneously, he argues, 'through the inscription of an authorial signature, the Indian writer places him- or herself in immediate tension with this communal, authorless, and identity-conferring source, at once highlighting the very questions of identity and authenticity the new literature attempts to resolve' (p. 11). This statement points to the way that complex issues of identity – how it should be characterised and defined – lie at the heart of contemporary Native American literature and literary criticism.

One of the difficulties experienced by non-Indian readers of Native American literature may well be their relative lack of knowledge of the oral tradition and, indeed, of Native cultures in general. James Ruppert foregrounds this problem in *Mediation and Contemporary Native American Literature* (University of Oklahoma Press, 1995). He describes mediation as 'an artistic and conceptual standpoint, constantly flexible, which uses the epistemological frameworks of Native American and Western cultural traditions to illuminate and enrich each other' (p. 3). In his readings of individual novels, Ruppert differentiates between the implied Native reader and the implied non-Native reader of works of fiction. Thus while on an initial reading of N. Scott Momaday's *House Made of Dawn* non-Native readers may well stress the novel's elements of social criticism, Ruppert reckons Native readers will be immediately alerted to the novel's mythic storyline. Since reading involves an active searching out of meaning by the reader, though, non-Native readers should become aware of how interpreting Momaday's novel calls into question the forms of knowledge and moral values with which they are most familiar and thus the act of reading moves them from a Western world-view into a far less familiar Native world-view. The advantage of this approach for non-Native readers is that it takes a sympathetic view of what Ruppert assumes is their distance from the cultural traditions featured in Native American literature and strives to find common ground between non-Native and Native readers of texts who each learn more of the other's culture through reading mediated works of fiction. For Ruppert, the readers who become aware of their *lack* of knowledge on reading Native American literature 'are now open to a Native epistemological pattern that they previously did not know how to see and to the new hybrid forms of meaning and knowledge that contemporary Native American writers can create' (p. 13).

Arnold Krupat also foregrounds the issue of the non-Native reader's estrangement from the 'reality' of tribal culture when he argues for an 'ethnocritical' approach to the study of American Indian literature that acknowledges differences between Native and Western conceptions of art, information and culture while simultaneously striving to discover a language that can mediate between the two. Krupat practises a cosmopolitan approach to the study of

Native American literature which sees Native fiction as a 'practice' and not a 'thing' that belongs to Indian people (*The Turn to the Native: Studies in Criticism and Culture*, University of Nebraska Press, 1996, p. 22). This approach has put Krupat at odds with certain Native critics, particularly Ward Churchill and Elizabeth Cook-Lynn, who advocate political sovereignty and cultural autonomy for Native Americans (see Churchill's *From a Native Son: Selected Essays on Indigenism, 1985–1995*, Beacon Press, 1996). Cook-Lynn, for example, argues that 'much modern fiction written in English by American Indians is being used as the basis for the cynical absorption into the "melting pot", pragmatic inclusion in the canon, and involuntary unification of an American national literary voice'. She concludes: 'To succumb to such an intellectual state is to cut one's self off as a Native American writer from effective political action. It severs one's link not only to the past but to the present search by one's native compatriots for legitimate First Nation status' (*Why I Can't Read Wallace Stegner and Other Essays: A Tribal Voice*, University of Wisconsin Press, 1996, p. 96).

For Gerald Vizenor, the 'Indian' *is* representation and he mocks those who purport to provide 'authentic' images of Native Americans, including radical activists within the Indian community. In his view all written representations of Native Americans, whether authored by non-Indians or Indians, are 'postindian simulations' that testify to the historical process of colonisation and linguistic and cultural dominance experienced by Native peoples in the United States. Against 'dominance' Vizenor posits the enabling term 'survivance' through which he proposes a new kind of presence for Indians, a presence created out of performative acts, such as naming and personal visions, that convey an individual identity while locating personhood within community (see Vizenor's *Manifest Manners: Postindian Warriors of Survivance*, Wesleyan University Press, 1994). Vizenor has become renowned as a trickster writer who uses post-structuralist and post-modern theories both to deconstruct dominant images of Indians and to reconstruct contemporary Indians *as* impure and thus 'inauthentic' crossbloods who nevertheless in their very hybridity best reveal the 'true' status of Native Americans today.

Case studies: three important works of Native American fiction

N. Scott Momaday, House Made of Dawn (1968)

N. Scott Momaday's novel *House Made of Dawn* (Harper and Row, 1989), which won the Pulitzer Prize for Fiction in 1969, has had a profound impact on Indian writers and critical interpretations of Native American literature. The novel tells the story of Abel, a Pueblo Indian, who after fighting in World War II returns to his home in New Mexico alienated from both Pueblo culture and white America. In an interview, Momaday comments on how Abel's trauma was shared by a 'tragic generation' of Indians who suffered 'a dislocation of the psyche'. He elaborates: 'Almost no Indian of my generation or of Abel's generation escaped that dislocation, that sense of having to deal immediately with, not only with the traditional world, but with the other world that was placed over the traditional world so abruptly and with great violence' (Laura Coltelli, *Winged Words: American Indian Writers Speak*, University of Nebraska Press, 1990, p. 94). Despite the novel's many images of alienation, the novel's final image suggests that Abel becomes reintegrated into Walatowa society as he runs through the high arid lands of the Southwest with his mind, body and soul in holistic harmony with the landscape that from time immemorial has sustained his people. Thematically complex and challenging in its use of aesthetic tropes associated with literary modernism, *House Made of Dawn* narrates Abel's renogotiation of his 'Indian' identity through his empowering embrace of ritualism and mythical precedent.

The novel is divided into a prologue and four sections. The prologue anticipates the end of the novel by showing Abel running at dawn in a ceremonial race. As Abel runs, he appears to become one with the 'still and strong' land. The prologue begins with the traditional invocation – *Dypaloh* – of a Walatowa (or Jemez) Indian storyteller and then announces the motif of 'a house made of dawn' which is associated with the Nightway Chant, a long and intricate healing ritual conducted by Navajo Indians. From the outset, Momaday evokes traditions of storytelling and healing within separate southwestern Indian cultures in a manner that suggests the

novel is a continuation of each tradition. Later it will transpire that
Abel is running seven years after the time setting of the novel's first
section, 'The Longhair'. In this section, set in the pueblo of Walatowa in 1945, readers are introduced to Abel when he stumbles in a
drunken stupor off the bus bringing him home from his army service. Abel is an isolated figure who can neither articulate the pain he
experiences in the aftermath of warfare nor find the right words to
renew the link between himself, the community and the land.
Through a series of memories that dramatise key points in Abel's
childhood and adolescence in Walatowa, readers learn more about
his character and the events that preceded his departure from the
pueblo. It becomes clear that his distance from the pueblo community predates his harrowing experience of combat during World War
II. However the fact that Abel has fallen out of sync with the rhythm
of pueblo life and no longer feels that he has a centred existence by
no means suggests he has rejected his own culture. But clearly Abel
is vulnerable to external influences on his return to Walatowa, as is
suggested by two key events: his relationship with Angela St. John,
a privileged white woman who is attracted to his 'primitive' masculine energy, and his murder of an albino Indian whom he understands to be an incarnation of evil.

The second section of the novel, entitled 'The Priest of the Sun',
is set in Los Angeles in 1952 and features a number of Indians who
have moved from their former homes on reservations to the city
under the federal government's policy of relocation. It transpires
that after a period of imprisonment, Abel has been relocated to the
city to continue his rehabilitation away from the reservation. This
section starts with Abel coming to consciousness after a terrible
beating inflicted by a corrupt policeman, Martinez, who represents
to Abel a second witch. Ironically, the beating proves to be the turning point in Abel's life as it pre-empts his return to Walatowa. The
section's title refers to Tosamah, a self-styled reverend and leader of
the Los Angeles Holiness Pan-Indian Rescue Mission. Simultaneously creative and disruptive, Tosamah is a trickster figure who
preaches a sermon on the Gospel according to St. John, conducts a
religious ceremony featuring the use of peyote, and tells the story of
the Kiowa Indians' migration from their former homelands in the
Rocky Mountains to the Southern Plains.

The third section, 'The Night Chanter', is also set in Los Angeles and begins with Benally, a Navajo Indian, telling the story of
Abel's departure from the city. The two have become close friends
while Abel lives in Los Angeles. Benally informs Abel about the
songs and chants associated with two Navajo healing ceremonies,
the Beautyway and Night Chant. Benally sings about the house
made of dawn, making a gift of words that will help Abel become
articulate again and so sing and pray into existence a symbiotic relationship with the land. Benally appears to undermine the worth of
his own words when he comments on the need for Indians to change
their ways once they move away from the reservation to cities: 'You
have to forget about the way it was, how you grew up and all' (p.
148). Although the events that have precipitated Benally's departure
from the reservation are not detailed, his sense of estrangement from
his home community is shared by many characters in Native American literature. Unlike Abel and Benally, Tosamah appears unable to
return to a reservation home; instead, while continuing to live in the
city, he seeks an imaginative connection between himself and his
Kiowa ancestry that is expressed through his story of the way to
Rainy Mountain.

'The Dawn Runner', the novel's final section, brings the narrative
full circle as Abel awakes at dawn, only a week after his return from
Los Angeles, to find his grandfather is dead. Abel prepares Francisco's body in ritual fashion and hurries away to run after the men
who have set off at sunrise. Struggling initially to keep his body in
motion – it is only a month or so since the beating – Abel runs
beyond pain to the point where 'he could see at last without having
to think' (p. 212). As he runs, so he sings under his breath the words
of the Night Chant. The novel ends with the Walatowa term *Qtsedaba*, indicating that the story is over.

I have provided this overview of *House Made of Dawn* to prepare
the way for a detailed examination of Abel's character and the events
in which he is involved. Apart from the image of the timeless runner
in the prologue, readers first see Abel reeling drunkenly off the bus
in pathetic contrast to Francisco's dignity. Indeed Abel shows no
recognition of his grandfather. As Louis Owens points out: 'In a
world in which identity is derived from community, to not know
one's grandfather is dangerous' (*Other Destinies*, p. 97). The imme-

diate explanation for Abel's dislocation might be his harrowing
experience of combat during World War II, but there is also reason
to believe that Abel's sense of alienation from both the white and
Indian worlds predates his enlistment. How, then, does Abel, from
the very moment of his birth, become a marginalised member of the
Pueblo community?

Abel never knows his father, only that the man was held in small
regard by members of the community: 'a Navajo, they said, or a Sia,
or an Isleta, an outsider anyway, which made him and his mother and
Vidal somehow foreign and strange' (p. 11). As a young boy he is
cursed by Nicolás *teah-whau*, a woman who is regarded as a witch by
Walatowa's population. An illegitimate child cursed by a woman
through whom evil is channelled, Abel also lacks a maternal uncle
who within Pueblo Indian communities traditionally takes the primary responsibility for a male child's instruction. Instead Francisco
assumes the role of instructing and, after his mother dies, caring for
Abel. By his adolescence, Abel is blessed with a deep sense of kinship to wild nature that simultaneously estranges him from fellow
Pueblos. He watches in awe the 'cavorting, spinning and spiralling'
(p. 17) of two golden eagles flying above the massive volcanic crater
of the Valle Grande in the Jemez Mountains. Such an experience
singles out Abel to be included in the Eagle Watchers Society to seek
the capture of an eagle for ceremonial purposes. On securing a large
female eagle, Abel follows the correct protocol by making a prayer
offering and singing. But he becomes tearful at the weight of the
sack containing the subdued bird, and during the night he kills it:
'Bound and helpless, his eagle seemed drab and shapeless in the
moonlight, too large and ungainly for flight. The sight of it filled
him with shame and disgust' (p. 22). This act excludes Abel from
further participation in the Eagle Watchers Society, and is further
indication of the tensions that come to exist between him and other
members of the Pueblo. Abel kills the eagle because he respects its
wildness and cannot bear to see its loss of independence. The profound longing he experiences for its power, independence and
beauty in motion reflects the wildness of his own being, and it is
hardly coincidental that the eagle's confinement in the sack is
echoed by Abel's incarceration in a prison.

Having pointed out the ways in which the younger Abel does not 'fit' into the Pueblo community, there is a more straightforward 'sociological' explanation for his alienation from both the Indian and white worlds on his return from World War II. In the days after his drunken encounter with Francisco, Abel's traumatic reaction to warfare continues. Contrasting with the memories of his childhood and adolescence, his memory of the years after his departure is chaotic: 'It was the recent past, the intervention of days and years without meaning, of awful calm and collision, time always immediate and confused, that he could not put together in his mind' (p. 23). Abel is unable to become reconciled to a non-Indian world where mass destruction has taken place. Significantly the single event during the war that Abel can remember in detail is coming to consciousness on the side of a wooded hill and finding himself among dead bodies. Mortar fire has ceased and it is the silence that awakens him, only for a German tank to encroach upon Abel. According to his commanding officer, Abel 'all of a sudden got up and started jumping around and *yelled* at that goddam tank' before 'giving it the finger and whooping it up and doing a goddam *war dance*' (p. 117). This farcical image of Abel taunting the tank contrasts images of the 'primitive' Indian and pastoralism with the destructive capacity of modern technology. On his return to Walatowa, Abel cannot simply remain the person he was at the start of his period of enlistment and a gap grows between his comprehension of pueblo life and his ability to act in appropriate ways. Yet despite his alienation from 'the old rhythm of the tongue', Abel retains a deep-set understanding of the significance of praying and singing: 'it was still there, like a memory in the reach of his hearing' (p. 58). Years pass, however, before he becomes attuned to pueblo life again because he kills an albino Indian and is subsequently imprisoned for murder.

Momaday's dramatisation of the violent encounter between Abel and the albino is enigmatic and open to various interpretations. The albino first appears on the Feast Day of Santiago, the Catholic patron saint of Walatowa, at the chicken pull. Initially he is described as 'large, lithe, and white-skinned' and referred to as a 'white man', but – as we see through Angela's eyes – there is 'something out of place, some flaw in proportion, or design, some unnatural thing' in his appearance that immediately becomes clear when she realises he is an albino, 'huge and hideous' (pp. 42–3; p. 44). The albino appears to pick on Abel after successfully pulling the chicken from the earth because he recognises how Abel is vulnerable to the enticement of shared violence. Abel's entrapment is complete when he kills the albino three days after the feast day. Outside Paco's bar in the darkness and rain, the snake-like albino embraces and kisses Abel who responds by driving a knife into the white man's torso and then castrating and disembowelling him. At the point of death, the albino 'seemed just then to wither and grow old' but there then appears to be an instant regeneration, for '[i]n the instant before he fell, his great white body grew erect and seemed to cast off its age and weight; it grew supple and sank slowly to the ground, as if the bones were dissolving within it' (p. 83).

Seven years later, after Abel has been moved to Los Angeles to continue the process of rehabilitation that began with his prison sentence, we learn from his confrontation with a second figure of evil, the corrupt cop Martinez, that he has failed to understand the need not to counteract evil with violence. Unlike Francisco, who tolerates the presence of evil when he senses the albino lingering on the fringe of his field of crops at Walatowa, and unlike the runners after evil who he will come to emulate, Abel, between the time leading up to killing the albino in 1945 and his spiritual epiphany as he lies broken-bodied near the shore in Los Angeles in 1952, remains out of sync with his fellow Walatowas' understanding of evil. Louis Owens argues that through 'attempting to destroy evil, Abel has become one with it, accepted its seed' (*Other Destinies*, p. 103). Kenneth Lincoln thinks 'Momaday portrays the albino more as symbol than character, the ancient evil in human nature serpenting into the kiva by way of invading Christianity', and then contends that through ritually killing the albino, Abel 'revers[es] the Christian myth of Abel's murder' (*Native American Renaissance*, University of California Press, 1983, p. 119). These interpretations indicate that accounting for Abel's motive in killing the albino takes readers into a realm of understanding with which many will be unfamiliar. Adopting the viewpoint of dominant white culture in regarding Abel's explanation in court for killing the albino, Tosamah mocks Abel by exclaiming: 'He killed a goddam *snake*!' (p. 149) Benally believes Abel did encounter genuine evil in the guise of the albino. Certainly we find in further allusions to evil in the novel evidence to support Benally's viewpoint. According to the diary of Fray Nicolás, a Catholic missionary who lived at Walatowa in the late nineteenth century, an albino child named Juan Reyes was born in 1875. If indeed this child and the albino are one and the same person, this would make Juan Reyes seventy years old at the time of the chicken pull and thus provide further evidence he is a witch. There is another explanation for Abel murdering the albino, namely the latter's association with whiteness and thus a history of European and American colonisation. Thus we might construe the albino as representing the external white world or the white man who exists inside Abel. However, as is the case if we understand the albino as a figure of malignant evil within the Pueblo community, even if the 'white man' is a wicked influence who derives from some place outside Pueblo society, he cannot simply be eradicated by Abel. Put another way, we may interpret Abel as having tried, through killing the albino, to purify both himself and the Pueblo community of white influence in the aftermath of his participation in World War II. But such an act would put the perpetrator at odds with the traditional world-view of Pueblo Indians, violate their code of appropriate conduct in the face of evil, and endanger their more subtle forms of resistance to pressures of acculturation within dominant American society by calling attention to the so-called 'primitivism' of Indians in the mid-twentieth century. The latter point is brought home by Tosamah when he labels Abel 'a longhair' and 'a real primitive sonuvabitch' who 'was too dumb to be civilized' (p. 148). Tosamah, though, speaks in a typically contrary fashion and there is good reason for us to consider that he is as much concerned with lampooning whites for their continuing fear of Indians in the era of relocation as with condemning Abel for his so-called primitivism.

Significantly, it is at the mid-point of the novel that Abel comes into an epiphanic understanding of the significance of ritual behaviour in accounting for and thus counteracting the negative influence of evil within the pueblo community. Lying 'racked with pain' on a rocky beach in a commercial yard in Los Angeles after being beaten by Martinez, images of the court hearing seven years earlier flash before him. Initially we learn that for Abel killing the albino was 'the most natural thing in the world' and that he would kill again if the same situation occurred (p. 102). But then an owl, a traditional harbinger of death, comes within Abel's range of vision. Striving to keep the owl 'away in the corner of his eye', Abel sees the old men running after evil, and so for the first time since his return from the war it appears possible that he can become centred again within Walatowa society. Momaday records Abel's vision of the men:

> The runners after evil ran as water runs, deep in the channel, in the way of least resistance, no resistance. His skin crawled with excitement; he was overcome with longing and loneliness, for suddenly he saw the crucial sense in their going, of old men in white leggings running after evil in the night. They were whole and indispensable in what they did; everything in creation referred to them. Because of them, perspective, proportion, design in the universe. Meaning because of them. They ran with great dignity and calm, not in the hope of anything, but hopelessly; neither in fear nor hatred nor despair of evil, but simply in recognition and with respect. Evil was. Evil was abroad in the night; they must venture out to the confrontation; they must reckon dues and divide the world. (p. 104)

Experiencing this vision proves a turning point for Abel and hence-forth he will be on the road to recovery. The meaning he perceives in the act of running 'hopelessly' leads him to start questioning how he has lost his way and wandered so far from home: 'He tried to think where the trouble had begun, what the trouble was. There was trouble; he could admit that to himself, but he had no real insight into his own situation. Maybe, certainly, *that* was the trouble; but he had no way of knowing' (p. 105). The hesitant and repetitive quality of these thoughts indicates that Abel has far to go before being healed mentally, but at least he is beginning to move away from an alienated perspective whereby both his mind and body have become 'his enemy' (p. 101).

It is through Benally instructing Abel in Navajo ideals of personal harmony and cosmic balance that Abel becomes prepared spiritually to travel home to Walatowa. Benally tells him about 'those old ways, the stories and the sings, Beautyway and Night Chant', singing from the latter about a house made of dawn (p. 146). Ironically, despite his intimate knowledge of Navajo ceremonial life Benally is estranged from life on the Navajo reservation, most of which lies in northern Arizona and northern New Mexico. Much of 'The Night Chanter', the third section of the novel, is narrated by Benally, while the remainder characterises his thought processes in a stream-of-consciousness style. He and Abel have much in common in addition to their friendship in Los Angeles. They both possess intimate memories of their childhood experiences, each was brought up by a grandfather, and they share the sense of having been '*right there at the center of everything*' at any early stage of their lives (p. 157). Benally, though, is inconsistent in his thinking about life on and off the reservation, and his narration is full of equivocation, ambivalence and uncertainty. He alternately longs for home and wants to become part of life beyond the reservation. He rejects the 'old' ways and embraces new forms of spirituality by participating in Tosamah's peyote ceremony. He claims the benefits of living in the city and in the heart of a culture of consumption – 'money and clothes and having plans and going someplace fast' – are far preferable to life on the reservation where 'there would be nothing there, just the empty land a lot of old people, going no-place and dying off' (p. 158; p. 159). He stresses the need to forget the way it used to be while consistently remembering the stories and experiences that gave meaning to his life on the reservation. All told, Benally's mindset suggests the difficulty of going 'home', both physically and metaphorically, and reflects the divided loyalties of a generation of Indians relocated to cities.

Contrasting with Benally's largely dualistic thinking about life at 'home' on the reservation and in the city, where he is part of a small pan-Indian community, is Tosamah's wizardry with words whereby he appears to occupy contradictory positions simultaneously without seeking to reconcile them. According to Louis Owens, Tosamah resembles the traditional trickster because he 'is in dialogue with himself, embodies contradictions, challenges authority, mocks and tricks us into self-knowledge' (*Other Destinies*, p. 110). Moreover the awkward relationship between Tosamah and Abel proves beneficial for the latter: 'As a trickster, Tosamah undertakes the appropriate trickster task of mocking and taunting Abel into self-knowledge, a painful process for Abel, but one that helps prepare him for his return to the pueblo' (p. 111). If we agree with Owens, Tosamah is as important a figure for Abel's recovery as Benally. Unlike Abel, or for that matter Benally, Tosamah appears unable to connect with a

geographical and metaphysical centre or middle of the sort alluded
to in their memories of Walatowa and the Navajo Reservation.
Owens contends that Tosamah has 'nothing except imagination and
language out of which to fashion his world' (p. 110). Nevertheless,
his sermon on the Gospel of St. John and the story he tells of the
Kiowa migration demonstrate the verve and creative adaptability of
the Indian's speaking voice.

In addition to Benally and Tosamah, the third character who
appears to contribute to Abel's healing in Los Angeles is Angela St.
Martin. Their paths cross again when she visits Abel in hospital
after the beating inflicted by Martinez. Angela recounts the story
she tells to her young son about an Indian brave born of a bear and
a maiden. For Benally, this is similar to the stories told to him by his
grandfather when he was a boy. Critical opinion, however, is divided
as to the nature of her treatment of Abel and the precise function she
plays in his recovery. According to Larry Evers, Angela's story is as
'rootless as a Disney cartoon' (Larry Evers, 'Words and Place: A
Reading of House Made of Dawn', Western American Literature vol.
11 (1983), p. 317). But for Louis Owens, through her earlier relationship with Abel, Angela 'has truly learned to "see" beyond' and
thus can aid his recovery when called upon (p. 107). This may be a
generous assessment of Angela's actions considering she visits Abel
a full two days after learning about his condition from Benally.
Owens's interpretation also leads us to query the extent to which
Angela could truly have become cured of her alienation from her
own body and soul in the years after departing New Mexico.
Although such a speculative query does not take us far, it does lead
toward the important issue of how interethnic relationships are
characterised not only in House Made of Dawn but also in the other
two novels I consider, Louise Erdrich's Tracks and Sherman Alexie's
Reservation Blues. To deny the efficacy of Angela's role in Abel's
cure has consequences for our larger understanding of the degree to
which Indians and whites form mutually beneficial personal relationships. For Kenneth Lincoln, in the scenes set in 1945 Angela
represents an 'insidious threat' to Abel's welfare because of her
'spiritual emptiness' and 'predatory sexuality' (Native American
Renaissance, p. 119). Pointedly, Lincoln does not moderate this hostile, and arguably misogynistic interpretation of Angela's character

with a concessionary assessment of her later visit to Abel in hospital. Neither does Kathleen Donovan achieve a positive view of
Angela's participation in Abel's recovery, although crucially Donovan is not judgemental about Angela's character but instead is at
pains to point out the gender politics of Momaday's writing (*Feminist Readings of Native American Literature: Coming to Light*, University of Arizona Press, 1998, p. 72). Donovan argues that 'Angela's
sexuality betrays Abel by removing him from the healing possibilities of ritual and landscape' (p. 77). She sees Milly, the white social
worker with whom Abel has a sexual relationship while living in Los
Angeles, as functioning in a similarly negative fashion: 'her attempts
to tie him through language, acculturation, and sexuality make her
as dangerous and manipulative as Angela' (p. 79). Donovan's con-
tentious criticism of Momaday's representation of women characters and both female and male sexuality in *House Made of Dawn* will
doubtless provoke divided reactions among readers, not least
because she regards the 'underlying misogyny' of Momaday's writing as 'inconsistent … with the search for harmony and balance
characteristic of Native American literature' (p. 72). This point
leads us to reconsider the degree to which Abel does in fact achieve
harmony and balance at the end of the novel.

Readers will recall how Abel returns to Walatowa to find Francisco ill and that his grandfather's death paves the way for him running at dawn in a final image of apparent completeness. Significantly
Abel, prior to Francisco dying and a week after his arrival from Los
Angeles, experiences a sense of alienation that echoes the estrangement he experienced on his return from World War II. Looking after
Francisco, he comes back to a room which 'enclosed him, as it always
had, as if the small dark interior, in which this voice and other voices
rose and remained forever at the walls, were all of infinity that he had
ever known'. Momaday continues: 'It was the room in which he was
born, in which his mother and his brother died. Just then, and for
moments and hours and days, he had no memory of being outside of
it' (pp. 195–6). This is an ambiguous image that suggests Abel feels
stifled and even imprisoned within the Pueblo community while it
also conveys a more benign sense of how Abel comes home to a sense
of continuity and familial connection in spite of, or perhaps because
of, the room's association with death. Bernard Selinger uses this

passage to argue that while 'Abel's travels off the reservation indicate that he is not at home in the non-Indian world, … there is nothing to indicate that he is at home on the reservation either' ('*House Made of Dawn*: A Positively Ambivalent Bildungsroman', *Modern Fiction Studies*, 45.1 (1999), p. 61). Karl Kroeber reckons that through showing Abel running behind rather than with the runners at dawn, Momaday acknowledges the 'ambivalently inconclusive and self-frustrating' nature of his fiction ('Technology and Tribal Narrative', in *Narrative Chance: Postmodern Discourse on Native American Indian Literatures*, ed. Gerald Vizenor, University of Oklahoma Press, 1993, p. 18). Kroeber further contends a fundamental incompatability lies between the novel's form and the 'authentically Indian imaginative form' of oral narrative invoked through the terms *dypaloh* and *qtsedaba*. He concludes: 'The variety of interpretations it has provoked, from disputes about the significance of details to arguments about whether its overall effect is optimistic or pessimistic, testifies to its being a novel by an Indian dramatizing the inappropriateness of the genre for the expression of his [Momaday's] Indianness' (p. 18). While Kroeber makes questionable assumptions about what forms an 'appropriate' mode of expression for Native American storytellers and what constitutes 'Indianness', nevertheless his criticism helps us evaluate the significance of the novel's ending by calling into question interpretations that assume Abel becomes successfully integrated into the pueblo community through the act of running. There are, however, many critics who do stress the holistic resolution of *House Made of Dawn*. For example, Kenneth Lincoln regards the final image of Abel running as 'an image of the native body as words-chanted-in-motion. It is a sunrise image of reintegration, of renaissance' (*Native American Renaissance*, p. 121).

Rival interpretations of the final images of *House Made of Dawn* indicate the richness and invention of Momaday's writing. One of the most useful approaches to the novel is employed by James Ruppert. As noted earlier in the discussion of recent literary theory, Ruppert uses a critical approach to Native American literature called 'mediation'. The term stresses the creative ways in which Indian writers draw upon distinct cultural traditions to produce their fiction. Although contemporary Indian writers may turn their attention to any subject matter of their choosing, Ruppert contends their 'mediational goals direct them ... toward Native concerns such as nurturing, survival, continuance, and continual reemergence of cultural identity' (*Mediation*, p. 4). Turning to *House Made of Dawn*, Ruppert argues that Momaday mediates the modernist elements of fragmentation, monologue and stream of consciousness with a non-Western world-view and sense of cyclical time. He then characterises the response of implied readers to the novel: 'The non-Native reader's uncertainty and confusion can only be resolved when he or she decides to pay attention to the new discourse context and establish a new meaning for chanting, running, and return. The Native reader is guided to see through the psycho-social turmoil to find the mythic pattern beneath the flux of modern existence' (p. 40). For Ruppert, the 'new meaning' non-Native readers may learn parallels the 'mythic pattern' he envisages Native readers discovering in their reading of the novel. By following the story of Abel's return to Walatowa and recognising that through ritual running Abel moves into mythic time and back into a centred existence, all readers can become aware of and share in the novel's 'healing effect' (p. 41).

This is an empowering vision of Native American literature's capacity to compel in both Native and non-Native readers a deep understanding of the holistic and ethical values that feature at the heart of Indian cultures. Having counterbalanced the cautious readings by Kroeber and Selinger of the ending of *House Made of Dawn* with Ruppert's argument that through imaginatively moving into mythic time and mythic meanings Abel, the novel's readers and even modern society can be brought 'back to primordial unity and eliminate what Momaday sees as the "psychic dislocation of ourselves in time and space"' (p. 41), I urge readers to evaluate these assessments and come to their own conclusion regarding the significance of the image of Abel running through the high arid lands of the Southwest.

Louise Erdrich, Tracks *(1988)*

Louise Erdrich's *Tracks* (HarperCollins, 1994) is the third in a sequence of four novels set on and around a fictional Chippewa reservation in North Dakota. The novel takes readers back to a crucial time in Native American history when the pressures of land loss, confinement on reservations, spread of epidemic diseases, forced assimilation efforts and intra-tribal conflicts had a profoundly unsettling impact on Indian communities. Covering the years 1912–24, the novel dramatises a time of deep division within tribal communities as they became factionalised along 'conservative' and 'progressive', or 'hostile' and 'friendly' lines in response to external pressures from the federal government to assimilate to white ways. Rather than dramatise in detail the machinations of Indian agents, logging company executives and tribal bureaucrats, Erdrich focuses on the experiences of an extended network of characters whose lives are dramatically changed as they struggle to come to terms with the social and economic forces that are undermining traditional Chippewa culture. The novel juxtaposes the voices of two alternating narrators, Nanapush, an elderly 'bush' Indian who tells his story to his adopted granddaughter Lulu, and Pauline Puyat, a younger woman of mixed Chippewa and white ancestry who strives to deny her Indian ethnicity and removes herself from the Indian community to become a nun. Erdrich dramatises familial rivalries and intricate revenge plots, pushes her characters to ecstatic and fevered states of sexual desire, traces the effects of love medicines and curing powers, and creates a tribal community filled with vibrant and fallible characters. She conjures an environment in which an animistic world-view prevails even as a growing proportion of the reservation's population distances itself from traditional Chippewa culture. Yet although individuals like Edgar Pukwan, the tribal policeman, become aligned with the white world, a deep-set conditioning into Chippewa ways prevails. Confronted with the task of burning buildings in which people have died of tuberculosis, Pukwan is scared of being being turned 'windigo' or crazy by the spirits of the dead; Boy Lazarre, whose family has signed a contract with the Turcot Lumber Company to log tribal land, dies convinced the horrible infection leading to his death was caused by Fleur Pillager when she touched his arm; and Pauline, in a beautifully realised scene, visits the Chippewa dead with Fleur during the time she is mortifying her own body in preparation for her full acceptance into the Catholic Church.

  Tracks begins with Nanapush's recollection of the time when consumption, or tuberculosis, devastated the Chippewa community.

This outbreak of disease, which follows an earlier epidemic of small-pox and outbreak of fever (probably measles), indicates the crucial role played by Old World pathogens in the conquest of Native Americans between the late fifteenth century and the twentieth century. In North America, over the centuries of European colonisation and westward expansion, Indians in countless numbers died of smallpox, measles, plague, influenza, typhus, diphtheria, cholera and tuberculosis. While this larger history of disease is only alluded to in *Tracks*, Nanapush acknowledges the corrosive impact of tuber-culosis on the local population: 'Our tribe unraveled like a coarse rope, frayed at either end as the old and new among us were taken' (p. 2). But disease is only one in a series of interrelated factors that have undermined Chippewa culture. Nanapush's life straddles the divide between the years when the Chippewas continued to subsist off the land and the time they became confined on a reservation and issued with government commodities in lieu of the food supplies they had created for themselves through hunting, gathering and horticulture. He states: 'I guided the last buffalo hunt. I saw the last bear shot. I trapped the last beaver with a pelt of more than two years' growth. I spoke aloud the words of the government treaty, and refused to sign the settlement papers that would take away our woods and lake. I axed the last birch that was older than I' (p. 2). These words indicate how throughout his life Nanapush has medi-ated between Chippewas and whites; when younger he served as a government interpreter and by the end of the novel he takes a promi-nent role in tribal bureaucracy.

Despite the earth's apparently limitless capacity to absorb the bodies of the Chippewa dead, Nanapush recognises that luck is always liable to change the fortunes of a dispirited people. He pos-sesses an animistic understanding of the world, believing actions in everyday life can both upset and correct the cosmic balance of life. He seeks to appease the spirits of the dead, prays to animal helpers and respects the power that reveals itself in dreams, visions and suc-cessful cures. Nanapush's name links him to the Chippewa trickster Naanabozho, who figures in traditional oral narratives as a culture hero. Paul Radin notes that '[l]aughter, humour and irony permeate everything Trickster does' (*The Trickster*, Schocken Books, 1972, p. xxiv), and there is plenty of evidence to support the view that

Nanapush displays these characteristics. His verbal parrying with Margaret Kashpaw (or Rushes Bear), the hilarious story he tells Pauline to make her urinate, and his ability to talk his way out of (and also into) trouble are facets that link Nanapush to the trickster. He recalls his father's explanation for the name: '"Nanapush. That's what you'll be called. Because it's got to do with trickery and living in the bush. Because it's got to do with something a girl can't resist. The first Nanapush stole fire. You will steal hearts"' (p. 33). It is no accident that Nanapush makes such a fine narrator, for, as Louis Owens explains, there is an implicit morality to his words: 'Respon-sible through his storytelling for remembering the way it was, and thus for preserving Indian identity, Nanapush clowns his way with wry and ribal humor through the tragic times for his tribe' (*Other Destinies*, p. 212). As a trickster, Nanapush proves able to improvise a way through awkward circumstances, rather like Naanabozho who is represented as a hare in many Chippewa stories. Nanapush's canny ability to evade those who would contain or injure him is not merely self-serving but used for the benefit of the tribe as a whole.

Significantly Nanapush refers to his people as the 'Anishinabe' (meaning First, or Original, People), the tribe's name for itself, rather than 'Chippewa', a term used by the US Government to refer to the tribe in legal agreements. Since Chippewa is the more com-monly used term in Erdrich's novel, I have employed it in this dis-cussion. Her characters live on the fictional counterpart of the real-life reservation of the Turtle Mountain Chippewa in North Dakota, from whom Erdrich is descended on her mother's side. They are part of a larger people, the Ojibwa, who nowadays have a total population of 200,000. Today the Ojibwa live in communities on either side of the US–Canadian border between southeast Ontario in the east and Montana and Saskatchewan in the west (Helen Tanner, 'Ojibwa', *Encyclopedia of North American Indians*, p. 438). At the outset of the novel, twelve years before making his crucial decision to adopt 'the new way of wielding influence' by run-ning for the position of tribal governor, Nanapush is scornful of bureaucracy and disdains those who would sell reservation land to a lumber company that exploits the reservation's rich timber resources. After the outbreak of disease takes the lives of many elders, Nanapush is considered an old man at the age of fifty. He comments that in the years of his own lifetime he has seen 'more change than in a hundred upon a hundred before' (p. 2). Although in 1912 Nanapush recognises the scale and rapidity with which Chippewa lifeways have been transformed, it will take him some years to realise precisely how to resist the wholesale purchase of allotted lands both by individuals within the tribe who are more oriented to white ways and by outsiders, principally the lumber company and local farmers who covet reservation land for the spread of arable agriculture. In order for us to understand the impact of the policy of allotment on both the Chippewas and tribes across the United States, we need to turn our attention to a crucial piece of legislation, the General Allotment Act.

Passed into law in 1887, the General Allotment Act divided reservation lands into allotments of 160 acres and 80 acres which were assigned, respectively, to the heads of families and all other individuals over the age of eighteen. Widely supported by both the administrators of Indian affairs and white reformers, the Dawes Act, as it was also known, was designed to hasten the integration of Indians into American society by promoting the growth of commercial agriculture on reservations. Allotted lands were held in trust for a period of twenty-five years, during which it was hoped Indians would learn to become efficient farmers and acculturate to white ways through converting to Christianity and pursuing formal education at off-reservation schools. As Francis Paul Prucha explains: 'With the incentive of a private farm to be cared for, developed, and then bequeathed to one's children, it was assumed that the Indians would enter into the economy and into the social and political life of the nation and thus be assimilated' (*The Indians in American Society*, p. 47). At the end of this period, a fee patent was issued and henceforth allotted lands were taxable if the individual land holder was deemed 'competent'. During the early twentieth century, administrators of Indian affairs tried to hasten Indians into independence and integration by greatly increasing the number of Indians who were regarded as competent. Unfortunately a great many Indians to whom fee patents were made failed to hold onto their lands. Prucha concludes: 'Instead of establishing the Indians as independent property owners and citizens, the policies pauperized the Indians. The great majority of Indians who received full control of their land quickly sold the land or lost it for failure to pay taxes or interest on their mortgages' (p. 50). Between 1887 and 1934, when federal Indian policy was transformed by the Indian Reorganisation Act, the total land holdings of Native Americans fell from 139 million acres to 48 million acres (statistic quoted in Nancy J. Peterson, 'History, Postmodernism, and Louise Erdrich's *Tracks*', in *Contemporary American Women Writers: Gender, Class, Ethnicity*, ed. Lois Parkinson Zamora, Longman, 1998, p. 182).

Evidence of the stark reality of land loss and the pressure to assimilate lies throughout *Tracks*. In the opening chapter, Nanapush warns Fleur 'the land will be sold and measured' (p. 8), and this proves true when at the end of the novel the Pillager allotments on the shore of Matchimanito Lake are logged. But Nanapush also alludes to Fleur's resistance to the encroachments of Indian agents and lumber company workers. Both characters consider the land sacred and are respectful of the manitous, or powers, that populate the natural world, especially the lake monster, Misshepeshu. (In a discussion of the world-view of the Ojibwa, Basil Johnson describes 'manitou' in the following way: 'Mystery, essence, substance, matter, supernatural spirit, anima, quiddity, attribute, property, God, deity, godlike, mystical, incorporeal, transcendental, invisible reality' (*The Manitous*, (p. 242).) In contrast to the Pillagers, Bernadette Morrissey, together with her brother Napoleon, son Clarence and daughters Sophie and Philomena, takes a very different view of the land. The Morrisseys are well-off mixed-bloods who have bought up the allotments of fellow Chippewas to create a large farm of 640 acres. Along with the Pukwan, Hat and Lazarre families, the Morrisseys are largely pro-assimilation in viewpoint and co-operate with the government agent administering local Indian affairs. Such actions indicate how the Morrisseys have internalised capitalist principles calling for land accumulation and productive use of arable land for agriculture while also co-operating with the Turcot Lumber Company to exploit timber resources for short-term financial gain.

Significantly in the last-but-one paragraph I have provided more 'facts' about the Dawes Act and the policy of allotment than is conveyed in *Tracks*. This observation brings us to the heart of a key issue, namely the way Erdrich regards the narration of history. In a perceptive discussion of *Tracks*, Nancy Peterson concludes

Erdrich's writing 'creates the possibility for a new historicity by and for Native Americans to emerge' ('History, Postmodernism', p. 188). Observing that Erdrich has spoken in interviews about the difficulty she experienced in directly confronting political and historical issues when writing *Tracks*, Peterson explores the ways that Erdrich uses both oral history and academic history to create a novel that 'works toward an understanding of history not as an objective narrative but as a story constructed of personal and ideological interests' (p. 183). She notes that while academic history can corroborate Nanapush's account of disease and land loss, it cannot 'fully acknowledge the horror of depopulation and genocide' (p. 180). Instead it takes Nanapush's fictional voice to articulate the pain and continuing suffering of the Chippewas from within their own culture and to provide an oral history that rivals Anglo accounts of westward expansion. Nanapush, however, cannot tell all, as he acknowledges himself, and his account is interpretive and idiosyncratic. Through juxtaposing accounts by the two narrators, Nanapush and Pauline, Erdrich provides readers with a fuller understanding of Chippewa culture during the early twentieth century. Crucially the events that dramatically change Chippewa livelihoods are, to quote Linda Hutcheon, 'given *meaning* ... by their representation in history' (quoted in Peterson, p. 177).

Erdrich, then, creates a multidimensional image of the various ways Chippewas respond to a period of crisis. Under the external pressure of a government policy of assimilation, the tribal members become divided among themselves. Factionalism gathers force, extended families become pitted against one another in rivalry, and individuals grow alienated from the traditional aspects of Chippewa society. In the case of Pauline, the urge to distance oneself from the Indian community is taken to an extreme. Indeed Pauline not only rejects her Indian ethnicity but actively seeks, through teaching at the Catholic sisters' school in Argus, the blinding and deafening of Indian children like Lulu. Unlike Nanapush's speech, which in being addressed to Lulu locates him in an extended family that lies at the heart of the Chippewa community, Pauline's narration is directed to no particular audience. Together with her sister Regina, Pauline hails from a family of mixed-bloods, 'skinners in the clan for which the name was lost' (p. 14). Nanapush refers to her as the last of a family 'who were always an uncertain people, shy, never leaders in our dances and cures' (p. 38). While Nanapush regards her as a misfit and an oddball for her fanatical embrace of Catholicism, he also recognises the power of her own storytelling voice, for Pauline is a gossip, liar and spreader of the Gospel, and in each of these capacities represents a threat to himself. Invisible to the Anglo men at Kozka's Meats in Argus, Pauline is also a marginalised figure within the Indian world who through claiming that she is 'wholly white' (p. 137) gains access to the convent and a home outside of the Indian community. In the process, she adopts white society's view-point on Indians – 'I saw that to hang back was to perish' (p. 14) – and denies her Indian ancestry.

Late in the novel, just prior to taking on the new name Leopolda, Pauline appears to recognise no kinship between herself and her ille-gitimate daughter, Marie, whom she merely refers to as 'the bastard child' (p. 198). In a tribal environment where the individual contin-ues to be located through family background and clan affiliation, a mother's rejection of her child is a profoundly unsettling act for the more traditional members of the tribe. It is also an unsettling act for Pauline herself and there will be a price to pay for maintaining her distance from Marie, namely a madness that grows in direct propor-tion to the amount she strives to suppress her physical appetites and cast off the beliefs she has internalised as a result of growing up within the Chippewa community. The extremity of Pauline's adopted faith, Catholicism, is demonstrated repeatedly. Regarding her pregnancy, she exclaims: 'Satan was the one who had pinned me with his horns' (p. 133). She chafes her skin by wearing a potato sack, walks with shoes on the wrong feet, and further mortifies her body by leaving pins in a headpiece to mimic Christ's crown of thorns and placing a rope about her neck to remind her of Christ's betrayal by Judas. For Pauline, Fleur represents one of the chief obstacles to the success of her missionary impulse to enlighten the benighted lives of Chippewas. Pauline recognises a similarity in their pivotal roles: Fleur is the hinge between the Chippewas, their traditional belief system and eternal damnation, while she is the hinge between the people, their salvation through Christianity, and their future as assimilated citizens. Having witnessed how whites claim all the advantages in society, Pauline regards the deaths of

Indians due to disease and their tendency toward alcoholism as signs of an inherent weakness that can only be remedied by turning away from their traditional lifeways. Yet as we have seen with Nanapush, the choice confronting Chippewas – the fiercely resistant tradition-alism of Fleur or Pauline's dismissal of the old ways for a 'progres-sive' future – is neither as stark nor as straightforward as Pauline contends. Indeed, in the midst of what appears to be her complete estrangement from the Chippewas, the extreme measures to which Pauline goes to deny her body and prove her new-found faith are a sign of how she can neither fully suppress her sexuality nor cancel out the animistic world-view of the Chippewas.

Given Pauline's deeply conflicted personality, her manipulation of Sophie and Eli, and the manner in which she rejects her own child, it is tempting for readers to demonise her character. Notably while she is a destructive influence on the Chippewa community, she is not ostracised by Nanapush and Fleur. Indeed Nanapush strives to return Pauline to her people. As Louis Owens observes: 'Nana-push's hilarious taunting of Pauline throughout the novel, laden with sexual comedy, may even be seen as typical of trickster's attempts to destroy hypocrisy and delusion and bring about self-knowledge. Just as traditional tricksters taunt and trick toward health, Nanapush is not willing to give up on even one soul as dera-cinated as Pauline's' (*Other Destinies*, p. 216). But Pauline's growing alienation from her fellow Chippewas cannot be prevented. Through providing an intricate portrayal of a woman of mixed-ancestry who grows progressively more hostile toward both her fellow Chippewas, Erdrich explores an integral part of tribal history. From the viewpoint of a later generation of Native Americans, the desertion of the Paulines of the Indian world must be accounted for. Thus we may see Erdrich's fiction as a recuperative effort through which errant individuals are brought back into the extended net-work of tribal and pan-Indian kinship.

While Pauline becomes the most alienated figure in the novel, clearly the figures who least compromise their understanding of the world when confronted by change are Fleur and Moses Pillager. Along with Nanapush and Pauline, Fleur is one of the novel's cen-tral characters. Her distant cousin Moses remains for the most part in the background, an enigmatic and shadowy presence at the margin of the community. As a child he cheated death, which alone would account for the fearful regard in which he is held by many Chippewas, but in addition to this he has a profound knowledge of powerful medicines. Similar to Moses, Fleur possesses creative and destructive powers. They each follow family tradition, for, as Nanapush comments, the Pillagers 'knew the secret ways to cure or kill' (p. 2). But where Nanapush has only respect for the Pillagers, Napoleon Morrissey refers to them pejoratively as 'Blanket Indians' (p. 91) whose lives appear to pro-assimilation Indians increasingly anachronistic in the face of modernisation.

As mentioned earlier, *Tracks* begins with Nanapush telling his granddaughter Lulu about the time when tuberculosis hit the reservation community hard. This was also the occasion when he discovered Lulu's mother, Fleur, among the dead bodies of her immediate family in the Pillager cabin. '[W]ild as a filthy wolf' (p. 3), the seventeen-year-old Fleur has, similar to Moses at an earlier age, tricked death. She appears to be at ease with the spirits of the dead, as is indicated by her return to the Pillager cabin after recovering in Nanapush's company. Further descriptions of Fleur in which she is compared to a wolf allude to her predatory abilities, her outcast status in a society that expresses its great fear of 'wildness' in both animals and Indians by killing them off ruthlessly, and her great capacity for survival against the odds. Early in the novel Pauline recalls how Fleur 'grinned the wolf grin a Pillager turns on its victims' (p. 19) when she entered the card game with the men at Kozka's Meats, while later, in the harrowing scene where Fleur visits the Chippewa heaven to resume her card game with the dead men in order to gamble for the life of her prematurely born baby, Pauline notes that Fleur is 'lean as a half-dead wolf' (p. 162). It is also Pauline who points out the ancient identification of the Pillagers with the bear clan and Fleur's kinship with the wild that compels fear and respect among fellow Chippewas:

> She got herself into some half-forgotten medicine, studied ways we shouldn't talk about. Some say she kept the finger of a child in her pocket and a powder of unborn rabbits in a leather thong around her neck. She laid the heart of an owl on her tongue so she could see at night, and went out, hunting, not even in her own body. We know for sure because the next morning, in the snow or dust, we followed the

tracks of her bare feet and saw where they changed, where the claws
sprang out, the pad broadened and pressed into the dirt. (p. 12)

Pauline's references to Fleur's shape-shifting abilities and her 'bear
cough' demonstrate how Fleur compels in Pauline a certain respect
even as she labels knowledge of medicine 'mess[ing] with evil'
(p. 12). Later, Lulu's birth will be prompted by the arrival of Fleur's
animal helper, a drunken bear.

The wildness Pauline perceives in Fleur is the wildness, albeit in
a diminished and residual state, that she roots out in herself but
cannot, ultimately, destroy. We find further evidence to support this
proposition in Pauline's characterisation of the water spirit, or manitou, Misshepeshu. That Pauline refers to it as a masculine 'devil'
who is 'love hungry with desire and maddened for the touch of
young girls' (p. 11) indicates she is jealous of Fleur's sexuality and
represses her own carnal desires. With the help of Moses Pillager's
love medicine, Pauline manipulates Sophie and Eli into passionate
coupling: '[Sophie] shivered and I dug my fingers through the tough
claws of sumac, through the wood-sod, clutched bark, shrank back-
ward into her pleasure' (p. 83). Pauline also describes the destructive
capacity of Misshepeshu – '[h]e's a thing of dry foam, a thing of
death by drowning, the death a Chippewa cannot survive' (p. 11) –
and suggests Fleur has a sexual relationship with the so-called monster. Fleur herself is reckoned by the end of the novel to have
drowned three times, her survival in each case strengthening her
identification with Lake Matchimanito and the land along its shore.
Nanapush explains the history of this tie: 'Pillager land was not ordinary land to buy and sell. When that family came here, driven from
the east, Misshepeshu had appeared because of the Old Man's connection' (p. 175). He also claims that 'the water thing was not a dog
to follow at our heels', indicating the way that people can never rely
on the power they invest in their animal helpers (p. 175). In the case
of Fleur, it appears that at a vital moment she is deserted by her
power: 'Her dreams lied, her vision was obscured, her helper slept
deep in the lake' (p. 177).

The fact that during a time of scarcity it is neither Fleur's dreams,
Nanapush's skill, Eli's hunting nor Margaret's preserves that saves
the household, but government commodities, suggests the necessity
of compromise if the Chippewa 'longhairs' or 'blanket Indians' are

to survive. Fleur's refusal to lend credence to the Indian agent's map which demarcates ownership of reservation land and her dismissal of the need to pay taxes on allotted lands indicates a fundamental unwillingness to comply with white authority. Heroic as such resistance is, it leads to the loss of the Pillagers' sacred land. For in the aftermath of the struggle to raise the money to pay taxes on both the Kashpaw and Pillager allotments and Nector and Margaret's subsequent betrayal of Nanapush and Fleur when only money for Kashpaw land is handed to the Indian agent, the Pillager land is sold to the Turcot Lumber Company. In a futile effort to raise sufficient money to purchase a new allotment, Eli goes to work for the lumber company, but such compromise is anathema to Fleur. Instead she seeks retribution on the employees of the Turcot Company through sabotage. Before being evicted from the former Pillager land, Fleur walks into the lake to drown for the third time, only to be saved by Eli and Nanapush. As she prepares to sacrifice herself in the water, so the water serpent's power – which prior to this Pauline claimed to have tamed – appears to be 'uncoiled' (p. 212). Thus Fleur again possesses the power that deserted her in the aftermath of her premature baby's death, and she uses it to bring down the trees surrounding her cabin on the men and equipment of the lumber company.

Fleur is last seen walking away from the old Pillager land, hauling a small wooden cart and carrying with her items which help situate her identity: stones from beneath the water of Lake Matchimanito, roots for medicinal purposes, the umbrella that shaded her baby's burial place, the markers for Pillager graves on which Nanapush etched the clan emblem of four crosshatched bears and a marten, and finally the charred patent leather shoes that once belonged to her daughter Lulu. Significantly Fleur does not walk further into the bush – what there is remaining of it – but toward the world outside the reservation. Nanapush watches her 'until the road bent, traveling south to widen, flatten, and eventually in its course meet with government school, depots, stores, the plotted squares of farms' (p. 224). Thus the character who hitherto has maintained a connection to the land that is more intimate and ardent than any other Chippewa's, leaves the reservation. Henceforth she will wander uprooted from the land but secure in her identity, a figure who continues to adhere to the old ways and maintain, as far as possible, an independent livelihood. There is an obvious tension at work in this representation, though. For even as Fleur appears to walk off social constraint, so she forsakes those members of the community who would like to claim her. Prior to setting out, Nanapush asks her to stay, but receives, as he expected, no answer. He understands the necessity of her departure even as he recognises the pain this causes her daughter Lulu.

Tracks concludes with an image of endurance and hope for the future. Acknowledging the debilitating forces of assimilation at work on the tribe, before leaving the reservation Fleur arranges for Lulu to be sent to the government school. During the ensuing years Nanapush is elected the tribal chairman, thus adapting to circumstances in which the Chippewas become 'a tribe of file cabinets and triplicates, a tribe of single-space documents, directives, policy' (p. 225). Although to some extent a compromise, becoming a bureaucrat enables Nanapush to challenge the pro-assimilation faction of the reservation community. In the process he gains the means to prove he is Lulu's legal father and thus has the right to call her home from an off-reservation boarding school. And so the novel ends with the image of Lulu's return. Her bright dress, shorn hair and scabbed knees mark her as a runaway from school and as resistant to control as her mother. But the lasting image is of Lulu rushing with abandon into the arms of Nanapush and Margaret. Through the novel's final line, Erdrich evokes the spirit and substance of cultural survival with a tender and enduring image: 'We gave against your rush like creaking oaks, held on, braced ourselves together in the fierce dry wind' (p. 226).

Sherman Alexie, Reservation Blues *(1996)*

Sherman Alexie is a young Spokane/Coeur d'Alene Indian who has published prolifically since the appearance of his chapbook, *I Would Steal Horses* (Slipstream Publications) in 1992 at the age of 25. In addition to three volumes of poetry – *The Business of Fancydancing* (Hanging Loose Press, 1992), *First Indian on the Moon* (Hanging Loose Press, 1993), *Old Shirts and New Skins* (American Indian Studies Center, UCLA, 1993) – he has written a collection of short fiction, *The Lone Ranger and Tonto Fistfight in Heaven* (Reed, 1998), and two novels, *Reservation Blues* (Reed, 1996) and *Indian Killer* (Random House, 1997). Most recently Alexie has worked in film, writing the screenplay for *Smoke Signals* (dir. Chris Eyre, 1998) adapted from one of the stories in *The Lone Ranger*, and directing a movie based on *Indian Killer*. While it has become commonplace for critics to comment on Alexie's young age – all of the aforementioned work was published before his thirtieth birthday – his publishing record is such that one surmises he is compelled to write by a sense of urgency and necessity. There is an immediacy and energy, as well as a certain raggedness, to *Reservation Blues* that contrasts with the measured tone and 'polish' of Momaday's *House Made of Dawn*.

In order for us to orient ourselves to the setting of Alexie's novel, we need to take account of how the reservation manifests the bicultural aspects of contemporary Indian lives. James Riding In points out that although reservations were imposed upon Native Americans by the US government, they are now regarded as homelands by a great number of Indians: 'Despite the reservations' grim origins, Indian people have been able to adapt to reservation environments while preserving many of their traditional values, beliefs, and customs'. He adds: 'Notwithstanding the oppression and land loss associated with their founding, reservations also represent a valiant struggle on the part of Indians for autonomy, self-sufficiency, religious freedom, and cultural integrity' ('Reservations', *Encyclopedia of North American Indians*, p. 546). Riding In's empowering definition of the reservation as home place helps orient readers to the following passage from *Reservation Blues*: 'The word *gone* echoed all over the reservation. The reservation was gone itself, just a shell of its former self, just a fragment of the whole. But the reservation still possessed power and rage, music and loss, joys and jealousy. The reservation tugged at the lives of its Indians, stole from them in the middle of the night, watched impassively as the horses and salmon disappeared. But the reservation forgave, too' (pp. 96–7).

Reservation Blues is set on the Spokane Reservation in the eastern part of Washington state, where three young Spokane Indians form an 'all-Indian rock and blues band' (p. 40) after the African American blues guitarist Robert Johnson miraculously arrives in their community. Johnson has travelled to the reservation in search of a

cure for a sickness he 'can't get rid of' (p. 6). Having made a deal
with the 'Gentleman' to become a great guitarist, he has been on the
run since faking his death in 1938. 'Old and tired' and unable to play
the guitar, Johnson is a tortured soul who has 'walked from crossroads to crossroads in search of the woman in his dreams' (p. 6).
Indeed Johnson does become cured of his sickness through the
attention of Big Mom, a mythological figure who appears to be ever-
present in Spokane Indian history. Reverting to playing the har-
monica, at the end of the novel he decides to remain among the
Spokanes because 'this Tribe's been waitin' for me for a long time'
(p. 303). In the meantime his guitar is adopted by Victor Joseph, who
along with singer and bassist Thomas Builds-the-Fire and drum-
mer Junior Polatkin, becomes a member of the band Coyote Springs.
The blues they play are 'ancient, aboriginal, indigenous' (p. 174).

Through describing the band's fortunes, Alexie dramatises the
tensions, ambivalences and inconsistencies Indians experience as
they call into question their sense of belonging to the Indian community. We see these ideas articulated in the rise and fall of Coyote
Springs and in the responses of Thomas, the novel's central character, to the band's fate. As Coyote Springs goes through its cycle of
early renown, near commercial success and subsequent collapse, so
Thomas experiences the initial excitement of creating music (largely
inspired by the magical qualities of Robert Johnson's guitar) and
finding an audience for his storytelling voice (prior to this, no-one
would listen to the stories he tells endlessly) and then coming to
terms not only with the band's disastrous encounter with the head
of New York City-based Cavalry Records, but also with the hostility
shown the band by members of its own community. The novel ends
with Thomas and Chess and Checkers Warm Water, two sisters
from the Flathead Reservation in Montana, who had earlier joined
the band, leaving the reservation in the company of magical horses,
spirits of the Spokane horses murdered by Colonel George Wright
some 130 years in the past. In the meantime Victor and Junior have
fallen into an alcoholic malaise and committed suicide respectively.
Judging by what happens to Victor and Junior, it would appear that
they have failed to transcend – either socially or imaginatively – the
debilitating conditions of the reservation. Thomas, on the other
hand, seems to be starting out on a journey at the novel's conclusion

– a journey, one suspects given his storytelling proclivities, into an emergent and dynamic sense of self and community.

Although I have glossed over the novel in order to convey a general sense of plot, in large part the strength of the novel lies in its 'feel' and its myriad wry observations on what it means to be an Indian in contemporary American society. Michael Gorra likens the novel to the performance of an American garage band: 'ragged and agreeable, digressive, picaresque, and as prolix as any drum solo', adding that as he reads it he is 'reminded of the anti-perfectionism of Seattle grunge, the belief that finish and form get in the way of an act's authenticity' ('Hopeless Warriors', *London Review of Books*, 5 March 1998, p. 21). Gorra also finds fault with Alexie's writing by describing the novel's missed notes, screechy reverb and popped strings. Gorra points out the sometimes 'preachy' quality of the omniscient narration when the thoughts of characters are articulated and contends that Alexie fails, when towards the end of the novel one of the characters commits suicide, to make 'the necessary tonal shift out of what has largely been a comic novel' (p. 21). While Gorra's criticisms are in some respects valid, in the remainder of this discussion I will point out the ways in which Alexie strives to create a multidimensional image of life on a contemporary Indian reservation. For although much of *Reservation Blues* is preoccupied with describing the day-to-day events, throughout the novel there are echoes of older and still enduring ways of understanding and acting in the world that remain distinctive to Spokane Indian culture. Always, then, images of loss, alienation and poverty are compensated for by scenarios in which characters hold on against the odds, find common purpose in the midst of domestic discord and manage to laugh – ironically, farcically, helplessly – at their collective fortunes.

Given the title of *Reservation Blues* and the central place of Robert Johnson in its plot, Ralph Ellison's eloquent statement about the place of the blues in African American culture has particular relevance to Alexie's novel: 'The blues is an impulse to keep the painful details and episodes of a brutal experience alive in one's aching consciousness, to finger its jagged grain, and to transcend it, not by the consolation of philosophy but by squeezing from it a near-tragic, near-comic lyricism' (*Shadow and Act*, Random House, 1964, p. 78).

Humour, along with the blues, is a salve on ancient wounds. Filling the novel's pages with dialogue, snappy one-liners, and caricatured characters, Alexie revels in the surface details of everyday life in and about the Spokane Indian Reservation. At times Alexie's storytelling resembles a stand-up comedian's performance as he focuses on the idiosyncracies of local life. Readers are shown a trading post that contains 'reservation staples: Diet Pepsi, Spam, Wonder bread, and a cornucopia of various carbohydrates, none of them complex' (p. 12); a son who on witnessing the miraculous survival of his alcoholic father concludes '[t]he only things that will survive a nuclear war are cockroaches and my father' (p. 119); and a character wearing 'a traditional Indian ribbon shirt, made of highly traditional silk and polyester' (p. 303). Such humour complements the many points in the novel where characters are faced with day-to-day poverty and poor quality food, alcoholism and domestic discord, and community factionalism that leads to outbreaks of violence. The reader unfamiliar with Indian humour may well wonder what there is to laugh at in such circumstances. Father Arnold, the reservation's Catholic priest, recalls his arrival among the Spokanes: 'He'd never thought of Indians as being funny. What did they have to laugh about? Poverty, suicide, alcoholism?' (p. 36). The answer to the Father's question lies in the fact that humour can bind people together, lift their spirits and help ameliorate their collective sense of selfhood. In a chapter of his landmark book *Custer Died For Your Sins: An Indian Manifesto* (Avon, 1970), Vine Deloria Jr. discusses Indian humour, noting '[t]he more desperate the problem, the more humor is directed to describe it' before concluding: 'When a people can laugh at themselves and laugh at others and hold all aspects of life together without letting anybody drive them to extremes, then it seems to me that that people can survive' (p. 149; p. 168).

Doubtless the alert reader will call into question the appropriateness of Deloria Jr.'s comments as a guide for comprehending *Reservation Blues*, because surely a number of Alexie's characters *are* driven to extremes? Furthermore, since Coyote Springs is formed during a temporary halt to the bullying of Thomas by Victor and Junior and given that from early on the band is pressured from without by community hostility, surely there is little evidence that the band members succeed in holding the aspects of their lives together?

Such observations are fair and I do not seek to dispute them, only to counterbalance them by reminding readers of Ellison's description of the 'near-tragic, near-comic lyricism' of the blues. Reading *Reservation Blues*, it is important to keep in mind the measured quality of Ellison's words, for throughout the novel Alexie interweaves elements of darkness and light, suffering and humour. That said, I do not wish to convey the impression that there is simple symmetry in the way that tragic and comedic elements are integrated into the story. Instead much remains in question by the end of the novel. Thomas's departure from the reservation suggests the uneasy relationship which has developed between himself and his fellow Spokanes will be the starting point of any future fiction that might feature the same characters. I will now explore three distinct aspects of *Reservation Blues* – Alexie's portrayal of Coyote Springs and the music the band plays, his characterisation of whites, and his representation of the reservation – before re-evaluating the novel's conclusion.

Two-thirds of the way through the novel, Robert Johnson sings for a brief time and on stopping '[t]he reservation exhaled'. The narrator continues: 'Those blues created memories for the Spokanes, but they refused to claim them. Those blues lit up a new road, but the Spokanes pulled out their old maps. Those blues churned up generations of anger and pain: car wrecks, suicides, murders' (p. 174). These words highlight a certain kind of cultural conservatism perceived to be at work within the reservation community. Thomas understands that for African Americans in the South during the 1920s and 1930s singing for joy and sorrow was a form of communal release and a means of expression that most whites could not comprehend. Looking at his fellow Spokanes, Thomas finds they have little music of their own or other forms of creative expression. Prior to the band forming, Thomas is an isolated figure. People won't listen to his stories – 'nobody believed in anything on this reservation' (p. 28) – and instead of telling their own stories or making their own music 'the Indians just dropped their quarters into the jukebox, punched the same old buttons, and called that music' (p. 28). The partial success of Coyote Springs provokes an ambivalent response within the community. On a rare visit to the reservation's Catholic church Thomas is told by a woman in the congregation what people have been saying about the band: 'The Christians don't like your devil's music. The traditionals don't like your white man's music. The Tribal Council don't like you're more famous than they are' (p. 179). Such reactionary criticism is, to a degree, a measure of the band's success in challenging staidness and complacency within the Spokane Reservation. For the band as a whole strives to break down the narrow parochialism of community prejudices by creating a form of 'tribal music' (p. 80) that draws on multiple influences and is in its articulation 'clumsy and terrifying' (p. 58). The band members start out playing cover versions of songs by Hank Williams, Buddy Holly, the Sex Pistols, Aerosmith and Kiss – even 'La Bamba' with Spokane words – but soon start producing their own material. (Thomas's lyrics preface each of the book's chapters.) Coyote Springs, then, perform songs that can remain within a distinctive idiom – Delta blues, country and western, punk, heavy rock – or cannibalise elements from each idiom, including that of traditional Indian music, to create songs that involve a '[l]ittle bit of everything' (p. 51). This energetic, eclectic and chaotic music is the most apt form of expression for a generation of Indians who have grown up watching 'bad television', eating commodity food, microwave burritos and 'wish sandwiches' – '[t]wo slices of bread with only wishes in between' – and dreaming traumatically about being deserted by alcoholic parents (p. 187). Playing it channels the violence of Victor who prior to joining the band 'roared from place to place, set fires, broke windows, and picked on the weaker members of the tribe' (p. 14). For Thomas, who 'tried to be as traditional as the twentieth century allowed', the band provides an ironic opportunity to express his storytelling voice (p. 49). Alone he sings Indian songs continually but never correctly: 'He wanted to make his guitar sound like a waterfall, like a spear striking salmon, but his guitar only sounded like a guitar' (p. 101). Hoping that his songs will light up a new road to the past and tradition, he wishes 'the songs, the stories, to save everybody' but this proves a forlorn desire (p. 101). Inevitably, given the fact that at the outset the band members' union 'wasn't a happy marriage', Coyote Springs's triumph over adversity is only partial and temporary and its members are always liable to fall into dispute with one another (p. 45). Falling into a pattern of excessive drinking and congratulating themselves on sleeping with white women, Victor and Junior's egotistical behaviour is less a demonstration of their male prowess than further evidence that they are both at heart 'fragile as eggs, despite their warrior guises' (p. 16).

One of the most obvious reasons for the band's failure to realise commercial success is its handling by the white agents of Cavalry Records. Through his characterisation of Colonel George Wright and General Philip Sheridan, Alexie makes a direct link between the victimisation of Native Americans during the Indian wars of before and after the Civil War and the commercial exploitation of Native American identity in the late twentieth century. Wright, who in 1858 ordered the killing of hundreds of Spokane horses, is portrayed somewhat sympathetically as a figure racked with guilt in the aftermath of warfare. The spirits of the murdered horses appear intermittently in the novel, suggesting that even as the pain of past events is acknowledged so the Spokanes persist through the capacity of their collective memory to revive the spirits of tribal members. Wright, after the Coyote Springs fails to perform coherently in the recording studio, sees in the band 'the faces of millions of Indians, beaten, scarred by smallpox and frostbite, split open by bayonets and bullets', and on gazing at his own hands finds 'the blood stains there' (p. 244). Sheridan, though, is seen in a different light. A Civil War hero who became one of the chief protagonists in the Plains Indian Wars of the 1860s and 1870s, and later succeeded William Tecumseh Sherman as the commander in chief of the US Army, Sheridan is represented as an unredeemed Indian hater. In sinister fashion he visits Checkers in her dreams, a brutal physical presence who ties her up and appears, given the way he fetishises her 'Indian beautiful' hair and 'tribal features', to want to abuse her sexually (p. 237). His physical desire to dominate the Indian woman, however, is clearly outmatched by the dominated woman's capacity to resist his encroachment. In exasperation, Sheridan cries, 'You never quit fighting. … When will you ever give up?' (p. 237)

In their guises as record company agents, Sherman and Wright initially exoticise the 'Indianness' of Coyote Springs. Reporting back to their boss, Mr Armstrong (whose name echoes that of another nineteeenth-century Indian fighter, George Armstrong Custer), the agents note the appeal of the Warm Water sisters – 'that exotic animalistic woman thing' – comment on Junior's appearance – '[v]ery ethnically handsome' – and conclude that although the band 'looks and sounds Indian' they advocate dressing its members in war paint and feathers to 'really play up the Indian angle' (p. 190). After Coyote Springs fails to conform to white expectations of Indian musical performance on their visit to New York City, Sheridan auditions Betty and Veronica, two white women who have attended the band's first gigs, and declares: 'We can still sell that Indian idea. We don't need any goddamn just-off-the-reservation Indians' (p. 269). Sure enough, Betty and Veronica appropriate signs of 'Indianness' to create their own approximation of tribal music. Thomas is appalled when he listens to their demo. He hears 'a vaguely Indian drum, then a cedar flute, and warrior's trill, all the standard Indian soundtrack stuff' before the women sing 'it don't matter who you are/ You can be Indian in your bones' (p. 295).

Alexie's biting satire on New Age 'wannabes' and the exoticising of Indian identity by non-Indians for commercial gain beckons the question of how the novel positions white readers. Vine Deloria Jr. points out that during the civil rights struggles of the 1960s the African American comedian Dick Gregory played an important role in building a bridge between African Americans and whites who also wished to challenge the entrenched racism of American society. Deloria Jr. reasons: '[Gregory] enabled non-blacks to enter into the thought world of the black community and experience the hurt it suffered. When all people shared the humorous but ironic situation of the black, the urgency and morality of Civil Rights was communicated' (*Custer Died For Your Sins*, p. 148). Alexie's humour serves a similar function insofar as it enables non-Indian readers to witness and emphathise with contemporary Native Americans as they continue to struggle not only for an improved standard of living but to exorcise the sense of failure that all too commonly haunts the mind. Witnessing and empathising with another person's pain compels an ethical responsibility on the part of the witnessing subject to try changing the conditions that give rise to the continuing social and economic inequalities which the other person experiences. Alexie, though, takes certain risks for an unsympathetic reader may find the novel's characterisation of reservation life confirms long-held prejudices of the sort articulated by Sheridan: 'I tried to help these god-

damn Indians. But they don't want help. They don't want anything'
(p. 229).

To understand further the social pathologies dramatised in *Reservation Blues*, it helps to return to Simon Ortiz's powerful introduction to *Woven Stone*. After stating that the child of colonialism is scarred for life by his or her experiences, Ortiz writes of his own childhood in the 1940s and 1950s: 'I was the silent, stoic child of a dysfunctional family, community, and nation' (p. 14). He explains this dysfunctionality by stressing the severe impact of the Federal Indian policy of forced assimilation on Native people of his generation: 'It was a severe and traumatic form of brainwashing, literally to destroy the heritage and identity of native people, ostensibly to assimilate them into an American way of life' (p. 8). This statement helps readers, Indian and non-Indian alike, to see into the mindset of an individual who knows only too well in relation to his own alcoholism how it is relatively easy to identify a problem but difficult to surmount it. While the terminology Ortiz uses to describe his own deep sense of dis-ease has only come into popular parlance over the past two decades, it could also, perhaps, be used retrospectively to describe the problems leading to Abel's alcoholism in *House Made of Dawn*. Turning to a Cherokee doctor's account of why there remains a high incidence of alcoholism in contemporary Native American communities helps us understand why images of drinking and alcohol abuse are so common in Native American literature. Dale Walker comments:

> There is tremendous pressure in this country to conform. And when a group like the Indian doesn't, there's a sense of failure. Wouldn't it be nice if [non-Indians] were right that Indian alcoholism is a genetic weakness? This ignores their tremendous cultural depression over many, many years. Their alcohol problems are huge. But the reasons are so perplexing. You hear … the sadness. (Quoted in Utter, p. 189)

The 'sadness' to which Walker alludes is found in much contemporary Native American literature, and particularly in representations of male characters. One has only to think of Abel and Benally in Momaday's *House Made of Dawn*, the World War II veterans of Leslie Marmon Silko's *Ceremony*, the nameless narrator of James Welch's *Winter in the Blood*, Gordie Kashpaw in Louise Erdrich's

Love Medicine, and the young men of the Spokane Reservation in Alexie's *The Lone Ranger and Tonto Fistfight in Heaven* as well as *Reservation Blues* to find characters struggling with the demons of alcohol and drug dependency. Some of these characters are depicted being pushed to extremes of violent behaviour, such as Emo in *Ceremony* when he murders Harley in the harrowing scene set at a disused uranium mine towards the end of the novel, or Junior Polatkin in *Reservation Blues* who climbs to the top of a water tower to put a shotgun to his mouth when in the aftermath of Coyote Springs's commercial failure he is no longer able to compensate for his deep-set sense of personal despair through the temporary salvation of alcohol. Obviously it would be erroneous to suggest that such grim images of social alienation predominate in Native American literature, and *Reservation Blues* is a case in point. For in the aftermath of Junior's suicide he returns in ghostly form, like a character come back from the dead in a low-budget horror film, to resume his friendship with Victor, his erstwhile colleague in the band. Humour, again, compensates for the painful realities depicted in the novel.

Investigating further

A great wealth of information on Native American cultures is available to students of literature who are also willing to read historical and anthropological sources on Native Americans. In addition, to even come close to an understanding of contemporary Native American literature it is important to enter into some comprehension of how modern writers use elements of the oral tradition in their work. A large amount of information about tribal stories, cosmologies and traditional livelihoods can be gleaned from works of fiction in which elements of the oral tradition are conspicuously featured, such as Leslie Marmon Silko's *Ceremony* (1977) and James Welch's *Fools Crow* (1986). Native Americans have been much represented in art, photography and film. Through viewing visual images with a critical eye, one quickly becomes aware of the ways in which through a tradition lasting since the early stages of European colonisation of the Americas, Indians have been constructed as 'savage' others in relation to 'civilised' whites.

While the publication of critical studies of Native American fiction has accelerated in recent years, it is important to note that currently much of the most up-to-date critical assessment is to be found in journals rather than books. In the Annotated Bibliography readers will find suggestions for full-length book studies of Native American literature. Note that some of these studies consider autobiography and poetry alongside fiction – hardly surprising when one considers the large proportion of Native writers who have published separate volumes of autobiography, fiction and/or poetry, or even blended all three genres together (along, sometimes, with art and photography) in certain texts (as in Leslie Marmon Silko's *Storyteller*). Articles on Native American literature feature in specialist journals such as *American Indian Culture and Research Journal*, *American Indian Quarterly*, *Studies in American Indian Literature*, *MELUS* (*Multi-Ethnic Literatures of the United States*) and *Wicazo Sa Review*. Critical discussion of Native writers is also featured in major American literature journals such as *American Literature*, *American Literary History* and *Arizona Quarterly* as well as in more narrowly defined journals such as *Journal of the Southwest* and *Western American Literature*. In addition, studies of individual Native American authors are featured in the 'Western Writers' series published by Boise State University Press.

Annotated short bibliography

Fiction

Alexie, Sherman, *Indian Killer* (Random House, 1997)
    Focusing on the character of an urban Indian brought up by adoptive white parents, this murder mystery cuts to the heart of contemporary debates about ethnicity and identity.
Erdrich, Louise, *Love Medicine* (HarperCollins, rev. edn., 1993)
    A powerful novel featuring multiple narrators who tell interweaving stories about their lives on and about a Chippewa reservation in North Dakota.
Hogan, Linda, *Mean Spirit* (Atheneum, 1990)
    Tells of how Osage Indians, after the discovery of oil fields on their reservation, endured a campaign of racial abuse from whites who coveted their lands and would murder Osages to possess them.

King, Thomas, *Green Grass, Running Water* (1993; Bantam, 1994)

    A comic novel featuring the trickster Coyote and a host of memorable characters heading for the Sun Dance gathering at a Blackfeet reservation in Canada.

McNickle, D'Arcy, *The Surrounded* (1936; University of New Mexico Press, 1978)

    A simply told but complex story of a young man of mixed Indian and European ancestry who becomes estranged from both the tribal community and white society.

Momaday, N. Scott, *The Ancient Child* (HarperCollins, 1990)

    The author's second novel combines tribal myth, Wild West lore and a contemporary setting to tell the story of how an Indian male born away from the reservation returns to tribal lands and becomes identified with the bear-boy of tribal storytelling.

Mourning Dove (Humishuma/Christine Quintasket), *Cogowea: The Half-Blood* (1927; University of Nebraska Press, 1981)

    The first novel written by a Native American woman writer. Flawed and fascinating.

Silko, Leslie Marmon, *Ceremony* (1977; Penguin, 1986)

    A key text. The novel interweaves narrative prose with oral poetry to dramatise the alienation and homecoming of its protagonist, Tayo, a veteran of World War II.

Vizenor, Gerald, *Bearheart: The Heirship Chronicles* (1979; University of Minnesota Press, 1990)

    A Rabelaisian novel that features a host of intriguing and bizarre characters travelling through the US in an oil-starved future.

Welch, James, *Fools Crow* (1986; New York: Penguin, 1987)

    Set in the 1870s, the decade Blackfeet Indians lost their autonomy on the northern Plains due to disease and US military pressure. A deeply moving yet ultimately uplifting story of a culture in transition.

Secondary sources

Allen, Paula Gunn, *The Sacred Hoop: Recovering the Feminine in American Indian Traditions* (Beacon Press, 1986)

    A highly informative – and somewhat controversial – series of essays that argues for a 'gynocratic' approach to the understanding of Native American cultures, religions and literature.

Berkhofer, Robert, *The White Man's Indian: Images of the American Indian from Columbus to the Present* (Random House, 1979)

Full of insights into the changing iconography of the Indian. Analyses a wide body of Euro-American representations, including literature, art and philosophy.

Castro, Michael, *Interpreting the Indian: Twentieth-Century Poets and the Native American* (University of New Mexico Press, 1983)

Although it focuses on poetry by non-Indians, this study provides an intelligent analysis of issues of translation and a brief but informative discussion of contemporary Native American literature.

Coltelli, Laura, ed., *Winged Words: American Indian Writers Speak* (University of Nebraska Press, 1990)

A useful series of interviews with major writers, such as Erdrich, Momaday, Silko and Welch.

Handbook of North American Indians, Vols. 1–20 (in progress), general ed. William C. Sturtevant (Smithsonian Institution Press, 1978 on-going)

A monumental series of volumes written by anthropologists, archaeologists and historians which provides a comprehensive understanding of Native American cultures.

Krupat, Arnold, *The Voice in the Margin: Native American Literature and the Canon* (University of California Press, 1989)

A key critical text. Provides an extended discussion of literary traditions in the US and argues for the incorporation of Native American texts in the literary canon.

Krupat, Arnold, ed., *New Voices in Native American Literary Criticism* (Smithsonian Institution Press, 1993)

An impressive range of well-written essays on fiction, poetry and oral literature.

Lincoln, Kenneth, *Ind'n Humor: Bicultural Play in Native America* (Oxford University Press, 1993)

An idiosyncratic and valuable discussion of the uses of humour in Native American literature and culture.

Pearce, Roy Harvey, *Savagism and Civilization* (1953; University of California Press, 1988)

An early intellectual history of Euro-American representations of the Indian. Essential reading.

Sarris, Greg, *Keeping Slug Woman Alive: A Holistic Approach to American Indian Texts* (University of California Press, 1993)

Combines autobiographical and critical writing to provide a series of meditations on cross-cultural communication.

Vizenor, Gerald, *Manifest Manners: Postindian Warriors of Survivance* (Wesleyan University Press, 1994)

Vizenor revels in demythologising the epistemological basis on which 'Indians' are understood. Challenging and essential reading.

Vizenor, Gerald, ed., *Narrative Chance: Postmodern Discourses on Native American Indian Literatures* (University of New Mexico Press, 1989)

An intriguing collection of essays that foregrounds post-structuralist and post-modern approaches to the study of Native American literature.

Wiget, Andrew, *Native American Literature* (Twayne, 1985)

One of the earliest surveys of Native American writing. Provides many valuable insights.

Wiget, Andrew, ed., *Dictionary of Native American Literature* (Garland, 1994)

Provides a well-balanced and informative series of essays on oral literatures and both historical and contemporary literature.

Wilson, James, *The Earth Shall Weep: A History of Native America* (Picador, 1999)

A comprehensive and well-written narrative history of Native Americans by an author who has also made television documentaries about Canadian and US Indian cultures.

3

African American fiction

Maria Lauret

Overview and antecedents: the evolution of African American fiction

Both of the major anthologies of African American literature published in the late 1990s, *The Norton Anthology of African American Literature* and *Call and Response: The Riverside Anthology of the African American Literary Tradition* come with a CD of songs, political speeches, and poems read aloud to supplement the written word. We might wonder why the editors found it necessary to do such a thing – after all, literary texts are usually assumed to be able to stand on their own feet and to function in their own right as forms of cultural expression. Yet in the case of African American literature this is both true and false: true, in the sense that African American novels, poems and plays were composed as written texts to be read, but false because another part of what is regarded as the African American literary tradition consists of, or derives from, oral forms such as songs or folktales or sermons which were meant to be heard and responded to there and then; that is, as they were being performed. 'Performed' here may even be the wrong term to use, for the songs and speeches, stories and verbal competitions had a use-value in African American daily life that was not primarily theatrical or aesthetic, but rather part of worship or work practices, the education of the young, or a means of maintaining community life. For much of literary history these 'vernacular texts' as they are called, these creative expressions from everyday life, did not have the status of literature at all – indeed, they were hardly recognised as a part of culture either by white or by black Americans. What we are faced with then from the outset in exploring African American literature are at least two strands of cultural production: one which is oral and performative (in the broad sense of having an element of improvisation in it which is unique to the occasion and which anticipates and demands a response from the audience) and another which is self-consciously part of a written tradition, designed to appear in print for an anonymous readership which is often interracial. All of these qualities in their opposing pairs (audience present and known or not, flexible performance versus stable and fixed printed form, community setting or public sphere, use-value or aesthetic appeal) are important in the interpretation of African American literature, as we shall see. It is equally important to realise however that these are not separate traditions, or forms of 'high' and 'low' culture which never mix. Rather, they are streams which at times have been quite separate, but at other times have merged in single texts, in a particular author's work, or in a whole literary movement – such as the Harlem Renaissance in the 1920s for example, or black women's writing since the 1970s. George Lipsitz puts this well when he writes that

> to talk about African-American writing separate from other forms of cultural expression misrepresents the guiding aesthetic behind black literature. Popular speech informs the poetry of Paul Laurence Dunbar and Langston Hughes, while blues and jazz influences pervade the writing of Ellison and Ishmael Reed … Toni Morrison's magnificent novels carry this inter-textuality and inter-referentiality to extraordinary heights, writing the history of an entire community through its stories and songs, through its rhymes and remedies. ('Race and Racism', in Mick Gidley, ed. *Modern American Culture: An Introduction*, Longman, 1993, p. 136)

We see the two strands of African American literary expression, the oral/musical and the written/literary, represented from the very beginning in the work of the first two black American poets, both of whom were women. Lucy Terry's 'Bars Fight' was a ballad, meant to be sung, about an Indian ambush on whites in Massachusetts in the mid-eighteenth century. 'Bars Fight' did not evince a distinctly African American presence, which immediately raises the question of what counts as African American literature: is black authorship enough? Phillis Wheatley, who was the first published African American poet, did include in her *Poems on Various Subjects, Religious and Moral* the now (in)famous 'On Being Brought from Africa to America'. This startling poem constructed the experience of slavery in an apparently positive light, because the poet credited America with saving her 'benighted soul' through conversion to Christianity. On more careful reading however it becomes clear that Wheatley protested white prejudice in this poem ('some view our sable race with scornful eye') and recognised the problem of her own credibility in the eyes of her reading public, which was inevitably white, educated, and very likely of the slaveholding persuasion ('On Being Brought From Africa to America' (1773) in Henry Louis Gates Jr. and Nellie Y. McKay, eds, *The Norton Anthology of African American Literature*, W.W. Norton 1997, p. 171). This is why her poems were published in Britain in 1773 preceded by various testimonials from prominent Boston dignitaries as well as from her master, John Wheatley, to prove their authenticity. As we shall see, this was to become the convention of publishing slave-narratives too, and even if by the early twentieth century African American writers did not need such patronage from whites anymore to be believed, they nevertheless still had to depend on endorsements by white critics at times to find their reading public. The structures of slavery and racism, in other words, cast their shadow long and wide for two centuries of African American cultural production, making it difficult for black writers to work with the measure of artistic freedom, the assumption of legitimacy, and the anticipation of recognition that white writers tend to take for granted.

The early to mid-nineteenth century

The first of the published slave-narrative writers therefore titled his autobiography *The Interesting Narrative of the Life of Olaudah Equiano, or Gustavus Vassa, the African, Written by Himself* (1789) to pre-empt incredulity at the fact that a black man could write his own story. Equiano's *Interesting Narrative* was unusual because it related,

like Wheatley's poem, the passage from Africa to America, something which is rare in the later, and better-known fugitive slave-narratives of the mid-nineteenth century. Unlike Wheatley, however,
Equiano made full use of his memories of Africa to depict a stark
contrast between the happiness of his childhood in (what is now)
Nigeria and the brutality, first of the Middle Passage and then of
slavery in colonial America and the Caribbean. Africa, in his autobiography, was not the 'pagan land' of Wheatley's poem, but the home
country whose manners and customs Equiano wanted to explain and
compare with the unChristian European *mores* of slavery in America. As his title indicates, Equiano was well aware of the erasure of
identity and individuality that the slave system was designed to
accomplish in its subjects: by naming himself twice – Equiano and
Vassa – he highlighted the doubleness of the slave's existence as both
self and property, a property named by the master.

It is also worth noting that Equiano designated himself 'an
African' in the title of his narrative and omitted the word 'slave'.
The significance of this becomes visible when we contrast Equiano's
title with that of what is probably the most famous nineteenth century African American text: *The Narrative of Frederick Douglass, an
American Slave, Written by Himself* (1845). Douglass's *Narrative*,
like Equiano's, is a vociferous and eloquent protest against slavery,
but unlike Equiano, who was writing in colonial times, Douglass
addressed the post-revolutionary United States government. By the
mid-nineteenth century the movement for the abolition of slavery
was gathering pace and abolitionist leaders such as William Lloyd
Garrison, impressed by Douglass's skills as a public speaker at a
protest meeting, encouraged him to act as a lecturing agent for the
Massachusetts Anti-Slavery Society. In this political, campaigning
context, then, it was important that the *Narrative* was read as that of
'an American slave', and the very structure, style and force of Douglass's autobiography are designed to reflect the reality *and* the
absurdity of that condition for one so eloquent, so cultured, and so
rational as the text revealed its author to be. A rip-roaring read in the
best tradition of the picaresque novel, *The Narrative of Frederick
Douglass* was a highly effective political tract, because Douglass continually analysed and commented on the events of his life as a slave
and of his escape to the North, as a political philosopher would.

Douglass distinguished between physical/economic slavery on one hand and psychic bondage on the other, and emphasised the importance of acts of resistance, however small, in order for the slave to retain his sense of personhood and spiritual freedom. The genius of Douglass's reasoning in the *Narrative* and also in a speech entitled 'What to the Slave is the Fourth of July?' (1852) was his ability to turn American rhetoric of democracy against itself, as Martin Luther King was to do a hundred years later. Independence Day, Douglass argued, exists to celebrate the founding of a republic and a constitution which says that 'all men are created equal' yet which, at the same time, holds in bondage 'a *seventh part* of the inhabitants of your country' ('What To the Slave Is the Fourth of July?', in Gates and McKay, eds, *The Norton Anthology of African American Literature*, p. 389). Note that he said 'your country', not 'our country', thereby exempting himself from membership of a nation which would not have him as a citizen, and of which he did not want membership unless and until the injustice of slavery were redressed.

Douglass, like Equiano and Wheatley, disproved in the very act of writing the racist adage that African Americans were not fit for anything other than to serve whites as beasts of burden. Yet his perspective was also a particularly masculine one which sought to meet its white readers on their own ground: that of reason, masculine pride, rhetorical skill and physical prowess. Harriet Jacobs's *Incidents in the Life of a Slave Girl*, written and published in 1861 under the pseudonym Linda Brent, complemented Douglass's *Narrative* because it came from a female perspective and privileged the bond between slaves and their children rather than the autonomous individual, as in Douglass's case. In so doing she appealed to the hearts as well as the minds of her intended readership. Jacobs's story, also framed by prefaces and testimonies of authenticity from white abolitionists like Amy Post and Lydia Maria Child, exemplified what has become known as the condition of double jeopardy: the protagonist Linda Brent suffers both as a slave and as a woman. The very reason why Jacobs did not publish under her own name had to do with the fact that she was a woman, not – as in England at the time – because women were not supposed to write, but because she knew from experience that black women under slavery were not in a position to protect their virtue from the advances, or assaults, of white men. Like Douglass, Jacobs was an expert at turning the values of her readers against themselves: if white women valued chastity and motherhood, how could they read Linda Brent's predicament (she becomes pregnant by a white man whom she has taken as a lover in order to protect herself from being raped by her owner) and still condone slavery? The subtext, of course, involved another question: how could white women condone the abuse of black women's bodies as labourers and mistresses, breeders of slaves and sexual servants, by their own husbands, their own fathers, their own brothers? Pointedly, Jacobs ended *Incidents* with a self-conscious reference to the conventions of nineteenth-century women's writing: 'Reader, my story ends with freedom; not in the usual way, with marriage' and she emphasised in the final lines both her gratitude to her grandmother and the fact that her struggle was fought for the sake of her children (*Incidents in the Life of a Slave Girl*, in Gates and McKay, eds, *The Norton Anthology of African American Literature*, p. 245). In privileging the connection between the generations, Jacobs thus restated an important theme in African American literature: that of family, and of family continuity in a history which has often made such continuity impossible, starting with the severing of the first link: that between the African mother and the black American child.

Douglass's and Jacobs's fugitive slave-narratives are regarded as the highest achievements in the genre, because they combined literary skill with didactic and rhetorical effectiveness in the abolitionist cause. Both texts continue to capture the reader's imagination *as stories* and it is because of this literary achievement that these self-representations enlist the reader's sympathy on their authors' side. Douglass and Jacobs did, however, have precursors in other African American writers who were not slaves, but who made their mark on the tradition as powerful political orators and essayists. Free blacks in the North such as Maria Stewart (*Religion and the Pure Principles of Morality, the Sure Foundation on Which We Must Build* (1831)), David Walker (*Appeal in Four Articles; Together with a Preamble, to the Coloured Citizens of the World, but in Particular and Very Expressly, to Those of the United States* (1829)) and Martin Delany (*The Condition, Elevation, Emigration and Destiny of the Colored People of the United States, Politically Considered* (1852)) published searing indictments of American democracy. Walker's *Appeal* was widely thought to have inspired Nat Turner's slave rebellion in 1831 and *The Confessions of Nat Turner*, written by Thomas Gray (a member of the Court which condemned Turner to death), far from belittling the motivation and the person of Nat Turner as intended, instead made his political voice and his spiritual justification for the uprising come through loud and clear. Delany and Walker were the first proponents of what was to become known as black nationalism, which insists on autonomy rather than integration, self-assertion, self-education, and black ownership of the means of production rather than dependence on whites. If all this sounds familiar from modern times, it is because such ideas were advocated by black nationalists in the 1960s too. And this is not the only echo of nine-teenth-century thought that resounded still a century later. Perhaps the most famous orator of the period, at least retrospectively, was Sojourner Truth, whose 1851 'Aren't I a woman?' speech can be regarded as the foundation of a black feminist discourse that is still pertinent today.

The late nineteenth century

With Sojourner Truth, who was illiterate and whose speeches were transcribed by white women's rights advocates, we return to the oral and musical tradition of spirituals, folktales and work songs which formed such a vital part of slave culture. Contemporary African American writers continue to draw on this musical and imaginative heritage of vernacular practices. Trickster tales appear in the work of Toni Morrison, Ishmael Reed and Walter Mosley, just as James Baldwin and Alice Walker in their early work often quote the spiri-tuals which inspired the Civil Rights movement also. More famously still, the mutation of work-songs into the blues of the early twenti-eth century found its way into the poetry of the Harlem Renaissance and became a trope of celebration and mourning of the African American condition in the work of writers like Langston Hughes through to Gayl Jones. Before the Harlem Renaissance however, that is, before Zora Neale Hurston elevated the black vernacular to a truly literary language in *Their Eyes Were Watching God*, two African American writers saw the potential of folk culture as an aesthetic resource: the novelist and short story writer Charles W. Chesnutt, and the poet Paul Laurence Dunbar. Both encountered the problem that Zora Neale Hurston would run into later on: how could they represent the vernacular voice of the people without being taken to pander to racist stereotypes, especially in a literary environment where Joel Chandler Harris's Uncle Remus stories had already 'mined' slave culture for the entertainment of a white reading public? Chesnutt's answer, for example in the famous story 'The Goophered Grapevine' (1887), was to use a device in which the framing narrator's conventional style is contrasted with the lively storytelling of the framed narrator, an ex-slave who explains the workings of conjuring or hoodoo in the vernacular. Dunbar's strategy as a poet was somewhat different: his aesthetic agenda for the valorisation of folk culture becomes clear only in the juxtaposition of his vernacular and high literary poems. 'When Malindy Sings' (1903), for example, celebrates the beauty of a black woman's voice: 'Oh, hit's sweetah dan de music/ of an edicated band' ('When Malindy Sings', in Gates and McKay, eds, *The Norton Anthology of African American Literature*, p. 894). But when this poem is read alongside the famous 'We Wear the Mask' ('We sing, but oh the clay is vile/ Beneath our feet, and long the mile/ But let the world dream otherwise/ We wear the mask'), the meaning of 'When Malindy Sings' is less 'sweet' and innocent than it might at first appear ('We Wear the Mask' (1896), in Gates and McKay, eds, *The Norton Anthology of African American Literature*, p. 896).

This drawing on specifically African American vernacular forms and tropes, however, was rather untypical of nineteenth-century African American writing. Black authors who aimed to advance the black cause usually observed the polite manners of conventional literary forms and wrote in standard American English. The first two novels of the African American tradition, William Wells Brown's *Clotel, or, The President's Daughter* of 1853 and Harriet E. Wilson's *Our Nig* of 1859, both wore the mask of conventionality, but only in form, not content – in fact, they made few concessions to a white readership. *Clotel* frequently quotes the Declaration of Independence to expose the hypocrisy of the United States government during slavery. The story concerns the degradation of the eponymous heroine, who is the daughter of Thomas Jefferson by one of his slaves. Although Clotel is as white as any free white woman, she is, of course, not free. One of many mixed race, white-looking, virtuous and beautiful heroines in nineteenth-century literature, Clotel ends up committing suicide (she jumps into the Potomac river, in close proximity to the seat of government in Washington DC), thereby epitomising the plight of the 'tragic mulatta' who is caught between black and white worlds, mother and father, slavery and freedom. In *Our Nig or, Sketches from the Life of a Free Black, In a Two-Story White House, North Showing that Slavery's Shadows Fall Even There By 'Our Nig'*, the protagonist Frado's tragedy was represented quite differently. Wilson made it clear in her title that Frado, a free black woman whom the white Bellmont family in the novel refer to as 'our nig', is both object of scorn and yet the subject of her own narrative. In the preface Wilson explained that Our Nig writes this story in order to provide for herself and her child, but in the process she exposes Northern racism – especially that of white women – in no uncertain terms. The double-voiced threat of Our Nig's authorship becomes clear at the end, when the narrator states that 'Frado has passed from their [the Bellmonts's] memories ... but she will never cease to track them till beyond mortal vision' (*Our Nig*, ed. R. J. Ellis, Trent Editions, 1998, p. 70). This last line promises a vengeful haunting of which the text itself is the material embodiment.

Writing is fighting, as Ishmael Reed would say more than a hundred years later, and if anything could sum up what African American literacy meant in the nineteenth century (and beyond), it would be this. Harriet Wilson knew it, as did Frances Ellen Watkins Harper, who expressed the same insight in a rather more genteel way in *Iola Leroy, or, Shadows Uplifted* of 1892. Adopting the same didactic method that William Wells Brown employed in *Clotel*, Harper interspersed the narrative action with political exposés in which she allowed her characters to discuss the race question. On one such occasion, the heroine Iola – again a white-looking, beautiful mulatta of virtuous character and possessed of great social decorum – voices her author's views on the importance of writing in the cause of racial uplift:

> 'Our enemies have the ear of the world, *and they can depict us just as they please.*'
> 'That is true ... but out of the race must come its own defenders. With

them the pen must be mightier than the sword. ... We cannot tell what
is in them until they express themselves.'
'Yes, and I think *there is a large amount of latent and undeveloped ability in the race*, which they will learn to use for their own benefit.' (my
emphasis) (*Iola Leroy*, ed. Hazel Carby, Beacon Press, 1987, pp.
115–16)

For Harper, as for Pauline Hopkins and a host of other women intellectuals who were involved in racial uplift, the temperance movement, and women's rights, that 'latent and undeveloped ability'
primarily concerned the potential of young black women. *Iola
Leroy*, as Hazel Carby explains, was therefore addressed to such
young women and not particularly to an interracial readership. The
use of a mulatta protagonist, she adds, was not 'a gesture of acquies-
cence to a racist social order' as is often supposed, but rather a way
of enabling the exploration of interracial social relations (which Jim
Crow laws and social convention rendered otherwise virtually
impossible) and at the same time highlighting the sexual exploitation
of black women by white men (Hazel Carby, 'Introduction', in *Iola
Leroy*, p. xxi). Iola has a fictional twin sister in Sappho Clark, the
heroine of Pauline Hopkins's novel *Contending Forces*, published in
1900. Again the tragic mulatta's plight is under discussion here, literally so as, in the famous chapter 'The Sewing Circle', a young
woman's view that the 'poor mulatto' is 'despised by the blacks of his
own race, scorned by the whites!' is countered by the elder Mrs
Willis's enlightened opinion that 'the fate of the mulatto will be the
fate of the entire race. ... It is an incontrovertible truth that there is
no such thing as an unmixed black on the American continent' (*Contending Forces: a Romance Illustrative of Negro Life North and South*,
Oxford University Press, 1988, pp. 150–1). This is a fairly radical
statement to make, and it is indicative of Hopkins's advanced political views. Masked as a family saga, which begins in Bermuda in 1790
and ends on an ocean liner to Europe a century later, Hopkins's
novel offers a panoramic survey of African American history and
makes sure that the most important contours of African American
political thought are stitched in: the 'contending forces' of the title
are represented in the Harvard-educated Will Smith and the black
educator Dr Arthur B. Lewis, fairly transparent portraits of W. E. B.
Du Bois and Booker T. Washington, respectively.

The early twentieth century

Washington's *Up From Slavery* (1901) and Du Bois's *The Souls of Black Folk* (1903) are two of the most influential socio-political texts of the twentieth century. But whereas Washington proposed a model of racial dignity through self-reliance, epitomised in his famous dictum 'Cast down your bucket where you are', Du Bois demanded recognition and equality from white society (*Up From Slavery*, in *Three Negro Classics*, Avon Books, 1965, p. 147). 'The problem of the twentieth century is the problem of the color line', Du Bois wrote prophetically in the 'Forethought' to *The Souls of Black Folk* (*The Souls of Black Folk*, in *Three Negro Classics*, p. 213). Only a couple of pages later, he diagnosed African American cultural identity as a matter of double consciousness, which he explained as 'this sense of always looking at one's self through the eyes of others … an American, a Negro; two souls, two thoughts, two unreconciled strivings; two warring ideals in one dark body, whose dogged strength alone keeps it from being torn asunder' (*The Souls of Black Folk*, in *Three Negro Classics*, p. 215). With this concept, and with his cultural activism as founder of the influential magazine *The Crisis*, Du Bois in effect became the first African American cultural theorist, whose influence during the Harlem Renaissance of the 1920s and early 1930s was considerable.

Du Bois's essay 'Criteria for Negro Art' of 1926 gained its notoriety chiefly for the following lines: 'Thus all Art is propaganda and ever must be … whatever art I have for writing has been used always for propaganda for gaining the right of black folk to love and enjoy' ('Criteria for Negro Art', in Eric J. Sundquist, ed., *The Oxford W. E. B. Du Bois Reader*, Oxford University Press, 1996, p. 328). Du Bois's criterion for African American art was thus a political one. Without neglecting aesthetic standards, he nevertheless felt that even if African Americans were to receive the same rights as those accorded to white American citizens, the legacy of slavery would still mean that they had different dreams, different aspirations for artistic expression. In his argument for cultural memory to be kept alive and to be used in the service of black emancipation, Du Bois differed from Alain Locke, another of the early black literary theorists. In 1925 Locke had asserted in his essay 'The New Negro', that African

American art should break with the past and confidently stride into an urban modernity no longer bound by the race problem. 'The Negro', Locke wrote, 'has American wants, American ideas' and progress was to be expected from inter-racial understanding through artistic work, from 'carefully maintained contacts of the enlightened minorities of both race groups' ('The New Negro', in Alain Locke, ed., *The New Negro: Voices of the Harlem Renaissance*, Atheneum, 1992, pp. 11–12; p. 9).

'The New Negro' is often regarded as the manifesto for the movement of black writers, intellectuals, painters, sculptors, actors and musicians in the 1920s and 1930s that became known as the Harlem Renaissance. Both Du Bois and Locke were instrumental in shaping this movement through their roles as mentors to young writers, editors of literary magazines, and their contacts with publishers. Although several white people such as Carl van Vechten and Mrs Rufus Osgood Mason were also involved in encouraging and funding black art, the African American press and the literary salons hosted by A'Lelia Walker and Jessie Redmon Fauset were crucial in creating an African American public sphere. It is important, therefore, to understand that Locke and Du Bois's disagreement was not about an authentic black versus a whitified art-for-art's sake artistic creed, but rather that it was a complex difference of opinion over African American cultural politics. The Renaissance was never a unified phenomenon but consisted more in a groundswell of artistic activity which converged in a particular time and place. Beginning after the First World War, when black veterans marched through the streets of Harlem in a victory parade, and ending in the mid 1930s as a result of the Depression, the Harlem Renaissance is commonly understood to have flowered as a result of the Great Migration which brought hundreds of thousands of African Americans from the Jim Crow South to the urban centres of the North. Harlem quickly became the negro capital of the world, as Claude McKay put it, inhabited by blacks for whom Harlem became a haven of safety at a time of vicious race-riots elsewhere in the country, and visited by white people who came to dance, drink, and generally to let their hair down. This was also the time of Prohibition, after all, and it was the era of untrammelled business expansion for moneyed white America. Music, of course, was the main attraction: jazz and blues

performers found an avid audience in Harlem, but literature also
flourished, first among older writers who were inspired by a high literary Romanticism and then among a younger generation who took
their aesthetic cues from the culture of the streets and clubs. Literary production was already underway when Locke and Du Bois
wrote their theoretical statements; Claude McKay's famous militant
poem 'If We Must Die' for example dates from 1919 and Jean
Toomer's *Cane* was published in 1923. *Cane* and 'If We Must Die'
captured the spirit of the Harlem Renaissance in very different ways.
Cane, in its formal mixture of prose, poetry and drama and its
textual journey from South to North and back again, examined
African American identity through the experience of migration.
Drawing on slave spirituals as well as European modernism (Imag-
ism), it explored African American gender relations, the opposition
between country and city, as well as the legacy of slavery and the
alienation of modernity to great aesthetic effect. McKay's poem, by
contrast, was written in response to the racist riots which broke out
in the Red Summer of 1919, and called in a highly conventional
poetic form for the 'we' in the poem, who are under attack, to fight
back. He never mentions race explicitly, however. Another well-
known poem of the mid 1920s, Langston Hughes's 'The Weary
Blues' (1925), was perhaps even more representative of the Harlem
aesthetic, because Hughes used blues and jazz rhythms and themes
in his work, thereby widening the appeal of his poetry to include
working class black people, and creating a poetic form in keeping
with his leftist political views. 'Jazz to me is one of the inherent
expressions of Negro life in America', Hughes wrote in the essay
'The Negro Artist and the Racial Mountain' , thereby signalling his
dissension from the aesthetic prescriptions of the older generation
in demanding the freedom to write as he chose, without concessions
to bourgeois respectability or white approval ('The Negro Artist and
the Racial Mountain' (1926), in Gates and McKay, eds, *The Norton
Anthology of African American Literature*, p. 1270). And indeed there
were intellectuals of the Harlem Renaissance whose agenda of 'racial
uplift', in the mould of earlier writers like Frances Ellen Watkins
Harper and Pauline Hopkins, demanded convention and
respectability in life as in letters. Often they did so, as Hughes
realised, at the expense of their working-class characters and at the

cost of ignoring the issue of black sexuality in their work. What Hughes himself ignored, however, was that women writers of the turn of the century had good reason to be silent on matters sexual, because black women were still suffering from the racist slur, propagated under slavery, that they were by nature lascivious creatures. Harlem Renaissance women writers like Jessie Fauset and Nella Larsen, who did explore women's sexuality in their work, were still constrained by that legacy, and although they used indisputably bourgeois settings they nevertheless were radicals in their own way by daring to address the issue at all. Renaissance women writers, therefore, were hardly the enemy, as indeed Hughes and his friends Wallace Thurman and Richard Bruce Nugent found out when their new literary magazine *Fire!!!* was thrashed by Du Bois and others in the black press, because they deemed it decadent and vulgar. Nugent's story 'Smoke, Lilies and Jade' (1926) had a large part to play in the *Fire!!!* controversy. Because it was a story of homoerotic desire, drugs and drink in the tradition of Oscar Wilde, it attracted the opprobrium of those race-leaders for whom respectability was a prime concern.

Zora Neale Hurston was also involved in *Fire!!!*, but her best-known work was not published until 1937. *Their Eyes Were Watching God* refreshed the parts previous black women writers had not been able to reach, in that it explored black women's identity through sexual desire, romance and women's friendship as well as giving the black vernacular a highly poetic and lyrical voice. Janie Starks's journey of self-discovery was, therefore, truly a modern story which validated black folk culture as much as black women's autonomy; Alice Walker's novel *The Color Purple* is but one of many more recent black feminist texts to pay homage to Hurston's creative genius.

The mid-twentieth century

Not everybody was so enchanted with *Their Eyes Were Watching God* as later writers like Walker would be, however. Richard Wright accused Hurston of pandering to white tastes in her stereotypical portrayal of 'laughing darkies' telling stories on the front porch. But then Wright's aesthetic philosophy, as laid down in his essay 'Blueprint for Negro Writing' of 1937, was urban and Marxist in outlook;

his novel *Native Son* (1940) exemplified his notion of the African American writer's social consciousness and responsibility to lay 'bare the skeleton of society ... [and] to plant flesh upon those bones out of his will to live' ('Blueprint for Negro Writing', in Gates and McKay, eds, *The Norton Anthology of African American Literature*, p. 1385). Bigger Thomas, Wright's protagonist, is caught on all sides by the forces of poverty in the urban ghetto and his story is a gripping and powerful indictment of American society. Wright locks the reader into Bigger's claustrophobic consciousness as the events of his young life roll inexorably towards their conclusion – fittingly, in prison, awaiting execution for the murder of a white woman. *Native Son* was to become a touchstone for later African American writers, whether they took it as a model for politically engaged writing, as the Black Arts movement of the 1960s did, or whether they rejected it as too restrictive for black self-expression, as did Ralph Ellison and James Baldwin in the 1940s and 1950s. Before that Ann Petry's *The Street* (1946), a novel about a single mother and her young son in Harlem during the Depression, had both echoed and revised Richard Wright's concerns in *Native Son*. Echoed, in that Petry's realist exploration of a working-class woman's existence in the urban ghetto followed Wright's lead both formally and politically: Lutie Johnson fails to realise her modest dreams of providing for herself and her son because of the same class- and race-determinants that Wright dissected in his novel. But Petry also took issue with Wright in showing a woman's additional vulnerability through her role as a single mother and as a sexually objectified woman. In this way, Petry exposed – by implication only – Wright's misogyny and that of many other African American men writers, until the advent of black feminism in the 1970s.

Naturalism and realism were not the only modes of representation prevalent during the period between the Harlem Renaissance and the 1960s, however, and neither was the novel. The poet Gwendolyn Brooks had a distinguished career from the 1940s onwards, and she was awarded the Pulitzer Prize for her collection *Annie Allen* in 1950. Lorraine Hansberry was likewise celebrated in her day, chiefly for her play *A Raisin in the Sun* of 1959. It is perhaps worth noting, therefore, that both women were writing to critical acclaim long before the current vogue for black women's fiction, although undoubtedly the relative lack of attention for Brooks and Hansberry today is also a reflection of their time, the time when Ralph Ellison and James Baldwin came to prominence as major essayists and novelists who made it into the American mainstream. Ellison's *Invisible Man* of 1952 still stands, with *Native Son*, as a classic text that no course in American literature of the twentieth century can do without. In that novel Ellison devised a whole new brand of African American writing, drawing on trickster tales and the blues as much as on Dostoevsky and European modernism, and presenting a run-through of African American race-thinking from Booker T. Washington to Marcus Garvey in a highly satirical vein. Ellison broke with the realist mould that Richard Wright had promoted in the 1930s, and forged his own brand of an African American modernism instead. James Baldwin likewise took issue with what he saw as the restrictive nature of Wright's 'Blueprint', notably in the essay 'Everybody's Protest Novel' of 1949. Baldwin was involved with the Civil Rights movement but had few illusions about the future of race relations in the United States. In his most eloquent and succinct volume of essays *The Fire Next Time*, he argued in his characteristic autobiographical voice and biblically inflected language that 100 years after emancipation white America had still not redeemed itself for slavery. If the Civil Rights movement failed, there would be 'no more water, the fire next time!' But if this sounds militant, it is not what Baldwin is chiefly known for today. Although he was not the first African American gay writer, his novels *Giovanni's Room* (1956) and *Another Country* (1962) openly addressed issues of black sexuality. Baldwin's work provided an analysis of race- and sexual oppression which shows astutely how black masculinity – gay and straight – is caught in the sexual myths of phallic power, myths which legitimised lynching earlier in the century and served as a projection of white men's insecurity and white women's fear and desire simultaneously. During the 1960s and 1970s however, Baldwin's rejection of black nationalism, his voluntary exile in Europe and the homophobia which was rife among African American activists (explicit and writ large in Eldridge Cleaver's essay on Baldwin and Wright in *Soul on Ice* (1968)) earned him the opprobrium of the Black Arts movement, to which we turn our attention next.

The 1960s

Twentieth-century African American literary history seems to move in cycles: just as the Harlem Renaissance was rejected, if not quite forgotten, by the realist writers of the 1940s and 1950s, so also did Ellison and Baldwin in turn wage an Oedipal battle with Richard Wright, only to see the Black Arts movement of the 1960s revive Wright and Langston Hughes as precursors to the Black aesthetic. Similarly, the writers of the Harlem Renaissance had had an interest, however ambivalent, in the notion of Africa as a homeland, which was rejected by the next generation and then again embraced by sixties radicals. In part the renewed interest in Africa came about because Africa itself had changed: many of the West African states which had been devastated by the slave trade and colonialism became independent in the late 1950s and early 1960s, and there was a sense of optimism about post-colonial black self-government. In part also the model of African independence provided political activists in the United States with a new theory of their own position: African Americans now came to conceive of themselves as an internally colonised nation engaged in a struggle for liberation. Culture was a vital battleground for independence: instead of seizing land and means of production – hardly a viable option – African Americans wanted to 'de-Americanise' their minds, their identities, their very notion of self. This entailed a searing critique of Western values and a concomitant celebration of Africanness, or of African Americanness, with a strong emphasis on 'indigenous' cultural forms like blues, jazz, and bebop. It also generated a mode of writing which took its inspiration from urban street culture and was designed to appeal to ordinary black people. The 1960s then became the era of black pride, of the founding of black studies departments in universities, of slogans like 'Black Power' and 'Black is beautiful', brought together in a new brand of cultural nationalism which was articulated by the theorists, poets and playwrights of the Black Arts movement. Preceded by the music and the political speeches of the Civil Rights movement (which did not really spawn a literature of its own), *The Autobiography of Malcolm X*, as dictated to Alex Haley (1965), was perhaps the first black text to articulate the righteous anger of young African Americans at the slow pace of progress and their desire for greater militancy. The literature and theory of the Black Arts movement followed this up by putting activism centre stage. As in the Harlem Renaissance, poets, playwrights and critics considered themselves part of a collective cultural effort for the benefit of black people in America; unlike the Harlem Renaissance this effort was to be explicitly allied with political agitation. Larry Neal put this very clearly in the opening paragraph of his essay 'The Black Arts Movement' of 1968: 'The Black Arts and the Black Power concept both relate broadly to the Afro-American's desire for self-determination and nationhood. Both concepts are nationalistic' ('The Black Arts Movement', in Gates and McKay, eds, *The Norton Anthology of African American Literature*, p. 1960). What Neal stressed here, and it is an important distinction to make, was that black art of the 1960s was not protest writing so much as an affirmative mode of cultural representation. It was not concerned with a white audience that needed to be persuaded of the justice of the African American cause, but addressed to black people whose lives and self-image should be enhanced by African American cultural production. If the connection with the vernacular tradition had been somewhat lost in the 1940s and 1950s, it was re-established and updated by poets and playwrights like Sonia Sanchez, Nikki Giovanni, Haki Madhubuti and – perhaps most of all – Amiri Baraka, who all employed urban slang and jive-talk in their work, making it into a literary language that everybody (at least, everybody familiar with the culture) could understand. In addition, these writers tended to present their work in public performance and to distribute and publish it in unconventional ways: on street corners, at demonstrations, and in political magazines. Poetic language changed accordingly, as Amiri Baraka showed in his (in)famous poem 'Black Art' (1969). Poetry was now an incitement to use *words* as weapons: 'We want "poems that kill"/Assassin poems, Poems that shoot/guns', he wrote ('Black Art', in Gates and McKay, eds, *The Norton Anthology of African American Literature*, p. 1883). Perhaps because longer prose did not lend itself to performance and to the quick-fire political appeal that Black Arts proponents wanted from literature, few novels were written during this period. But the wheel turned again by the time the 1970s came around, when black women veterans of the Civil Rights and black nationalist movements began to write themselves into existence. Partly they did so in protest against the sexism of African American cultural-political activism of the 1960s, when race was the dominant concern and issues of gender, except insofar as they pertained to black masculinity, were regarded as divisive and white-identified. More importantly however, the black women writers of the 1970s wanted to forge a positive African American female identity, in concert with the new black feminism, and to make their voices heard in the novel.

The late twentieth century

Gloria Hull and her fellow editors put the dilemma facing black women very well, when they entitled their textbook of black women's studies *All the Men are Black, All the Women are White, But Some of Us are Brave*. Another, less polite way of putting this is that African American women had suffered from the double jeopardy of sexism in the black movements and racism in Women's Liberation. The remedy, as Toni Cade recognised in her preface to *The Black Woman*, a path-breaking anthology of poetry, short stories and essays published in 1970, was that women should now be 'turning toward each other', and this is exactly what African American women writers would do (Toni Cade, *The Black Woman: an Anthology*, New American Library, 1970, p. 7). Toni Cade turned to her own ancestors first, adding her grandmother's name – Bambara – to her own. That name appeared on the cover of a fine short story collection, *Gorilla, My Love* (1972), about a feisty young black girl who is trying to survive in the city. Maya Angelou was to treat the same subject and apply it to the rural South in the extremely popular first volume of her autobiography *I Know Why the Caged Bird Sings* (1970). Toni Morrison's *The Bluest Eye* (1970) addressed the question of how self-love is to be achieved for a black girl in a society which hardly values her very existence, let alone her thoughts or her beauty. As she moved on to become probably *the* major writer of the late twentieth century, Morrison's thematic range was to broaden out from the issue of female friendship in *Sula* (1974) to black people's relation to the African American past: she explored their folk heritage in *Song of Solomon* (1977), slavery and motherhood in *Beloved* (1987) and black modernity in *Jazz* (1991). Despite its difficulty, Morrison's work has attracted a popular readership and in 1993 she received the Nobel Prize for literature for her whole œuvre, the first African American to do so. Besides Morrison and Angelou, Alice Walker also published her first book in 1970: *The Third Life of Grange Copeland*, a story of poverty and family violence spanning three generations in the American South. Of what we might call 'the big three' in African American women's writing – award-winners, best-sellers and critical successes all – Walker is easily the most controversial. In her fiction and essays she has taken on not only sexism in the black movements of the 1960s (*Meridian* (1976)), domestic violence and father-daughter rape, but also female genital mutilation in her 'African' novel *Possessing the Secret of Joy* (1992). Most famously, *The Color Purple* (1982) drew fire from black community groups for its depiction of a lesbian relationship and for its purportedly negative representation of black men.

I said before that African American literary history tends to move in cycles, and we see this again in the renaissance of women's writing since the 1970s. Whereas the Black Arts generation was chiefly concerned with black masculinity, the city, and the vernacular language of the street, women writers are interested in mother-daughter relationships, family and community, and the rural 'folk'. Very distinctively this is a literature of place, of small towns, neighbourhoods, and of home – whether that home is a literal or a spiritual one. Gloria Naylor's writing is a good example of this: her novels *The Women of Brewster Place* (1982), *Linden Hills* (1985), *Mama Day* (1988) and *Bailey's Cafe* (1992) are formally diverse and increasingly complex, but they all 'belong' to their particular setting. Naylor's sources of inspiration, such as folk culture, jazz, and spirituality, are shared by many other black women writers, such as Audre Lorde (*Zami* (1982)), Paule Marshall (*Praisesong for the Widow* (1983)) and Gayle Jones (*Corregidora* (1975)). Many creative writers who are veterans of sixties black movements and of black feminism have carried this activist stance over into their work, and are insightful literary critics and political essayists as well as poets and novelists. This is true of Morrison, whose slim but invaluable collection of lectures *Playing in the Dark* (1990) has re-drawn the map of the white American literary canon, and it is true of Walker, who has published several essay collections, among them the well known *In Search of Our*

Mothers' Gardens (1982) where she outlines her literary and political ancestry. The novelist Sherley Ann Williams (*Dessa Rose* (1986)) is a sensitive and subtle literary critic, and poets June Jordan and Audre Lorde have contributed much to the understanding of the politics, as well as the aesthetics, of black women's lives and – in Lorde's case – of black women's lesbian existence. Although the custom is to speak of African American women's literature as 'new', it will be clear that most of the writers discussed so far have been publishing for at least thirty years. The same is not true of younger writers like the poet Rita Dove and the novelist Terry McMillan, whose best-seller *Waiting to Exhale* (1992) broke new ground in the genre of romantic fiction for black women.

Amidst the current wealth of black women's creative production, African American men's writing has been receiving rather less attention. Ishmael Reed, about whom I shall say much more later, is a case in point: he has been writing for decades and is undoubtedly one of the most versatile, interesting and influential novelists today, yet his fiction and his essays are regularly allowed to go out of print. John Edgar Wideman is another prolific novelist; *The Homewood Trilogy*, *Philadelphia Fire* (1990) and his autobiographical *Brothers and Keepers* (1984) share themes with black women's writing in that they address family bonds in relation to place, but they are not getting as much critical attention as might be expected. Charles Johnson, similarly, has dealt with slavery in *The Middle Passage* (1990) and *The Oxherding Tale* (1974), but his work is not as well known as Morrison's *Beloved* or Williams's *Dessa Rose*. In contrast to Reed, Wideman, and Johnson, the star of Walter Mosley, author of a series of detective novels set in LA which chart an African American counter-history of that city, is rapidly rising. Apart from *Devil in a Blue Dress* (1990) and its successors in the Easy Rawlins series, Mosley has also published the intriguing blues novel *R.L.'s Dream* (1995) and *Blue Light* (1999), both of which venture outside the detective genre and show completely new sides to his creative talents.

It will be clear from this rather lengthy overview that the history of African American writing has as long a pedigree as Americans of African descent themselves have in the new world. And if anything is distinctive of African American writing today, it is the constant revision of, and dialogue with, the tradition I have sketched out above. Obviously there is much more to be said, and read, by and about African American writers, but what has been surveyed so far should equip us with a reasonable map to explore the relation between writing and theory, fraught as this expedition will be with the problems and controversies that come, so to speak, with the territory of African American literature.

African American fiction and recent literary theory

We have seen that there is a good deal of African American literary theory before the advent of recent theory, but most of it tended to be programmatic and prescriptive rather than analytical and retrospective. Du Bois, Locke, Wright, and the theorists of the Black Arts movement were all looking for an appropriate mode of representation for black *writers* to employ in order to advance the cause of African American creative expression, but they were on the whole less interested in advancing a theory of *reading*, or of criticism. From about the mid-1970s onwards all this changed with the advent of various European schools of thought in the American academy, and the change did not come smoothly. Deborah E. McDowell describes the arrival of theory in African American literary study, *pace* Houston Baker and Thomas S. Kuhn, as a paradigm shift:

> While 'Criticism' had stakes in close analysis and interpretation, 'Theory' had stakes (and imperatives) in grand frameworks – semiotics, structuralism, poststructuralism, psychoanalysis – and methodological systems. ... People responded variously to the quake. Some ignored it and kept right on doing what they were doing before it hit. Others experienced conversions. ... Still others set about crawling from underneath the rubble to see what they could salvage while trying to rebuild. I place myself in this latter camp. (*'The Changing Same': Black Women's Literature, Criticism and Theory*, Indiana University Press, 1995, pp. xi–xii)

In other words: the reaction to theory was no different among African American critics than it was anywhere else in the academy at the time: a mixture of panic, hostility, enthusiasm and ambivalence. Initial mistrust of 'white' theory of European descent was, at the very least, to be expected from black scholars who had only just managed to establish a field of their own; what was remarkable was the comparatively rapid rise of theory in African American studies. In part, this was due to the conservative backlash in American politics under the Nixon, Bush, and Reagan administrations which forced various forms of activism – feminist, gay, black and ethnic – into a retreat during this period, and in many cases that retreat led into the academy, where the climate for radical change was perceived to be less hostile than it was in policy making, legislation, or direct action. Although some black academics saw the new theory as a threat to their activist credentials, others perceived its potential as a philosophical foundation for -precisely – social change. In addition, the 1980s saw a whole new generation of African American students enter higher education and graduate from prestigious white universities where they came into contact with theory, and these beneficiaries of the Civil Rights gains of the 1960s were to shape African American studies for the next generation. This new breed of academic critics of African American literature often encountered difficult conditions of work and received little respect for what was then still regarded as a field of limited interest and range. Nevertheless, they set about the task of recovering a broken, if not quite lost, tradition, creating new theoretical approaches by drawing on Marxism, post-structuralism, feminism and psychoanalysis, and generally establishing African American literary criticism as a discourse to be reckoned with.

Ironically, the first theoretical essay in African American literary study positioned itself explicitly *against* the incursion of theory in the academy. Barbara Smith's seminal 'Toward a Black Feminist Criticism' of 1977 opened with the line 'I do not know where to begin', because 'merely by writing about Black women from a feminist perspective and about lesbian Black writers from any perspective at all' Smith felt she was undertaking 'something unprecedented, something dangerous' ('Toward a Black Feminist Criticism', in Angelyn Mitchell, ed., *Within the Circle: An Anthology of African American Literary Criticism from the Harlem Renaissance to the Present*, Duke University Press, 1994, p. 410). The black feminist criticism that Smith forged in this dangerous enterprise nevertheless proved to be highly influential – so influential, that from today's vantage point it seems almost commonplace. For one, she postulated that the intertwining of gender, class and racial politics was essential for a black feminist perspective. Secondly, the black feminist critic should have a good knowledge of, and be committed to, black women's writing as 'an identifiable tradition' ('Toward a Black Feminist Criticism', in Mitchell, ed., *Within the Circle*, p. 416). Thirdly, she should have a good eye and ear for black women's language, and she would 'think and write out of her own identity and not try to graft the ideas or methodology of white/male literary thought upon the precious materials of Black women's art' ('Toward a Black Feminist Criticism', in Mitchell, ed., *Within the Circle*, p. 417). Finally, Smith demonstrated these principles in a daring – and still controversial – lesbian reading of Toni Morrison's *Sula*, in order to counter homophobia in literary representation as well as in life.

As the caution against the adoption of 'white/male literary thought' indicated however, such thought (chiefly post-structuralism) was already exerting its influence on black feminist criticism, as much as it was also changing the work of African American male critics, including those such as Houston Baker who had previously been proponents of the Black Aesthetic. Robert Stepto and Dexter Fisher's edited collection *Afro-American Literature: The Reconstruction of Instruction* (1979) took issue with the Black Arts Movement for its overtly political stance on cultural expression and for its neglect, as they saw it, of the formal properties of literary texts. One of the main contributors to this collection was Henry Louis Gates Jr., soon to become *the* African American post-structuralist critic and theorist-in-waiting. However, his later collaborator and friend Houston Baker still had reservations about theory at this stage. In *Black American Literature Forum*, the journal that became the focus of the theory debate, Baker responded to Stepto and Fisher's book with an article entitled 'Generational Shifts and the Recent Criticism of Afro-American Literature'. In a long and detailed analysis of African American critical movements, Baker conceded the critical weakness of the Black Arts movement and the need for a new theoretical paradigm, but he argued against 'a sometimes uncritical imposition upon Afro-American culture of literary theories borrowed from prominent white scholars' ('Generational Shifts and the

Recent Criticism of Afro-American Literature', in Mitchell, ed., *Within the Circle*, p. 303). Against Gates's post-structuralism and that of other 'new breed' critics, Baker maintained his allegiance to the 'holistic, cultural-anthropological approach' that he felt was implicit in the Black Aesthetic ('Generational Shifts and the Recent Criticism of Afro-American Literature' in Mitchell, ed., *Within the Circle*, p. 324). He did so only for the time being, though: by 1984, when his *Blues, Ideology, and Afro-American Literature* was published, Baker's conversion to post-structuralism was evident. He subtitled this book *a Vernacular Theory*, thereby signalling his commitment to both the vernacular black tradition and to a systematic mode of thinking about texts as linguistic and aesthetic artefacts rather than as socio-political documents 'about' African American life, as previous critics – black and white – had so often done. Adopting a post-Marxist perspective informed by post-structuralist arguments about the indeterminacy of literary signification, Baker took the blues as his matrix for a vernacular theory, arguing that the blues 'are the multiplex, enabling *script* in which Afro-American cultural discourse is inscribed' (*Blues, Ideology, and Afro-American Literature: A Vernacular Theory*, University of Chicago Press, 1984, pp. 3–4). Perhaps the most persuasive use Baker has made of this blues matrix was *Modernism and the Harlem Renaissance* (1987), where he argued for a wholesale revision of modernism in light of African American artforms such as the blues and the literature of the Harlem Renaissance.

Also in 1987, Henry Louis Gates published *Figures in Black*, followed by his path-breaking *The Signifying Monkey: A Theory of African-American Literary Criticism* a year later. Gates had for some time been engaged in the project of translating post-structuralist insights for a specifically African American critical use, and in these two books he presented the results of that effort. Gates's theory takes as its starting point the black vernacular practice of 'signifyin(g)', a term which has obvious resonances with the post-structuralist theory of signification. 'Signifyin(g)' can mean various things. In the story of the signifying monkey, it means a kind of verbal trickery: by spreading rumours, the monkey tricks the lion into having a fight with the elephant, as a result of which the king of the jungle is humiliated in full view of the laughing monkey, safely out of reach high up in the tree. 'Signifyin(g)' can also just mean making fun of a person, or talking around a subject without quite getting to the point. In every case, it is an indirect means of expression that involves a play with, or on, power-relations and as such, Gates explains, 'one does not signify something; rather, one signifies *in some way*' (*The Signifying Monkey: A Theory of African-American Literary Criticism*, Oxford University Press, 1988, p. 54). 'To signify on' somebody or something furthermore is to use language in order to change the meanings by which that somebody or something knows it – or herself; it is, in other words, a technique of *significa-tion* in the post-structuralist sense which makes the ambiguous, stretchable, subversive workings of language – of all language – visible. It is this self-consciousness, this self-reflexive 'knowing' quality of African American signifying that appeals to Gates, and that enables him to take it as a figure for the African American literary tradition: texts 'signify on' other texts, revise them, talk back to them, repeat them, often with parodic, critical effect. Obviously this is a highly suggestive schema for African American criticism, and Gates has been tremendously successful in making it stick, both through his own prodigious writing on and editing of African American literature and in the critical following that his work has generated.

That work has by no means been uncontroversial, however. A bruising encounter between him and the critic Joyce Ann Joyce in *New Literary History* in 1987 illustrates just what was at stake in Gates's promotion of theory in African American studies: institutional power versus allegiance to ordinary African Americans as well as the very notion of blackness itself were the bones of contention in this debate – no less, and a lot more besides. It was Joyce A. Joyce who fired the first shots. In 'The Black Canon: Reconstructing Black American Literary Criticism' she attacked Gates for, in effect, denying his race by adopting 'white' theory. Not only did she find his writing style sterile and elitist (many others who are opposed to theory have said that too), but she also took issue with Gates's view of language 'as merely a system of codes or as mere play', which ignores the fact that in African American history language has had a vital role in resistance and emancipation ('The Black Canon: Reconstructing Black American Literary Criticism', *New Literary His-*

tory, 18:2, 1987, p. 341). 'Rather than being a "linguistic event" …
independent of phenomenal reality', Joyce concluded her argument,
'Black creative art is an act of love which attempts to destroy
estrangement and elitism by demonstrating a strong fondness or
enthusiasm for freedom and an affectionate concern for the lives of
people, especially Black people' ('The Black Canon', p. 343). Gates
responded at length in '"What's Love Got to Do with It?" Critical
Theory, Integrity and the Black Idiom', interpreting – predictably –
Joyce's attack first of all as resistance to theory and then answering
some of her more serious charges point by point. He bats away
Joyce's accusation that theory is abstract and elitist with the (familiar) retort that it is a discourse in its own right, a specialist and pro-
fessional language which one would not expect to be accessible to a
mass audience. Importantly though, he outlines where he stands
when it comes to Joyce's assumed alliance between black literary
criticism and African American politics: 'I do not think that my task
as a critic is to lead people to "freedom". My task is to explicate black
texts' ('"What's Love Got to Do with It?" Critical Theory, Integrity
and the Black Idiom', *New Literary History*, 18:2, 1987, p. 358). But
to deny such 'race leadership', and to insist that blackness is a signi-
fier and a trope, rather than simply a biological or even a cultural
given, as Joyce seems to assume, is not to betray one's own African
American identity nor to deny the critic's responsibility to African
American culture: 'My charged advocacy of the relevance of contemporary theory to reading Afro–American and African literature
closely has been designed as the prelude to the definition of principles of literary criticism *peculiar to the black literary traditions themselves*', Gates insists (my emphasis) ('"What's Love Got to Do with
It?"', p. 351). Indeed, probably no contemporary African American
scholar has done more to promote access to this tradition than
Henry Louis Gates has, as an editor (of the Schomburg Library of
Nineteenth Century Black Women Writers, for example) as well as
in his critical and theoretical work. And if this defence of his
integrity was not convincing enough, Gates adds for good measure
that his theory of signifying is no mere matter of 'linguistic play', but
a validation of the black vernacular: 'only a black person alienated
from black language use could fail to understand that we have been
deconstructing white people's languages – as "a system of codes or

as mere play" – since 1619. That's what signifying is all about'
('"What's Love Got To Do With It?"', p. 359). I have found it necessary to summarise this debate in some detail, because it represents,
I think, not simply an attack on versus a defence of theory, but rather
a crucial division in African American criticism between those who,
like Joyce A. Joyce, position themselves as cultural nationalists and
those who do not. 'The blackness of blackness', in Gates's phrase, is
central to this debate: is blackness, as Joyce assumes, a material
entity, or it is a sign or even a metaphor whose meanings – therefore
– are not fixed, as Gates believes? Confusion arises, and it happened
in this exchange, when people think that if blackness is a metaphor,
then the existence of race is denied and the reality of racism with it.
But to deny the objective existence of race is not to deny the dis-
criminatory and pernicious *effects* of a belief in racial inferiority (or
even difference), and Gates certainly recognises that fact.

Another confusion arises, however, when 'theory' is left to fend
for itself as a single and homogeneous entity in such for-or-against
arguments, rather than being discussed as a plurality. In the
Gates/Joyce exchange, as in Barbara Christian's 'The Race for
Theory' (1987) which also questioned the uses of 'white' (particularly French-derived) feminism and deconstruction, the issue was
one of competing theor*ies*. Deborah McDowell makes this clear in
her analysis of both the Joyce/Gates debate and Christian's essay,
when she points out two important slippages in the theory wars
which are of specific relevance to African American studies. First of
all 'theory' functions as shorthand for post-structuralism, thereby
equating the two as if other systematic modes of conceptualising
general trends in culture somehow do not count. Secondly, McDowell argues, the opposition between theory and resistance to theory is
not a neutral one, but is 'often racialized and gendered especially in
discussion of black feminist thinking, which … gets constructed as
"practice" or "politics", the negative obverse of "theory"' ('Trans-
ferences: Black Feminist Thinking: the "Practice" of "Theory"' in
'*The Changing Same*', pp. 157–8). Barbara Christian's main objection in 'The Race for Theory' was that theoretical work, which as
she saw it merely reinforces the power of whites and males, gained
its current high status in the academy *at the precise historical moment*
when black women were beginning to forge a critical discourse and

a tradition of their own. She feared that the theory 'takeover' would jeopardise black feminist criticism because 'theory has become a commodity ... that helps determine whether we are hired or promoted in academic institutions – worse, whether we are heard at all' ('The Race for Theory', in Mitchell, ed., *Within the Circle*, p. 348). In the controversy which 'The Race for Theory' generated, Christian's fear was often dismissed as simply an anti-intellectual response to new developments, but in my view this is a little too easy. Instead, her argument should be read for what it is: a legitimate objection to the hegemonic status of a narrowly defined body of theory, which she feels is imposed upon texts in often flat-footed and counterproductive ways. Christian calls this a fixing of methods which has in fact hampered innovation, and relegated exploratory, text-specific readings to the realm of the untheorised or naive. As Deborah McDowell has also observed, the underlying question in all of this is not for or against theory therefore, but what counts as theory: does it have to be 'white', Eurocentric and based on grand systems of thought? In a later essay entitled 'Fixing Methodologies', Christian herself demonstrated that the answer is 'no'. Taking issue with psychoanalytic readings of Toni Morrison's *Beloved*, which she argued left too many important aspects of that text out of account, Christian presented an Afrocentric approach in order to highlight the importance of African rituals such as ancestor worship in the novel, as well as Morrison's representation of the Middle Passage. It is in the use of an Afrocentric methodology that Christian's critique of 'white' psychoanalytic criticism of *Beloved* is articulated: because she believes that, as a black woman, she shares Morrison's cultural memory and heritage, she is better equipped to read *Beloved* in its proper frame, a frame which is furthermore authorised by Morrison's own frequent references to the role of the ancestor in African American culture.

Afrocentrism, as a distinctive theoretical paradigm which starts from the premise that African American people are essentially of African descent despite their centuries-long existence in the United States, differs fundamentally from any other theory-informed critical approach to African American writing. As Christian's use of it shows, Afrocentrists believe that all the peoples of the black diaspora share a common heritage, whether that heritage is conceived in terms of African culture or as African survivals in American culture. Molefi Kete Ashante, Professor of African American Studies at Temple University, is the best known theorist of Afrocentricity. He explains it as follows:

> There are some people around who argue that Africans and African-Americans have nothing in common but the color of their skin. This is not merely an error, it is nonsense. There exists an emotional, cultural, psychological connection between this people that spans the oceans and the separate existence. It is in our immediate responses to the same phenomena. ... We are not African-Americans without Africanity; *we are an African people* ... And quite frankly our politics, like the expressiveness of our religion, is more often similar to that of Africa than of white America. (my emphasis) (*Afrocentricity*, Africa World Press, 1988, p. 67)

New students of black American culture often adopt this approach almost automatically, when they assume that the difference, or rather the specificity, of African American culture must lie in its Africanness. Second thoughts however reveal something not quite so simple: 500 years of history in colonial and post-revolutionary America have left their mark on African American culture – a brutal mark, it is true, but part of its brutality consisted precisely in tearing people away from their African lands, their diverse cultures, their languages and depriving them of their proper names and sense of self. However much Ashante wants to promote the idea, therefore, of an essentially African identity – and certainly there is no denying the richness and the range of African American cultural forms whose origins can be traced back to Africa – he can only do so at the expense of an Americanness which is, in its turn, shaped by the history of slavery. None of this is to say that Afrocentric thought is therefore to be dismissed out of hand. It continues to be tremendously influential, especially in popular cultural practices such as rap music, and in African American studies departments which research Africanisms in language, spirituality, dance, and in formal patterns of music and speech such as call–and–response. Although the theoretical premises upon which Afrocentric thought is based conflict with the tenets of theory originating in Western culture, in practice African American criticism which is informed by such theory often draws on Afrocentric scholarship as well, thus creating a hybrid critical discourse which recognises the contributions of both traditions.

Since the 1980s the most influential critics of African American writing have used theory in a variety of ways. Apart from Gates's and Baker's transformative work in post-structuralism, and Barbara Smith's black lesbian feminist criticism, other approaches such as psychoanalysis, materialism, cultural studies, queer theory and post-colonial theory have begun to shape African American criticism. Hortense Spillers's critical interrogation of psychoanalysis is a good example of this productive interplay. In 'Mama's Baby, Papa's Maybe: an American Grammar Book' (1987) Spillers examines what the Middle Passage and slavery did to African American relations of kinship, to gender definitions and to the notion of African American history itself. Spillers traces a symbolic order which is radically different from Lacan's or Kristeva's, because it is built not on patriarchal relations and the Name of the Father – how could it be when, under the law of slavery, 'the condition of the child follows that of the mother' – but on rupture. Spillers writes: 'The massive demographic shifts, the violent formation of a modern African consciousness, that take place on the subsaharan Continent during the initiative strikes which open the Atlantic Slave Trade in the fifteenth century of our Christ, interrupted hundreds of years of black African culture' ('Mama's Baby, Papa's Maybe: an American Grammar Book', in Mitchell, ed., *Within the Circle*, p. 460). Nothing of the Lacanian, or indeed the Freudian schema holds in this 'raced' symbolic order, which is one of namelessness, kinlessness, and in an important sense also genderlessness. Under slavery, the orders of reproduction and production coincide, Spillers points out, not only in the slave-woman's childbearing but also in the slave-master's 'fathering' of labour power. 'Under these arrangements, the customary lexis of sexuality, including "reproduction", "motherhood", "pleasure", and "desire" are thrown into unrelieved crisis' ('Mama's Baby, Papa's Maybe', in Mitchell, ed., *Within the Circle*, p. 473). One of the ways in which Spillers puts this figure of rupture to use is to read the African American literary tradition in its image. In *Conjuring: Black Women, Fiction, and Literary Tradition* (1985), she sees the history of black women's writing as *dis*continuous, marked by repeated ruptures and forgettings and very real differences between women writers. Of Zora Neale Hurston's work Spillers says for example that it bears little or no relation to that of her immediate predecessors or contemporaries, that it is 'as though Hurston had never heard of either [Jessie Fauset or Nella Larsen]'; the same goes for the discontinuity between Hurston and Ann Petry ('Cross-Currents, Discontinuities: Black Women's Fiction', in Hortense J. Spillers and Marjorie Pryse, eds, *Conjuring: Black Women, Fiction, and Literary Tradition*, Indiana University Press, 1985, p. 252). Traditions are not born, but made – by critics and educators – and the single unified tradition that Barbara Smith called for and which Marjorie Pryse, in her introduction to *Conjuring*, apparently believes in, comes at the cost of forgetting 'a matrix of literary *discontinuities* that partially articulate various periods of consciousness in the history of an African-American people' ('Cross-Currents, Discontinuities', in Spillers and Pryse, eds, *Conjuring*, p. 251). Hazel Carby has argued along similar lines in *Reconstructing Womanhood* that a tradition of women's writing which privileges rural and folk themes and has the work of Zora Neale Hurston and Alice Walker at its centre, 'has effectively marginalized the fictional urban confrontation of race, class and sexuality' that Carby finds in Nella Larsen, Dorothy West, Ann Petry, and Toni Morrison (*Reconstructing Womanhood: The Emergence of the Afro-American Woman Novelist*, Oxford University Press, 1987, p. 175). Carby's materialist analysis emphasises contradiction rather than a romanticised notion of a unified tradition, and this insight applies to the state of feminist criticism too. She is interested in the ways that conditions of cultural production are structured by power-relations of race, gender, and class, and this means that neither sisterhood between African American and white women, nor that between black women, should be automatically assumed – or even necessarily desired – in black feminist critical practice.

Carby's approach bears the imprint of British cultural studies, which over the past few years has had quite an impact in the United States. Cultural critics and theorists such as Stuart Hall, Kobena Mercer, and Paul Gilroy all started in the so-called 'Birmingham school' of cultural studies. Broadly speaking, all three have been engaged in the kind of cultural critique that exposes race as an essentialist category *par excellence*. In contrast to American Afrocentrists, their theoretical project (which is also an historical one) highlights the complexities of a black identity which consists in the criss-crossings of ethnicity, nationality, class and gender. Building on Stuart Hall's pioneering work in this respect, Gilroy's *The Black Atlantic* (1993) conceptualises a diaspora culture that is shared among peoples of African descent in Britain, the Caribbean and the United States. But it is important to realise that unlike the Afrocentrists, he sees this not as an African culture, nor as one mainly characterised by African survivals, but as a culture which itself has undergone transformations due to the experiences of the Middle Passage and slavery, and its contact with 'white' Europe and America. This diasporic culture, then, is truly a hybridised formation which transcends the national or ethnic particularities of British, Caribbean or American blacks on one hand, without falling back into a notion of pure 'black' authenticity unsullied by 'white' Eurocentric thought on the other. Whereas Gilroy's book is primarily concerned with modernity and with black music, Kobena Mercer's *Welcome to the Jungle* (1994) extends the black cultural studies approach to post-modernism and to popular cultural forms such as film, photography, and fashion.

The 'Britpack' readings of African American culture have found their match, however, in the work of critics like bell hooks, Susan Willis and Michele Wallace, which could be characterised as African American cultural studies. hooks in particular is a prolific writer, a teacher and autobiographer as well as a critic, and her subjects range from literature, popular cinema and TV to African American spirituality and the politics of post-modernism. From the profoundly influential *Ain't I a Woman: Black Women and Feminism* of 1981 to *Outlaw Culture: Resisting Representations* (1994) and beyond, hooks has sought to reach audiences outside as well as within academe with a plain-speaking style and a level of theoretical engagement that recognises no boundaries between the intellectual and the everyday. Although her work has become increasingly informed by theory, it is characteristic of hooks's approach that she sees psychoanalysis, post-structuralism, post-colonial and queer theory on a continuum with modes of theorising that originate in African American vernacular culture. In an interview where she talks about her experience of cross-dressing, hooks explains:

> I think that a lot of what's going on in my work is a kind of *theorizing through autobiography* or through storytelling. ... So a lot of my work views the confessional moment as a transformative moment – a moment of *performance* where you might step out of the fixed identity in which you were seen, and reveal other aspects of the self . . . as part of an overall project of *more fully becoming who you are*. ('Moving into and Beyond Feminism', in *Outlaw Culture: Resisting Representations*, Routledge, 1994, pp. 209–10)

'Theorizing through autobiography' strikes me as a characteristic phenomenon in non-dominant writing. Not only does hooks here emphasise the process, the activity ('theoris*ing*') rather than a fixed outcome, but she also relates this activity to events in everyday life which can offer insights of a general and analytical nature. To do this in the autobiographical mode is equally well rooted in African American thought: after all, Frederick Douglass theorised the psychic and the material condition of slavery in his *Narrative*, and Alice Walker often uses her autobiographical essays to theorise issues in cultural politics. The passage quoted above also illustrates another new development in African American studies: the advent of queer theory. hooks 'reads' her own experience of stepping out in drag as a performance, along the lines set out by Judith Butler in her path-breaking book *Gender Trouble*. Butler reconceptualised gender- and sexual identity as acts of perpetual mimicry, repeat performances of patterns of behaviour which have no ultimate origin, or original, in a biological or cultural identity that exists prior to discourse or to norms and regulations. The bit of queer theory that hooks draws on here is beginning to inform literary criticism too; Butler's own reading of Nella Larsen's *Passing*, for example, takes off from Deborah McDowell's original highlighting of that novel's lesbian undercurrent, but she then extends it into a queer reading informed by psychoanalysis.

With Butler's take on Nella Larsen we have come, in a sense, full circle: from Barbara Smith's pioneering lesbian reading of *Sula* to a queer reading of *Passing*. At the same time, this circular movement also traces a journey of expansion: where Smith was anxious to keep black feminist criticism black, Butler's essay is part of a growing body of work on African American culture by white theorists. It is published, furthermore, in a collection entitled *Female Subjects in*

Black and White: Race, Psychoanalysis, Feminism, which explores not just the virtues and problems of psychoanalytic theory in African American criticism, but which also addresses the tensions between black and white critics – around such uses of 'white' theory and around the institutional politics of academe. Despite the increasing involvement of non-African American scholars in the study of black culture (or because of it?) these institutional issues have not gone away. African Americanist Ann duCille for example critiques the incursion of – this time – post-colonial theory into the study of black women's writing. Her particular target is the common usage of the theory of 'the Other':

> Within and around the modern academy, racial and gender alterity has become a hot commodity that has claimed black women as its principal signifier ... Why are black women always already Other? I wonder. To myself, of course, I am not Other; to me it is the white women and men so intent on theorizing my difference who are the Other. ('The Occult of True Black Womanhood: Critical Demeanor and Black Feminist Studies', in Elizabeth Abel et al., eds, *Female Subjects in Black and White: Race, Psychoanalysis, Feminism*, University of California Press, 1997, p. 21)

duCille's provocative interrogation of the paradigm of the Other is both pertinent ('To myself I am not Other') and unproductive, for the question 'why are they [the others] so interested in me?' reproduces the fixed assumptions of self and other, identity and difference, that she is critiquing in the very same paragraph. Toni Morrison avoids this problem when she turns the tables of identity against the concept of the Other, no less sharply than duCille but more insightfully so, in 'Unspeakable Things Unspoken' of 1988:

> We are the subjects of our own narrative, witnesses to and participants in our own experience, and, in no way coincidentally, in the experience of those with whom we have come into contact. We are not, in fact, 'other'. We are choices. And to read imaginative literature by and about us is to choose to examine centers of the self and to have the opportunity to compare these centers with the 'raceless' one with which we are, all of us, most familiar. ('Unspeakable Things Unspoken: the Afro-American Presence in American Literature', in Mitchell, ed., *Within the Circle*, p. 375)

I want to close my survey of African American literature in relation to theory with this quotation, because Morrison here, it seems
to me, offers a way out of the dilemma that essentialisms of any kind
always get themselves caught in. Cross-racial, cross-cultural scholarship does not necessarily entail either a falling into assumptions of
categorical difference or a subsumption into sameness, a so-called
'universality' which has all too often masked its Eurocentric definitions of literary excellence and human importance. Morrison's 'all
of us', who can choose to examine centres of the self, addresses
African Americans and readers who are outside the culture alike. In
so doing, it opens up the possibility of cross-racial, cross-cultural
scholarship: the distinction between 'white' culture and 'black' is
perhaps not so clear-cut. Or rather, it is yet to be discovered in a
critical and theoretical enterprise that does not objectify African
American writing as the 'discourse of the Other', but regards it as
a subject in its own right.

Case studies: three important works of African American fiction

I have chosen three relatively contemporary novels to look at more
closely, in order to demonstrate what can be done with literary
theory in our reading of African American literature and to show
that, if anything is characteristic of black writing, it is its self-conscious engagement with what has gone before. Ishmael Reed's *Flight
to Canada* is satirical, postmodern and seriously funny, whilst Toni
Morrison's *Jazz* presents a stylish high-literary experiment with
narrative point of view, in stark contrast to Gloria Naylor's linear
and pared-down urban realism in *The Women of Brewster Place*.
These different modes of representation are intimately related to the
ways in which each writer hooks up with different parts of the tradition. Reed for example draws on the work of Zora Neale Hurston
and the parodic tendencies in Ellison's *Invisible Man*, as well as the
nineteenth-century slave-narratives. Morrison's *Jazz* offers a critical take on the Harlem Renaissance in a murderous alternative story
of African American modernity, and *The Women of Brewster Place*
revises the writing of place in the work of Richard Wright, Ann
Petry and also Toni Morrison. All three then write fictions which

enter into a dialogue with the African American literary tradition in more or less explicit ways, and I shall highlight that intertextual conversation by drawing on the historical overview above, to show how a reading of contemporary literature is enhanced by a familiarity with that of the past.

Ishmael Reed, Flight To Canada *(1976)*

Of the three writers I want to examine here, Reed undoubtedly engages with the African American tradition in the most explicit fashion. *Flight to Canada* is a wild romp through not only the stereotyped landscape of the Old South with its Gothic mansions, abusive slave-masters and self-deluded 'uppity' house-slaves, but also through the literature of slavery from Harriet Beecher Stowe's *Uncle Tom's Cabin* to Frederick Douglass and William Wells Brown's slave-narratives. Besides these, other literary figures such as Phillis Wheatley, Henry Bibb, Edgar Allan Poe, T. S. Eliot and Ezra Pound, Paul Laurence Dunbar and Nat Turner also make their cameo appearances. The diversity of this motley crew already indicates that Reed's text is not exactly a conventional historical novel which wants to go over old ground in order to uncover some new truth. On the contrary, *Flight to Canada* is perhaps best described as a text which interrogates the very possibility of truth, historical, (re-)visionary or otherwise: 'Strange, history', the narrator tells us at the beginning. 'Complicated, too. It will always be a mystery, history. New disclosures are as bizarre as the most bizarre fantasy' (*Flight to Canada*, Random House, 1976, p. 8). The mystery of history is revealed through a mixing up of fact and fiction; or rather, a stirring up of what is on and what is off the record, and this makes the historical record itself look, if not ridiculous, then certainly less serious than we thought it was. This is particularly true of the canonical literary record; Harriet Beecher Stowe is turned into a figure of fun when we are told that she wrote *Uncle Tom's Cabin* primarily in order to buy a few more silk dresses. Shapers of American history such as President Lincoln get the same caricaturing treatment, for he is alternately portrayed as an illiterate bumpkin and as a canny political player who suffers from the occasional bout of moral confusion.

In the mid-1970s, when the prescription of the black aesthetic that art should be political was still in force in African American letters, this level of satire meted out to iconic whites associated with the abolition of slavery was to be expected. But for Reed to also intimate that Nat Turner, leader of a slave uprising, was a bit of an impetuous fool, and William Wells Brown an opportunist writer/entrepreneur desperate to get a job on the Abolitionist lecturing circuit, is a different matter. This was a daring thing to do in 1976, but then Reed has always courted controversy and more particularly so where it concerned the Black Arts movement, whose blueprints for African American writing he found stifling and ultimately counterproductive. Quoting Reed himself, Bernard Bell writes in *The Afro-American Novel and its Tradition* that Reed wants 'to destroy the myth "that Afro-American or Black writing is conformist, monolithic, and dictated by a Committee" and to demonstrate that the new generation of Afro-American writers "will not be consigned to the cultural slaves' quarters as were our geniuses of the past"' (*The Afro-American Novel and Its Tradition*, University of Massachusetts Press, 1987, p. 330).

Using an escapee slave writer named Raven Quickskill as his narrator in *Flight to Canada*, then, is an apt literalisation of the metaphor Reed used in this quotation. Raven, like Reed, is given to flights of imagination and Reed, like Raven, is indeed not content to be bound by the rules of the black aesthetic which he feels would consign and confine him to the slave quarters of cultural marginality. Reed's novel is irreverent in every respect, but he doesn't don the mask of bizarre fantasy simply for laughs – although there is that too. As Richard Walsh has pointed out, the chief method Reed employs to produce his effects of the comic and bizarre is anachronism, or 'Hoodoo time', as Reginald Martin calls it (*Ishmael Reed and the New Black Aesthetic Critics*, Macmillan, 1988, p. 98). There are airplanes and telephones in this story, and President Lincoln's murder is televised: 'When the cameras swing back to the balcony, Miss Laura Keene of *Our American Cousin* is at Lincoln's side "live". Her gown is spattered with brain tissue. A reporter has a microphone in Mary Todd's face. "Tell us, Mrs Lincoln, how do you feel having just watched your husband's brains blown out before your eyes?"' (*Flight to Canada*, p. 103). This passage gives a good impres-

sion of Reed's not–too–subtle humour: the image of a brain–bespat-
tered First Lady is clearly reminiscent of the Kennedy assassination
which was to be televised a century later, and if it is absurd to think
of Lincoln's murder on TV, it might be equally absurd (and taste-
less) to construct historical truth around television images of the
Kennedy shooting – 'live', yet endlessly repeated, with blood and
brain–tissue as 'evidence' of 'what actually happened'. Reed is never
very interested in what actually happened, but rather in what historical events mean in the popular imagination. Because of the fact that
both presidents were murdered, both also came to be remembered
as martyrs to the cause of racial progress and as friends of the
African American people, a reputation which is not entirely
deserved in either case. This, however, is not quite Reed's point. As
Richard Walsh writes, '[h]is basic strategy is an equation between
the Civil War itself and the civil unrest of the 1960s' ('"A Man's
Story Is His Gris-Gris": Cultural Slavery, Literary Emancipation
and Ishmael Reed's *Flight to Canada*', *Journal of American Studies*,
27:1, April 1993, p. 59). By implication then, the critique that the
novel stages of the notion of freedom after emancipation applies to
the Civil Rights struggle during the 1960s as well: political progress
must be accompanied by cultural progress, and this does not happen
automatically. As long as African Americans are still bound by the
slavemaster's thinking, religion, or material aspirations, freedom
remains out of reach. 'Canada' encapsulates this idea: it represents
as much a geographical location to the narrator (cold, inhospitable,
and in thrall to American capital, as Quickskill discovers by the end)
as a mental space of 'exile, death, art, liberation or a woman. Each
man to his own Canada' (*Flight to Canada*, p. 88). This double meaning for 'Canada' is matched by the 'flight' of the title, for not only
does Quickskill escape to Canada, he does so in a jumbo jet. More
importantly still, he travels in style: in a poem, also entitled 'Flight
to Canada', which precedes the narrative and which in many ways
prefigures what happens to Quickskill subsequently. It is this travelling in style, in figuration, to a Canada of the mind, a Canada of writing, that is Reed's subject in this novel, but it is a paradoxical one.
For just as Canada turns out to be American–owned ('They just
permit Canadians to operate it for them', the down–to–earth Car-
penter tells the narrator) so also is Quickskill's writing a mixed

blessing which offers no ultimate escape to freedom, but only to a
way-station, a town called Emancipation (*Flight to Canada*, p. 161).
On one hand, the poem catches up with Quickskill in that it enables
the slave-catchers to trace him to his refuge, but on the other it also
functions, together with his subsequent parody of the slave-narrative, as a self-inscription which thumbs its nose at the slave-master
and signifies on him. Raven is therefore in the end caught by and in
his own words, which is why he eventually returns to the Virginia
plantation where he came from. There he joins Uncle Robin, an
Uncle Tom-type of figure who is another slave-trickster with a bird
name. Uncle Robin's alternative strategy for freedom is to stay put
and to play the master at his own game: he inherits, albeit fraudu-
lently, his former master's plantation. In a peculiar twist of fate
therefore it is Uncle Robin's subversion from within which wins the
day. Not only does he poison the dyslexic slavemaster with Coffee-
mate, but he also wheedles his way into the master's will by becoming his literacy assistant, 'his reading and writing ... Property
joining forces with property' (*Flight to Canada*, p. 171). This last
phrase, and the ones which follow it ('I left me his whole estate. I'm
it, too. Me and it got more it') are indicative of Reed's signifying
style, and they offer an astute analysis of property relations under
slavery into the bargain (*Flight to Canada*, p. 171). As Hortense
Spillers notes, for the slave 'there is no separation between economic
and private status' ('Changing the Letter: the Yokes, the Jokes of
Discourse, or, Mrs.Stowe, Mr.Reed', in Deborah E. McDowell and
Arnold Rampersad, eds, *Slavery and the Literary Imagination*, Johns
Hopkins University Press, 1989, p. 28). What does it mean for a
person to become a commodity? *Flight to Canada* asks insistently.
And the answer is consistently absurd yet true, as Leechfield,
another of the escaped slaves illustrates: '"Look man" – he pulled
out a wad of bills – "I sent the money to Swille. I bought myself with
the money with which I sell myself. If anybody is going to buy and
sell me, it's going to be me"' (*Flight to Canada*, p. 71). Indeed Swille,
the slave-master, himself illustrates the absurdity of the trade in
human property too: '"Look Robin, if they'd came to me and if
they'd asked to buy themselves, perhaps we could have arranged
terms. But they didn't; they furtively pilfered themselves.
Absconded. They have committed a crime, and no amount of

money they send me will rectify the matter'"(*Flight to Canada*, p. 19). The idea of 'pilfering oneself' is indeed bizarre, but it is the bizarre truth of slavery parodically articulated in the voice of a Mafia boss in some Scorsese movie. Throughout the novel Reed manipulates such anachronistic rhetorical styles for comic effect. In the passage preceding this one, for example, Robin and Swille discuss the possibility that runaway slaves suffer from *drapetomania*, a 'scientific' term for the compulsion to run away. Here again we are on the trail of something which is both a joke and not: like his irreverent attitude to historical figures and canonical texts, Reed's eclectic and often cartoon-like borrowings from diverse discourses and cultural traditions serves his polemical purpose of escape from the cultural slaves' quarters. Who would *not* want to run away from oppression, cultural or otherwise? As Richard Walsh lucidly explains, *Flight to Canada*, in its mapping of the contemporary on to the slave-narrative, argues that 'the forms of slavery still exist in modern America, under the guise of the monoculture's institutionalized subordination of all other cultures' ('"A Man's Story Is His Gris-Gris"', p. 63).

Reed's advocacy of multiculturalism is well documented; in his Foreword to the Literary Mosaic series of ethnic American literature he writes for example that the series (which he edits) is designed 'so that students can become acquainted with more than the few Europeans and European Americans covered by traditional texts or the same lineup of token ethnic writers found in the policy issue multicultural books' ('Foreword', in Shawn Wong, ed., *Asian American Literature: A Brief Introduction and Anthology*, HarperCollins, 1996, p. x). This commitment to multi-culturalism and critique of what Reed terms mono-culturalism – broadly speaking Western culture in its dominant forms of rational thought, Christian religion and classical literature – is more eloquently expressed in his 'Neo-HooDoo Manifesto' of 1972, where he says:

> Neo-HooDoo believes that every man is an artist and every artist a priest. You can bring your own creative ideas to Neo-HooDoo. … Whereas at the center of Christianity lies the graveyard the organ-drone and the cross, the center of Neo-HooDoo is the drum the ankh and the Dance. So Fine, Barefootin, Heard It Through the Grapevine, are all Neo-HooDoos. … Neo-HooDoo borrows from the ancient Egyptians

... Neo-HooDoo borrows from Haiti Africa and South America.
Neo-HooDoo comes in all styles and moods. ('Neo-HooDoo Mani-
festo', in Gates and McKay, eds, *The Norton Anthology of African
American Literature*, p. 2298)

It is perhaps important to emphasise that although for Reed Neo-
HooDoo (or Jes Grew, as he calls its epidemic manifestation during
the 1920s in his earlier novel, *Mumbo Jumbo)* is 'a black thing', it is
not necessarily nor exclusively for or about African Americans, nor
is it 'owned' by them. Any such pretension to cultural purity is
anathema to Reed's aesthetic, and this is why in *Flight to Canada* we
find a long sub-plot set in ancient Egypt and an important Native
American character (Quaw Quaw), as well as Native American
tropes such as that of the Raven, a trickster figure who appears in
various tribal mythologies – Richard Walsh mentions the Tlingit in
particular ('"A Man's Story Is His Gris-Gris"', p. 65). In typical signifying style, Raven of course also alludes to Edgar Allan Poe's most
famous poem, as well as connoting blackness and flight. Raven
Quickskill's surname furthermore sounds vaguely Indian and syn-
thesises the words 'quick', 'skill' and 'quill', thereby encrypting
Raven's identity as a writer. If you were to write the three words very
quickly, you would get quickskill, who is always a bit ahead of himself – as his premonitory poem shows. Much fun can be had with
such decoding of names and images, and the search for buried references is potentially endless in Reed's work. It is probably useful
nonetheless to also heed Henry Louis Gates's warning in *The Signifying Monkey*, that to read Reed's figures literally is to 'be duped by
figuration, just like the Signified Lion': nothing quite fits neatly, and
to assume that it could or should is to misunderstand the nature of
Reed's use of black vernacular culture as a poetic mode of representation (*The Signifying Monkey*, p. 238).

   That said, what remains stable in the general un-fixing of language and historical order is Reed's critique in *Flight to Canada* of
the slave-narrative as a genre of white-controlled and therefore
unfree confessional writing. The novel reveals that the canonical
status of, say, Frederick Douglass's *Narrative*, now regarded as the
archetypal text of African American emancipation, is purchased at
the cost of obscuring the ways in which Douglass had to please his
white audience and his Abolitionist sponsors in order to be heard at

all. As the critic Patrick McGee notes, Quickskill's slave-narrative does not suffer from such limitations. Unlike Douglass, Brown, Jacobs and others, Quickskill 'does not write to prove his humanity ... he does not seek recognition of his master or masters' (*Ishmael Reed and the Ends of Race*, Macmillan, 1997, p. 38). Instead, as Quickskill's master Swille recognises, he uses literacy 'like that old Voodoo – that old stuff the slaves mumble about' (*Flight to Canada*, p. 36). Swille is well aware of the trickery and treachery of Quickskill's signifying activities: 'Fetishism and grisly rites ... Not one of them with the charm and good breeding of Ms Phillis Wheatley, who wrote a poem for the beloved founder of this country, George Washington' (*Flight to Canada*, p. 36). This satirical reference to Wheatley shows that Reed can be as vicious about other African American writers as he usually is about white modernists like Eliot and Pound, his favourite (pardon the pun) *bêtes noires*. Wheatley wrote in the service of powerful whites, Reed suggests, which is almost as bad as Harriet Beecher Stowe's appropriation of an existing slave-narrative, *The Life of Josiah Henson, Formerly a Slave* for the plot of *Uncle Tom's Cabin*. Both practices (literary prostitution and literary theft, respectively) in Reed's view have a long history in African American culture, and they are criminal because they violate the sacred power of a person's writing as not a mere expression, but a realisation of self. In connection with Josiah Henson Quickskill tells us: 'A man's story is his gris-gris, you know. Taking his story is like taking his gris-gris. The thing that is himself. It's like robbing a man of his Etheric Double. People pine away. ... Somebody has taken their story' (*Flight to Canada*, p. 8). This oft-quoted passage articulates the author's views, and there is little doubt that the criticism of Wheatley and of Harriet Beecher Stowe also emanates from Reed himself.

The alert reader will notice that if a man's story is his gris-gris, a woman's is evidently either stolen or faked for the pleasure and delectation of whites. Reed's misogynist tendency is as apparent here as it is in his representation of Princess Quaw Quaw, the Native American character with 'suffragette' leanings who refuses politics and wants to be 'universal'. In relation to black women writers like Phillis Wheatley, his charge is more specifically that they are in cahoots with the white establishment in order to advance themselves at the expense of black men. *Reckless Eyeballing* (1986), his deeply controversial novel about the rise of black feminist literature, made the same argument, and Reed's very public accusation of Alice Walker for selling out when she let Steven Spielberg direct *The Color Purple* has not endeared him to feminist readers and critics. As a result, the reception of Reed's work has been frequently dominated by the issue of gender; as Patrick McGee notes, 'he probably receives more recognition from the press and media for his remarks on feminists and black women writers ... than he has received from critics for his literary achievement' (*Ishmael Reed and the Ends of Race*, p. 58). If this is so, and if it is to be deplored, then it is certainly not for want of provocation on Reed's part, and we might do better to see what women writers have had to say about the sexual politics of African American writing.

Gloria Naylor, The Women of Brewster Place *(1982)*

> Perhaps African-American writers have been particularly interested in setting, because displacement, first from Africa and then through migrations from South to North, has been so much part of our history. ... [W]e know how critical our location is to the character of our social creations, of how place helps to tell us a great deal about who we are, and who we can become. ('Gloria Naylor's Geography: Community, Class, and Patriarchy in *The Women of Brewster Place* and *Linden Hills*', in Henry Louis Gates Jr., ed., *Reading Black, Reading Feminist: A Critical Anthology*, Penguin, 1990, p. 348)

Barbara Christian is not the only critic who has noted the importance of place in black women's writing, but it is helpful here to remind ourselves of its origins in the experience of *dis*placement, if only because it is often too easily assumed that the writing of place is about rootedness (including African roots) and women's community. Gloria Naylor's first novel is a good counterexample to this clichéd view, for *The Women of Brewster Place* depicts instead an urban, ghettoised existence in which Africa hardly figures and where community, amongst poor and divided people, cannot be taken for granted. The novel opens with an unequivocally unromantic statement of place as a material entity conceived in political corruption: 'Brewster Place was the bastard child of several clandestine meetings between the alderman of the sixth district and the managing director of Unico Realty Company' (*The Women of Brewster Place*, Minerva, 1992, p. 1). Built shortly after the First World War to serve the political and business interests of both white men, the street's history follows that of successive waves of Irish and Italian immigration, until the city elders decide to wall it off in order to protect adjoining wealthier neighbourhoods from the smell of 'ethnics' in their midst. Brewster Place becomes a dead-end street in more ways than one. By the time black people arrive from the segregated South in the mid-1950s, 'ethnics' have become 'whites' and have moved on to better things, whilst African Americans 'clung to the street with a desperate acceptance that whatever was here was better than the starving southern climate they had fled from. Brewster Place knew that unlike its other children, the few who would leave forever were to be the exception rather than the rule, since they came because they had no choice and would remain for the same reason' (*The Women of Brewster Place*, p. 4). In this way – upfront in a prelude chapter entitled 'Dawn' – Naylor announces that this is a novel about class, about the downward mobility of a neighbourhood and its people, cut off from the lifeblood of the city and of mainstream society. The sense of dead-endedness is exacerbated by the proximity of Linden Hills, a wealthy black area which hovers as a ghostly presence on the periphery of vision for the inhabitants of Brewster Place – so near, and yet so far. *Linden Hills* is the title of Naylor's second novel, and it is significant that there is little, if any, overlap between the two: the class divide is that strong. As Barbara Christian also observes, it is remarkable for a black American writer to posit class division in intraracial terms; usually, class and race are collapsed into one as writers 'tend to portray black communities as distinct from white society' ('Gloria Naylor's Geography', in Gates, ed., *Reading Black, Reading Feminist*, p. 349). Naylor does not do this: white society here is of no more than historical interest, and the focus of attention is on gender relations and homophobia amongst poor and working-class African Americans. Both class- and race-unity are problematised in this novel.

The women of Brewster Place are less a community than a collection of different types: there are the older migrants from the South and a younger generation of city girls, women of good and bad sexual repute, childless women and mothers, married and single. They are introduced to us chapter by chapter, each one bearing a woman's name, with the exception of 'The Two' (about a lesbian couple) and 'The Block Party', which brings all the characters together – albeit only in a dream. Originally, the disjointedness of this structure was emphasised in the subtitle *A Novel in Seven Stories*, but for reasons unknown this has been omitted from the British edition. Only one of the seven main characters lives in Brewster Place by choice. Kiswana Browne, college-educated and born in Linden Hills, moves to Brewster because she has ideals: she wants to organise the women so that they can act collectively and demand improvements in their living conditions from landlords and local politicians. Kiswana's role as a binding force is in many ways mirrored by that of Mattie Michael. Mattie is what black feminist theorist Patricia Hill Collins would call an 'othermother', a woman who mothers other people by giving them comfort and support. In a sense she is therefore an older and more informal version of the community activist (*Black Feminist Thought: Knowledge, Consciousness and the Politics of Empowerment*, Routledge 1991, p. 10). Mattie's friend Etta Mae Johnson, the lesbians Theresa and Lorraine, and the welfare mother Cora Lee are 'bad' women, at least according to the neighbourhood gossips. They refuse to, or can't, conform to the standards of what a good black woman is supposed to be: married, virtuous, and able to control her children. Yet being a good mother and wife does not necessarily bring rewards: Lucielia Turner is such a model of virtue, yet her husband deserts her all the same, and she loses her only child in a domestic accident.

If I make it seem as though these women are merely types, then I should add that the third-person narrative perspective allows each woman her individual view on the situation that she finds herself in. More often than not this perspective prevents the reader from making easy (and hasty) judgements. In *The Women of Brewster Place* Naylor is concerned with what is often called the feminisation of poverty. More particularly she presents a feminist argument, enhanced by the text's realism, to the effect that it is not only African American men who have a hard time in America's inner cities but that women struggle too. If black women survive it is because they have better support systems, the narrative seems to suggest, but it also shows that black women's reputation for strength and endurance is hard earned and not simply there to be celebrated or idealised. Because the novel puts women centre stage, the men of Brewster Place are represented only insofar as they have an impact on women's lives. Ben, the caretaker and oldest resident on the street, is an alcoholic defeated by his experiences of racist abuse in the South. When he arrives on a still all-white Brewster in the 1950s, 'There was little protest over his living in the block because it got around that he was a nice colored man who never bothered anybody. And when ... the radiators leaked, or the sink backed up, ... it was convenient to have someone around to take care of those things, even this man with strange hair and skin and hints of stale liquor on his breath' (*The Women of Brewster Place*, p. 3).

Ben lives in a dingy basement flat and befriends Lorraine, one of the two lesbians, in a surrogate father-daughter relationship which is unexpected, yet genuine. It is doubly bitter and ironic therefore that it is Ben who is killed by the desperate force of Lorraine's rage against black men after she has been gang-raped by local youths. In a passage which revises Richard Wright's portrayal of Bigger Thomas and his friends in *Native Son* (1940), Naylor does not mince words when she launches her feminist critique of black masculinity:

> C. C. Baker and his friends ... always moved in a pack. ... They needed the others continually to verify their existence. When they stood with their black skin, ninth grade diplomas, and fifty-word vocabulary in front of the mirror that the world had erected and saw nothing, those other pairs of tight jeans, suede sneakers, and tinted sunglasses imaged nearby proved that they were alive. (*The Women of Brewster Place*, p. 161)

But neither does she lose sight of the dismal conditions under which black male self-identity is formed, and of how that identity compares to white male power projected in the media. A few pages on these same young men are described as 'dwarfed warrior-kings' defending their pitifully small territory. They will not be fighter pilots, astronauts or politicians; ' – and they knew it. They only had that three-hundred foot alley to serve them as stateroom, armored tank, and executioner's chamber' (*The Women of Brewster Place*, p. 170). In a discussion of the criticism that black women writers like

Alice Walker have received for their purportedly hateful representation of black men, Deborah McDowell reports that Gloria Naylor by her own account was extra careful in this novel 'not to have a negative message come through about the men' ('Reading Family Matters', in Cheryl A. Wall, ed., *Changing Our Own Words: Essays on Criticism, Theory, and Writing by Black Women*, Routledge, 1990, p. 94). We can only suppose that Naylor regarded Ben (who is a benevolent old man like so many who appear in Alice Walker's fiction) as a sufficient counterbalance to the likes of C. C. Baker, Mattie's shiftless son Basil, and Lucielia Turner's irresponsible husband Eugene, but it is a delicate balance at the very best. Instead of defending Naylor and other African American women writers against the man-hating charge, it is probably more accurate and more productive to recall the many woman-hating representations of mothers, lovers and wives that we find in black men's fiction. Ishmael Reed's *Reckless Eyeballing* and Richard Wright's *Native Son* are but two exemplars of this, and black feminist writing such as Naylor's stands as a useful corrective to the – often unacknowledged – misogyny in classic African American men's novels.

Nor is it the case that Naylor lays the blame for the difficult lives in Brewster Place simply at the door of men. Much more important a theme in the novel concerns the relation between desire and reality for African Americans, a theme which Langston Hughes addressed in his famous poem 'Harlem', where he asked 'What happens to a dream deferred?' Naylor uses this question as her epigraph to suggest a connection between the dreams and hopes of the Harlem Renaissance and those of the present day, but also to question their validity. Her answer regarding black women's specific dreams and realities is complex and variegated. For a woman like Lucielia, deserted by her husband, the dream of a happy family life explodes when her only child is accidentally electrocuted and she herself is barely saved by the ministrations of Mattie Michael, her 'othermother'. The passage in which Mattie rocks Lucielia like a baby back to life is worth quoting because, as Farah Jasmine Griffin has observed, '[t]he laying on of hands ritual serves not only as a safe space where Ciel is healed, but also as a discursive retreat within the text itself' (*'Who Set You Flowin'?' The African-American Migration Narrative*, Oxford University Press, 1995, p. 120).

Ciel moaned. Mattie rocked. Propelled by the sound, Mattie rocked
her out of that bed, out of that room, into a blue vastness just underneath the sun and above time. ... She rocked her on and on, past
Dachau ... They flew past the spilled brains of Senegalese infants
whose mothers had dashed them on the wooden sides of slave ships.
... She rocked her into her childhood and let her see murdered
dreams. And she rocked her back, back into the womb, to the nadir of
her hurt. ... It would heal. (*The Women of Brewster Place*, pp. 103–4)

This uncharacteristically visionary passage suddenly ruptures the
text's realism and takes it into a whole other dimension. Naylor was
to make the power of African American women to get 'underneath
the sun and above time' a major theme in her third novel, *Mama Day*
(1988), but here we get an early intimation of its healing force in a
scene which evokes a long history of maternal suffering and which
uncannily foreshadows Toni Morrison's *Beloved*. Mattie Michael's
own dream of mothering a son who can make his way in the world
had been shattered when that son betrayed his mother's faith in him,
yet she manages to make a way out of no way by moving to Brewster
Place and acting as a mother to Lucielia and to others who need her
help. Her friend Etta Mae needs it when her romantic fantasy of
marrying a silver-tongued preacher ends in the cold morning light
of a room where '[t]here would be two or three small rectangles of
soap wrapped in bright waxy covers that bore the name of the hotel'
(*The Women of Brewster Place*, p. 72). Etta Mae knows that she, like
the hotel room, has only been rented for the night and it is Mattie's
love that she comes home to, Mattie and the Billie Holiday records
which articulate the pain of abandoned women in the black vernacular of the blues.

Unlike Mattie and Etta Mae who learn to face up to disillusion-
ment, women like Cora Lee, who has six children and is pregnant
again, never get to the stage where they can distinguish between
dream and reality. Cora Lee keeps getting pregnant because in her
mind she is still the child that wants another baby doll for Christ-
mas, even though it is patently obvious that she cannot look after the
children she already has as a single mother on welfare. Only when
she takes them to a performance of Shakespeare's *A Midsummer
Night's Dream* is she confronted with an alternative vision of the
future – as a mother of children who could become actors, doctors

or lawyers. Naylor sails rather close to the wind of stereotype in her portrayal of Cora Lee, the black-mother-on-welfare-with-too-many-children, but again this rather dismissive representation gains more depth when we read it in dialogue with another text in the African American literary tradition. Michael Awkward does so in *Inspiriting Influences*, where he points out that the profound impact Toni Morrison's *The Bluest Eye* had on Naylor when she first read it is still visible in *The Women of Brewster Place*. In a close comparison of both novels, Awkward argues quite convincingly that Cora Lee's obsession with dolls (and they are emphatically black dolls) stands in contrast to the destructive effect that white dolls have on Claudia's sense of self in *The Bluest Eye*, because they reflect an ideal of beauty that black girls can never aspire to. These passages about Cora Lee's dolls, says Awkward, 'represent perhaps the signal moment of critical revision in the Afro-American woman's narrative tradition' (*Inspiriting Influences: Tradition, Revision, and Afro-American Women's Novels*, Columbia University Press, 1989, p. 106). What he means by this is that Naylor takes Morrison's concern with the psychic health of black girls in a racist culture further: Naylor is interested in black women's position in a world which offers them few options *but* mothering, which is valued amongst African Americans but not outside. Whilst *The Women of Brewster Place* on one hand affirms this valorisation of mothering, it also asks what future black children can realistically aspire to in a working-class urban ghetto. '*But babies grow up*', the Cora Lee chapter hypnotically repeats and this, ultimately, is the problem that Naylor addresses.

Kiswana Browne's upper-middle-class mother articulates the same issue in a different way, when she comes to visit her daughter and criticises her for not making enough of her talents by living amongst 'these people' in Brewster Place. Mrs. Browne's apparent snobbery is gradually deconstructed in the chapter as it becomes clear that she is trying to do the best by her daughter and that she herself is not lacking in race-consciousness or social responsibility. What is more, in making Kiswana aware of African American women's long history of community activism, she disabuses her of the idea that sixties revolutionary slogans such as 'black is beautiful' are particularly insightful, or that taking an African name, as Kiswana has done, is a revolutionary act in itself. The mother explains:

I am alive because of the blood of proud people who never scraped or begged or apologized for what they were. ... It broke my heart when you changed your name. I gave you my grandmother's name, a woman who bore nine children and educated them all, who held off six white men with a shotgun when they tried to drag one of her sons to jail for 'not knowing his place'. Yet you needed to reach into an African dictionary to find a name to make you proud. (*The Women of Brewster Place*, p. 86)

So much for African roots. Like Alice Walker's short story 'Everyday Use', Naylor here critiques the 1970s vogue for Afrocentrism as superficial and misguided. And like Walker's work also, Naylor stresses the importance of black women's free expression of their sexuality in *The Women of Brewster Place*. When Kiswana's mother is embarrassed by an African statue with protruding breasts, she is exposed as a hypocrite, as are the women who point the finger at Etta Mae for being a 'loose woman' at a tenants' meeting.

In that same meeting a row breaks out over the presence of Lorraine, a lesbian, and it is in Naylor's treatment of black lesbians that we see both the limitations and the political courage of her intraracial thematics. Barbara Smith's essay 'The Truth That Never Hurts' makes clear that, in portraying Theresa and Lorraine as the most isolated characters in Brewster Place and Lorraine as the most victimised, Naylor succeeds admirably in critiquing homophobia among African Americans but fails miserably in another important respect: 'Lorraine and Theresa are classically unhappy homosexuals of the type who populated white literature during a much earlier era, when the only alternatives for the "deviant" were isolation, loneliness, mental illness, and death' ('The Truth That Never Hurts: Black Lesbians in the Fiction of the 1980s', in Barbara Smith, *The Truth That Never Hurts: Writings on Race, Gender and Freedom*, Rutgers University Press, 1998, p. 60). In the 1970s and 1980s, Smith argues, such a representation of lesbians is not only retrograde but also inaccurate, since black lesbians have struggled – not least in literature – to make their voices heard and the existence of lesbian community is something Naylor chooses to ignore. Whilst this may be true, I think that Smith in turn ignores a subtler and more theoretical dimension of Naylor's approach to lesbianism, which is that she uses Mattie and Etta Mae's close friendship to highlight what

Adrienne Rich has termed 'the lesbian continuum' ('Compulsory Heterosexuality and Lesbian Existence', in Ann Barr Snitow, Christine Stansell and Sharon Thompson, eds, *Desire: The Politics of Sexuality*, Virago, 1984, p. 229). During the tenants' meeting, Mattie and Etta Mae try to come to terms with Theresa and Lorraine's relationship, and what they discover in the course of their discussion is something more than – simply – that they can live with it. Mattie realises that she has loved, and has been loved by, women more than any man, and when Etta Mae agrees but still wants to insist that it's 'different', Mattie responds: 'Maybe it's not so different. … Maybe that's why women get so riled up about it, 'cause they know deep down it's not so different after all' (*The Women of Brewster Place*, p. 141). This is a direct echo of Rich's theory of the lesbian continuum, and it gives Theresa and Lorraine a history in black women's age-old close bonding of which they themselves remain tragically unaware.

Here again we see that we gain a lot more from *The Women of Brewster Place* if we bring our knowledge of previous African American and feminist writing to bear on what at first appears to be a straightforward urban realist novel. True, Naylor is concerned with class and with black feminist themes such as woman-bonding, motherhood and sexist abuse, but I think we can also conclude that below the surface runs an intertextual current which draws on and takes issue with writers like Wright, Morrison, Walker and also Jean Toomer's *Cane* (in the Southern part of Mattie's story, for example). What emerges too is a lyrical element in Naylor's writing, faintly reminiscent of the opening of Zora Neale Hurston's *Their Eyes Were Watching God*, at the end when Brewster Place is finally shut down: 'But the colored daughters of Brewster, spread over the canvas of time, still wake up with their dreams misted on the edge of a yawn. They get up and pin those dreams to wet laundry hung out to dry, they're mixed with a pinch of salt and thrown into pots of soup, and they're diapered around babies. They ebb and flow, ebb and flow, but never disappear' (*The Women of Brewster Place*, p. 192). Perhaps it is not accidental that Naylor was to develop this poetic and visionary dimension of her writing in *Mama Day*, a novel set on an island removed from everyday American urban reality and therefore a place of imagination.

Toni Morrison, Jazz (1992)

Just as in Reed's *Flight to Canada* Quickskill's poem encapsulated all of the action that was to follow, you only have to read the first page of *Jazz* to get the gist of the story that ensues: Joe Trace, a middle-aged man, kills his young lover Dorcas 'to keep the feeling going'. When his wife Violet interrupts Dorcas's funeral and cuts the dead girl's face, she is thrown out of the church. Violet then runs home, opens the window and releases her birds from their cages. Strange plot, you might think, obviously crazy people, and probably something symbolic to do with the birds – freedom? catharsis maybe? the satisfaction of revenge? Characteristically for Morrison, the opening sequence of her sixth novel makes us wonder about the absurdity of the actions of the characters and curious about their motivation. More puzzling still is the gossipy voice which tells us this story-in-a-nutshell, beginning with a hush: 'Sth, I know that woman. ... Know her husband, too' (*Jazz*, Picador, 1992, p. 3). Why the secrecy? Who is speaking, and how does this mysterious voice know what it claims to know? The fact that the voice gives her secret away so readily becomes even more paradoxical when in the course of the novel she changes her mind repeatedly about what happened next and how to explain it. Near the beginning for example, the voice rhapsodises about the city in which these strange events take place, and she is fully confident of her own power to account for them:

> I'm crazy about this city. ... A city like this one makes me dream tall and feel in on things. Hep. ... Alone, yes, but top-notch and inde-structible – like the City in 1926, when all the wars are over and there will never be another one. The people down there in the shadow are happy about that. At last, at last, everything's ahead. The smart ones say so and people listening to them and reading what they write down agree: Here comes the new. Look out. There goes the sad stuff. The bad stuff. ... Forget that. History is over, you all, and everything's ahead at last. (*Jazz*, p. 7)

But by the end, once Joe and Violet's story of city and country, North and South has been told and they don't appear to be so crazy after all, the voice is much less self-assured:

> It was loving the City that distracted me and gave me ideas. Made me
> think I could speak its loud voice and make that sound sound human.
> I missed the people altogether. ... I was sure one would kill the other.
> ... That the past was an abused record with no choice but to repeat
> itself at the crack and no power on earth could lift the arm that held
> the needle. (*Jazz*, p. 220)

Like the narrator of Ellison's *Invisible Man*, who realises when he
sees three boys on the subway that he has missed a vital element of
reality, Joe and Violet have apparently defeated the narrator's design
for their lives, because they refuse to conform to the historical pattern of violence and emotional deprivation that the past had laid out
for them. They do not kill each other or break apart, and neither do
they leave the city which has wrought such havoc on their lives.
Instead, they settle down to a comfortable middle age and befriend
another young girl, Dorcas's best friend Felice (whose name means
'happiness'), as a sort of adoptive daughter. But this ending does not
come easy. What the narrative shows is that history is not over, but
very much alive in the present: Joe and Violet's past in the rural
South has everything to do with their messed-up city selves, and this
new start cannot be made by wiping the slate of history clean but –
paradoxically – only by reading and understanding what is written
there.

Morrison has said time and again that it is important to her 'To
make the story appear oral, meandering, effortless, spoken – to have
the reader *feel* the narrator without *identifying* that narrator, or hearing him or her knock about' ('Rootedness: The Ancestor as Foundation', in Mari Evans, ed., *Black Women Writers: Arguments and
Interviews*, Pluto Press, 1985, p. 341). In an interview with Alan Rice
she likened that appearance of effortlessness to the jazz musician's
performance ('Jazzing It Up a Storm: The Execution and Meaning
of Toni Morrison's Jazzy Prose Style', *Journal of American Studies*,
28:3, December 1994, p. 424). *Jazz* does appear oral, but we certainly hear the narrator 'knock about' even if we still cannot identify
her. Her presence is particularly obtrusive at the end, when the voice
addresses the reader like a lover would, demanding attention and
touch: '*I love the way you hold me, how close you let me be to you. I like
your fingers on and on, lifting, turning. I have watched your face for a
long time now, and missed your eyes when you went away from me. Talk-*

ing to you and hearing you answer – that's the kick' (Jazz, p. 229). The book itself is talking to us here, self-consciously and coyly demanding to be read *and re-read* right down to the final lines: 'Say make me, remake me. You are free to do it and I am free to let you because look, look. Look where your hands are. Now' (*Jazz*, p. 229). What is this all about? Obviously, once we have got to the final full stop we are 'free' to make what we can of the novel, but does it need stating quite so blatantly? Is this a gimmick, a post-modern ploy to make us as readers aware of the manipulations that the narrative voice, any narrative voice, inflicts on us?

As many critics have noted, the title *Jazz* gives us a clue as to why this manipulation of style and form by an unstable narrative voice is highlighted. Improvisation is of the essence in jazz performance, and this is what Morrison's narrator seems to do, elaborating and changing the tune, varying the beat, and creating the breaks for other instruments or voices to come in. Like jazz then, *Jazz* is less about story than style. If the narrator knows the score she doesn't play it straight, and we as first-time readers lose the plot, swept up as we are by the virtuosity of Morrison's language and imagery, for this novel is stuffed with domestic details, the sights and sounds of the streets, intricate descriptions of women's work, the tastes and smells of food. All of these realistic signifiers of city life have layers of meaning, but only on a second reading, the 'remake', does *Jazz* reveal its complex design *as* a design, and not mere improvisation. As Alan Munton notes in an essay which cautions against a too-easy assumption that Morrison's writing is structured on a jazz aesthetic, both writer and musician 'must work hard at their respective arts in order to make them appear effortless, whether upon the printed page or upon the bandstand' ('Misreading Morrison, Mishearing Jazz: A Response to Toni Morrison's Jazz Critics', *Journal of American Studies*, 31:2, August 1997, p. 238). Improvisation only gives the appearance of spontaneity when in fact it is highly structured; analogously, the voice's narrative improvisation is a stylistic conceit. That *Jazz* is so highly stylised is not to say, of course, that the novel has no substance; as in jazz, and as in African American vernacular culture more generally, style *is* substance – the two are coterminous.

As Morrison herself has said in her invaluable essay 'Unspeakable Things Unspoken', what makes a literary work 'black' is its language, 'its unpoliced, seditious, confrontational, manipulative, inventive, disruptive, masked and unmasking language' ('Unspeakable Things Unspoken: the Afro-American Presence in American Literature', *Michigan Quarterly Review*, Winter 1988, p. 11). We get plenty of this from the narrator in *Jazz*, unreliable and inventive as she is, but crucially we get such 'masked and unmasking' language before that, in the novel's epigraph from *The Nag Hammadi*. There, the goddess Thunder gives a good indication of what is to come: 'I am the name of the sound/ and the sound of the name./I am the sign of the letter/ and the designation of its division' (*Jazz*, n.p.). We can take this epigraph as a post-structuralist statement of the treacherousness of the sign 'I' (which is letter and sound, the meaning of which shifts according to who utters it) and of the division of the subject (I, me); or rather, of the subject-in-language, which is always already divided from itself. Later on, Morrison's narrator plays on the sound (and sight) of I/eye, again a familiar theoretical pun which here highlights the disembodied narrator's voyeurism: 'I watch everything and everyone and try to figure out their plans, their reasonings, long before they do' (*Jazz*, p. 8). As Eusebio L. Rodrigues notes, 'Perhaps this "I" is an all-seeing eye, all-piercing too, one that can penetrate human motives and plans' ('Experiencing *Jazz*', in Linden Peach, ed., *Toni Morrison: Contemporary Critical Essays*, Macmillan, 1998, p. 164). Believing her own divine eye, the voice tells what she sees, but unlike the omniscient narrator of old, she comes to realise that history and people have an inside story which is, so to speak, off the record: appearances are not everything. It is often said that the hallmark of the modern consciousness is its splitness, its self-consciousness which can both be and observe the self at the same time. This self-surveillance is particularly characteristic of city life, in which a person is constantly reflected in the mirrors of consumer society and in the eyes of others. Both theoretical insights of the *Nag Hammadi* epigraph – that of the division of the subject in language and that of deception by the gaze – are important themes in modernity, as indeed they are in *Jazz*.

What migrants such as Joe and Violet have to deal with in becoming city people is the exact opposite of what they expect and hope for. When they 'dance into' the North on a train, the green curtain

which had divided 'whites only' from the black carriages is removed
to give everybody equal access to the dining car – but most of the
black people do not take the opportunity, having brought their own
food and being, in any case, too poor to pay extra. We can read this
as a sign of what African Americans expected to find in New York:
the spoils of consumer society are in principle open to all, but in
practice segregation still rules and Harlem is the only place, a city of
refuge, where African Americans can truly be themselves. That, at
least, is the idea, but it doesn't work out that way for the Traces.
Instead, they learn through their obsessive involvement with Dorcas
and the grief it brings them, that 'the City spins you … Makes you
do what it wants. … All the while letting you think you're free'
(*Jazz*, p. 120). It takes them away from themselves and splits them
in two, one who acts and one who observes, as it does with Violet.
After Dorcas's death she thinks of herself as *this* Violet and *that*
Violet, or rather Viole*nt* – as the neighbours then begin to refer to
her. Like the narrator, Joe and Violet get distracted by the city and
'what they start to love is the way a person is in the City' – which is
about desire, not love (*Jazz*, p. 33). The very way in which they
make their living – he as a cosmetics salesman, she as a hairdresser –
is bound up with the consumerism of the Jazz age and the new
industries it brings with it, like Madame C. J. Walker's cosmetics
empire of hair straighteners and skin-whitening creams. Joe, in his
fifties, seduces Dorcas with presents from his cosmetics case, not
because he does not accept her as she is, but because *she* doesn't. And
since Dorcas, despite her strict upbringing by the prudish Alice
Manfred, is a true city girl, she rejects Joe Trace for the much
younger Acton, who wants to change her: 'Acton, now, he tells me
when he doesn't like the way I fix my hair. Then I do it as he likes it.
… Joe didn't care what kind of woman I was. He should have. I
cared. I wanted to have a personality and with Acton I'm getting
one' (*Jazz*, p. 190). 'Getting a personality' for Dorcas means to
shape herself in the image of advertising, in Acton's idea of the kind
of woman he can show off and possess. This is what gets her killed
and what sets Violet on her trail, and on the trail of that other light-
skinned creature who was loved at Violet's expense: the mysterious
Golden Gray of her youth in Virginia.

The self-division which Violet experiences in the city is only

healed when she has confronted her past in the South. Violet articulates this very clearly when she explains to Felice why she lost her
self and became obsessed with Dorcas, cutting the dead girl's face
and then falling in love with her portrait: 'I messed up my own life.
... Before I came North I made sense and so did the world. We
didn't have nothing but we didn't miss it' (*Jazz*, p. 207). She
remembers how her grandmother True Belle told her adoring stories about Golden Gray, the blonde son of True Belle's white mistress and a black woodsman, Henry Lestroy (or Lestory, another
textual pun). Farah Jasmine Griffin explains that both Joe and Violet
are 'motherless children', Violet since Rose Dear committed suicide
and Joe because his mother, Wild, abandoned him at birth (*'Who Set
You Flowin'?' The African-American Migration Narrative*, Oxford
University Press, 1995, p. 185). The Traces are scarred by their histories of maternal neglect and by the valorisation of light-skinned
African Americans over darker ones. At one point Violet speculates
that, having been taught to love Golden Gray's blonde beauty, what
she wanted was a lover in his image, whereas Joe was all the time
looking for Wild but found her own dark-skinned self, and then the
light-skinned Dorcas. 'Which means', Violet concludes, 'from the
very beginning I was a substitute and so was he' (*Jazz*, p. 97). This
is not a great foundation to build a happy marriage on – it is, if anything, a recipe for disaster. As Jill Matus puts it, '[t]he Golden Gray
fable works economically ... to suggest the psychic freight that Joe
and Violet bring to the City – that great expectorate of what is dor-
mant inside its "new" inhabitants' (*Toni Morrison*, Manchester University Press, 1998, p. 137). And that 'psychic freight' does indeed
demand its toll. Joe and Violet Trace's 'crazy' crimes against Dorcas
are represented in the novel as also, or perhaps primarily, crimes
against themselves. Their grief takes them, in remembering, to the
South where grief began. Once they realise that city life cannot erase
their pain but merely provides a temporary distraction from it, they
can put the pieces together again, with new birds to remind them of
the South, and a new girl who visits because she wants to. A happy
ending to a sad and involved story – inevitably simplified in my
account, because it is impossible to recapture the virtuoso performance of Morrison's text with all its nuances, blue notes, and the
trickster voice that is so difficult to pin down.

What will be clear however is that *Jazz* is no rhapsody on Harlem life; in Morrison's representation of the Great Migration, African Americans paid a high price for black modernity. There is, as Brian Jarvis points out, 'no sentimentalisation of nature and the rural South' in this novel (*Postmodern Cartographies: The Geographical Imagination in Contemporary American Culture*, Pluto Press, 1998, p. 135). Yet I think there is a nostalgia for the South's way of life, grounded in 'honest' manual labour and able to sustain an unself-conscious, undivided black identity. However much that identity might have been rooted in pain, *Jazz* seems to suggest, it was also nurtured by a collective historical experience of slavery. And this is what is absent in the city, for Morrison – though it can be heard in its music: jazz. Even prim and proper Alice Manfred, who initially abhors 'the dirty, get-on down' songs of Bessie Smith and others, comes to realise that 'The history is in the music and the music is in the history', as Jill Matus puts it (*Jazz*, p. 58; *Toni Morrison*, p. 137). Certainly there is no nostalgia for the Jim Crow laws which drew that green curtain across the interstate train. But neither does *Jazz* validate the optimism of Alain Locke's New Negro, nor the sense of excitement about a modernity which accords African American art forms a rightful and distinctive place in metropolitan culture. Indeed, as several critics have noted, the Harlem Renaissance is not mentioned at all in *Jazz* and the City itself is never named, although there are plenty of clues which enable us to identify it as Harlem. One of these is that, as in *Beloved*, Morrison started with an historical document, a photograph of a young black girl's funeral in Harlem by James VanderZee, and set her imagination to work on it. There are various references to other VanderZee photographs in *Jazz* too, such as the protest march against the East St. Louis race-riots and the parade of the black veterans of World War I. Yet and still, these Harlem references do not a renaissance make and the question arises why Morrison chose to ignore it so studiously. One answer lies in what Langston Hughes also observed at the time: the Harlem Renaissance was hardly representative of African American life in the 1920s and it passed most ordinary Harlemites by. Besides, as we saw in the overview, much of Harlem's cultural production was in any case consumed by whites. Another, not unrelated, reason why *Jazz* ignores the Renaissance may be traced back to Morrison's own experience of having been taught by Alain Locke at Howard University in the 1950s. According to *The Norton Anthology of African American Literature*, 'Morrison has said that much of the African American literature she encountered while at Howard left her "feeling bereft" for it seemed to be written to someone other than herself or the black people she knew' (headnote to 'Toni Morrison' (unsigned), in Gates and McKay, eds, *The Norton Anthology of African American Literature*, p. 2095). It seems reasonable to assume then that in *Jazz* Morrison wanted to imagine a Harlem inhabited by ordinary, working-class people, not the 'niggerati' (as Zora Neale Hurston called them) of Locke and his circle. And undoubtedly the preferred reader at the end to whom the narrative voice addresses her declaration of love, is African American rather than white – as readers of Harlem Renaissance literature often were.

But although *Jazz*'s side-stepping of the Harlem Renaissance is, of course, valid in these respects, it is not unproblematic in others. To explore this further, we have to return to Golden Gray and to Dorcas, the mixed-race characters in the novel. The first problem is that, as Farah Jasmine Griffin remarks, Dorcas is painted throughout 'as a character who does not deserve our sympathy, as a selfish, uncaring young woman' (*'Who Set You Flowin'?'*, p. 196). Dorcas never really stands a chance in this narrative and she ends up, in Jill Matus's words, 'a sacrificial victim' to Joe and Violet's contentedly restored marriage (*Toni Morrison*, p. 141). This is troubling both because of the racial politics implied in her victimisation and because – as Linden Peach rather generously puts it – '[Morrison's] own improvisation on love celebrates monogamy and faithfulness; a counterpoint to the so-called new morality of the Jazz Age' (*Toni Morrison*, Macmillan, 1995, p. 127). If we read *Jazz* against, say, F. Scott Fitzgerald's *The Great Gatsby*, then Peach is undoubtedly right in his interpretation of it as a counterpoint, but I find his judgement generous because it fails to note how conservative *Jazz*'s sexual politics are – you only have to imagine what Alice Walker would have done with the developing friendship of Violet and Alice Manfred, for example, to see this point. My second problem can illustrate this conservatism further. Golden Gray, the other mixed-race character, is also portrayed very unsympathetically by the narrator, because he is (at least to begin with) white-identified,

arrogant, and repulsed by Wild's blackness. The voice changes her
mind and her tune about Golden Gray when he meets his (very
black) father, Henry Lestroy/Lestory, and starts to imagine a whole
new character for him: 'I have to alter things. I have to be a shadow
who wishes him well' (*Jazz*, p. 161). This narrative fantasy ends
with Golden Gray accepting, or rather, choosing his blackness and
maybe following Wild into the woods – Joe finds his clothes in
Wild's deserted cave later. Unlike Joe and Violet, who resist the
voice's construction of their characters, we don't get to know anything about Golden Gray (or Dorcas) that is not blatantly manipulated by what the narrative voice wants to see him as: now bad,
because white-identified, and now good because he rescues a dark-
skinned black woman and thereby redeems himself. At one point
Golden Gray is described, from Henry's point of view, as 'this queer
man … who knew so little of the rules of hospitality' and the narrative voice in her 'bad' phase takes great pains to represent him as
vain and effeminate, changing his outfits all the time and worrying
about dirtying his clothes (*Jazz*, p. 170). Can 'queer' be an innocent
word in this text, a contemporary novel after all? More importantly,
can it be innocent in the context of the Harlem Renaissance, many
of whose leading figures (Alain Locke among them) were both light-
skinned and 'queer'? Can the story of Golden Gray, who is brought
up as white but discovers a yearning for authenticity, for a black
father's love and approval, be read as an allegory for the Harlem
Renaissance leaders's yearning for a black authenticity whose
traumatic southern history they had not lived through? Such a
reading in terms of the 'absent presence' of the Harlem Renaissance
is supported by the voice's early reference to 'the smart ones', cited
at the beginning of this essay, who believe that history is over
and 'everything is ahead at last'; Alain Locke wrote words to
similar effect in 'The New Negro' (*Jazz*, p. 7). If the answer to
this last question can be 'yes', then *Jazz* shows Locke and his
circle to have been badly mistaken. In presenting Joe and Violet's
story as a polemical counter-construction of African American
modernity, Morrison emphasises – with due benefit of hindsight –
the murderous legacy of history rather than the relative optimism of
the black Jazz Age. That such a revision of history brings a rein-
statement of a conservative racial and sexual politics in its train

is, perhaps, ironic: *Jazz* may be more a novel of the 1920s than the 1990s after all.

Investigating further

There is no substitute for reading around in African American literature, and the two anthologies I used in my overview are the best places to start and to continue in order to get a sense of the writing of a particular period or movement, or to see the continuity as well as contrasts within and between different strands of the tradition. *The Norton Anthology of African American Literature* (1997) and *Call and Response: The Riverside Anthology of the African American Literary Tradition* (1998) do not vary greatly in their selections nor in volume, but the *Norton* has the virtue of consistency in the quality of headnotes whereas those of *Call and Response* are uneven – to say the least. *Call and Response* does, however, include some reprinted theoretical and critical essays and is therefore more comprehensive in its coverage of both primary and secondary material. For other further reading I refer back to my historical overview and to the secondary literature mentioned in the case studies and the theoretical section, above.

Beyond the literary, the student of African American literature should read up on history. Peter Parrish's overview of the historiography of slavery entitled *Slavery: History and Historians* (1989) is invaluable, as is Manning Marable's *Race, Reform and Rebellion: The Second Reconstruction in Black America, 1945–1982* (1984) for African American activism since World War II, and his *Beyond Black and White: Transforming African-American Politics* (1995) for the contemporary period. A chronological introduction to African American history might consist of Vincent Harding, *There Is a River: The Black Struggle for Freedom in America* (1981) or Eugene Genovese's *Roll, Jordan, Roll: The World the Slaves Made* (1975), followed by Eric Foner's *A Short History of Reconstruction 1863–1877* (1990), Nicholas Lehman's *The Promised Land: The Great Migration and How It Changed America* (1989) and C. Vann Woodward's *The Strange Career of Jim Crow* (third edition, 1974). Lerone Bennett's *The Shaping of Black America* (1975) is a good basic introduction. There are some fascinating oral history collec-

tions and anthologies of political manifestos too: Clayborne
Carson's *Eyes on the Prize: The Civil Rights Reader* (1991) for example, or Joanne Grant's edited collection *Black Protest: History, Documents, Analyses 1619 to the Present* (1968) which outlines the
African American militant tradition. In Studs Terkel's *Race* (1992)
you can hear the voices of people who lived through radical changes
in the social climate. David Levering Lewis's *When Harlem Was in
Vogue* (1981) is one of many social histories of the Harlem Renaissance which give a good insight into the cultural scene and its material contexts.

Lawrence Levine's *Black Culture and Black Consciousness: Afro-
American Folk Thought from Slavery to Freedom* (1977) still provides
a solid introduction to what I called in the overview 'vernacular culture', especially when read alongside Geneva Smitherman's *Talkin'
and Testifyin': The Language of Black America* (1977), an excellent
source for those who want to study both the poetry and the structure
of black vernacular language. In addition, Walter Ong's *Orality and
Literacy: The Technologizing of the Word* (1982) lucidly explains the
characteristics of oral cultures versus those which rely on print, and
study of it should prevent readers and critics of African American
literature from reiterating the all-too-current cliché that black writing is somehow 'oral' in essence or origin.

Also at a more theoretical level, students of black literature may
want to reflect on the concept of race and its historical evolution.
Howard Winant and Michael Omi's *Racial Formation in the United
States from the 1960s to the 1990s* (second edition, 1994) should be a
good start, as well as Martin Bulmer and John Solomos's recent and
more wide-ranging collection *Racism: a Reader* (1999). K. Anthony
Appiah's *In My Father's House: Africa and the Philosophy of Culture*
(1992), together with *Race Matters* (1994) by Cornel West are more
philosophical reflections on the importance – and the fictionality –
of race as a concept and a lived reality in the contemporary United
States. For those interested in the relation between African American and African cultures, John Mbiti's *African Religions and Philosophy* (1969) and *Africanisms in American Culture*, edited by Joseph
Holloway (1991) are illuminating.

On gender, there is a wealth of critical and historical writing relating to black women. bell hooks's *Ain't I a Woman? Black Women and*

Feminism (1982) is a modern classic, whereas Paula Giddings's *When and Where I Enter: The Impact of Black Women on Race and Sex in America* (1984) is particularly informative about black women at the turn of the nineteenth and twentieth centuries, and should be better known. Patricia Hill Collins's *Black Feminist Thought* (1990) gives an Africanist perspective on black feminist theory, in contrast to *But Some of Us Are Brave: Black Women's Studies* (1981) edited by Gloria Hull *et al.* which still stands as an excellent introduction to African American feminism. Recently, black masculinity has also received systematic attention from cultural critics, and *Representing Black Men* (1996) is a valuable contribution by editors Marcellus Blount and George P. Cunningham to African American gender studies. Film is another avenue to explore in this regard; Spike Lee's *Jungle Fever* (1991) is notorious for its essentialist racial/sexual politics, whereas other films such as John Singleton's *Boyz 'n the Hood* (1991) are more concerned with the reconstruction of black masculinity and fatherhood. Isaac Julien's *Looking for Langston* (1989), in contradistinction to these, goes in search of a black gay masculinity by paying homage to Langston Hughes and Richard Bruce Nugent.

And finally, but not least, there is music. Again, there is no substitute for listening to it, and for listening to the variety of African American musical forms from gospel to rap and from bebop to soul, with everything in between. Reading about it helps, but remains ancillary. Paul Oliver, *Blues Fell this Morning: Meaning in the Blues* (second edition, 1990) and Sally Placksin's *Jazzwomen 1900 to the Present: Their Words, Lives and Music* (1982) are founts of information, historical and biographical as well as musical. On jazz, two collections edited by Krin Gabbard *Representing Jazz* and *Jazz among the Discourses* (both 1995) are but recent additions to the copious literature already available on this, the foremost of American musical forms. For rap, Tricia Rose's *Black Noise: Rap Music and Black Culture in Contemporary America* (1994) is an authoritative source; Houston Baker's *Black Studies: Rap and the Academy* (1993) is less insightful on the music, but useful for analysis of rap's social and political significance.

Annotated short bibliography

*Primary texts**

*Details of original publication are given, but all are available in modern editions.

Angelou, Maya, *I Know Why the Caged Bird Sings* (Random House, 1969)
  Classic narrative of a young girl's growing up in the South in the 1930s. The first of her five-volume autobiography and the most accomplished.

Baldwin, James, *The Fire Next Time* (Penguin, 1965)
  Autobiographical essays about African American politics in the 1960s in the best tradition of the oratory of the black church.

Ellison, Ralph, *Invisible Man* (Random House, 1952)
  A must-read modernist retrospective of twentieth-century African American identity.

Gaines, Ernest, *The Autobiography of Miss Jane Pittman* (Bantam, 1972)
  Fictionalised memoirs of an ex-slave spanning a century of African American experience from the Civil War to Civil Rights.

Gates, Henry Louis Jr. and McKay, Nellie Y., eds, *The Norton Anthology of African American Literature* (W. W. Norton, 1997)
  Broad coverage of the history of African American writing, with excellent headnotes and a CD of music and oratory.

Hill, Patricia Liggins, ed., *Call and Response: The Riverside Anthology of the African American Literary Tradition* (Houghton Mifflin, 1998)
  Similar coverage to the *Norton* but edited from a cultural nationalist perspective. Includes some major critical and theoretical essays and also comes with a CD.

Hurston, Zora Neale, *Their Eyes Were Watching God* (J. B. Lippincott, 1937)
  The uplifting story of a young black woman's self-discovery. Regarded as a classic for its feminist theme and its innovative use of the vernacular as a poetic language.

Larsen, Nella, *Quicksand* & *Passing* (Alfred A. Knopf, 1928; 1929)
  Two novellas about light-skinned black women's search for identity and sexual expression. Key texts in black feminist criticism of the 1980s and 1990s.

Lewis, David Levering, ed., *The Portable Harlem Renaissance Reader* (Penguin, 1994)

Essays and memoirs, fiction and poetry introduced by one of the major historians of the Harlem Renaissance.

Malcolm X, *The Autobiography of Malcolm X* (Grove Press, 1965)

As told to Alex Haley, who edited it. Essential reading for an understanding of this charismatic and continually influential figure.

Marshall, Paule, *Brown Girl, Brownstones* (Random House, 1959)

Forerunner of the renaissance in women's writing which came with feminism. Another growing up story, this one is about immigrants in New York of Caribbean descent.

McMillan, Terry, *Waiting to Exhale* (Doubleday, 1992)

'The number one international bestseller' which made McMillan's name as an innovative writer of popular fiction for black women. Also made into a (dismal) feature film.

Morrison, Toni, *Beloved* (A. Knopf, 1987)

Groundbreaking novel of slavery and reconstruction, the latter of which here means the reconstruction of a traumatic past through the agency of a murdered child. Later made into a (reasonable) feature film, instigated by Oprah Winfrey.

Morrow, Bruce and Rowell, Charles H., eds, *Shade: an Anthology of Fiction by Gay Men of African Descent* (Avon, 1996)

First anthology devoted to writing by black gay men, incorporating work of writers from the African diaspora outside the United States as well as from within.

Mosley, Walter, *Devil in a Blue Dress* (W. W. Norton, 1990)

Another first, this time of the Easy Rawlins detective series. Set in the Los Angeles of the late 1940s, Mosley revises the genre of crime fiction as well as urban space.

Reed, Ishmael, *Mumbo Jumbo* (Doubleday, 1972)

Like Morrison's *Jazz*, set during the Harlem Renaissance. A 'signifying' novel which is the centrepiece of Gates's argument in *The Signifying Monkey*.

Toomer, Jean, *Cane* (Horace Liveright, 1923)

A 'novel' in a fragmented form of stories, poems and a play about North and South, men and women, history and modernity. A classic of twentieth-century literature.

Walker, Alice, *The Color Purple* (Harcourt Brace Jovanovitch, 1982)

Pulitzer Prize-winning epistolary novel of a black woman's survival of abuse and her liberation through the love of a woman blues singer. Made

into a major feature film (dismal) by Steven Spielberg, with Oprah Winfrey and Whoopi Goldberg..

Wideman, John, Edgar *Brothers & Keepers* (Holt, Rinehart and Winston,
1984)

Insightful autobiographical account of the relationship between an academic and his brother, who is a convict. Examines the condition of African
American masculinity.

Wright, Richard, *Native Son* (Harper, 1940)

Unmissable naturalist novel tracing the inexorable demise of Bigger
Thomas, a young black man trapped in the web of a racist society.

Secondary texts

Abel, Elizabeth, Christian, Barbara and Moglen, Hélène, eds, *Female Subjects in Black and White: Race, Feminism, Psychoanalysis* (University of
California Press, 1997)

Innovative collection of essays by African American and white scholars,
examining the (mis-)uses of psychoanalysis in African American studies
and the (im-)possibilities of inter-racial feminist scholarship.

Baker, Houston A., *Blues, Ideology, and Afro-American Literature: a Vernacular Theory* (University of Chicago Press, 1984)

Theorisation of a 'blues aesthetic' in African American literature from
Olaudah Equiano through to Ralph Ellison. Somehow manages to combine materialist and post-structuralist approaches.

Bell, Bernard W., *The Afro-American Novel and Its Tradition* (University of
Massachusetts Press, 1987)

Invaluable chronological survey of African American fiction from
William Wells Brown to Ishmael Reed. Not so strong on women's writing.

Braxton, Joanne M. and McLaughlin, Nicola, eds, *Wild Women in the
Whirlwind: Afra-American Culture and the Contemporary Literary Renaissance* (Rutgers University Press, 1990)

There are many other collections of black feminist literary criticism, but
this one is duly eclectic and gives attention to spirituality as well as more
hard-nosed materialist readings.

Carby, Hazel V., *Reconstructing Womanhood: The Emergence of the Afro-
American Woman Novelist* (Oxford University Press, 1987)

Puts the writing of African women from slavery to the 1920s on the map.

Crucial for an understanding of the history of women's writing before Zora Neale Hurston.

Christian, Barbara, *Black Women Novelists: The Development of a Tradition, 1872-1976* (Greenwood Press, 1984)
Very accessible and path-breaking essays in black feminist criticism.

Collins, Patricia Hill, *Black Feminist Thought: Knowledge, Consciousness and the Politics of Empowerment* (Unwin Hyman, 1990)
Feminist theory from an Afrocentric perspective. Not specifically about literature, but insightful about common patterns and themes in black women's writing.

Ellison, Ralph, *Shadow and Act* (Random House, 1964)
Essays and interviews on literature and music in which Ellison makes his analysis of African American culture crystal clear.

Evans, Mari, ed., *Black Women Writers: Arguments and Interviews* (Pluto Press, 1985)
Still a classic of black feminist criticism, combining interviews with short essays by and about a wide range of black American women writers.

Fabre, Geneviève and O'Meally, Robert, eds, *History and Memory in African-American Culture* (Oxford University Press, 1994)
Examines the importance of this crucial theme in ethnic writing, starting from Pierre Nora's concept of 'sites of memory' (*lieux de mémoire*). Requires some theoretical foreknowledge.

Gates, Henry Louis Jr., *The Signifying Monkey: A Theory of African-American Literary Criticism* (Oxford University Press, 1988)
Key text in the critical canon of African American studies. Not for absolute beginners in literary theory, but relative beginners will find this study well worth the effort.

Harris, Trudier, *Exorcising Blackness: Historical and Literary Lynching and Burning Rituals* (Indiana University Press, 1984)
Examines the trope of lynching and other forms of ritualised racist violence in men's and women's writing from Chesnutt to Morrison.

Lauret, Maria, *Alice Walker* (Macmillan, 1999)
Comprehensive chronological coverage of Walker's essays and fiction, as well as a useful guide to the reception of Walker's work.

Lee, A. Robert, *Designs of Blackness: Mappings in the Literature and Culture of Afro-America* (Pluto Press, 1998)
An encyclopaedic survey of African American literature, inevitably superficial when it comes to discussion of individual texts, but unrivalled

in range and knowledge of the tradition.

Matus, Jill, *Toni Morrison* (Manchester University Press, 1998)
The best and the most up-to-date of monographs on Morrison's fiction and the critical industry it has generated.

Mitchell, Angelyn, ed., *Within the Circle: An Anthology of African American Literary Criticism from the Harlem Renaissance to the Present* (Duke University Press, 1994)
A gem of a collection, bringing together key critical essays which are otherwise hard to find, because they are out of print or scattered in journals.

Morrison, Toni, *Playing in the Dark: Whiteness and the Literary Imagination* (Harvard University Press, 1992)
The William E. Massey Sr. Lectures in American Civilization, given in 1990, in which Morrison turns the tables on the white American canon from Poe and Twain to Melville and Willa Cather.

Pryse, Marjorie and Spillers, Hortense J., eds, *Conjuring: Black Women, Fiction, and Literary Tradition* (Indiana University Press, 1985)
Offers a good range of articles on black women's writing, in which the question of whether this body of literature constitutes a tradition is itself debated.

Tate, Claudia, *Black Women Writers at Work* (Oldcastle Books, 1985)
Oft-cited collection of interviews with contemporary African American women writers.

Walker, Alice, *In Search of Our Mothers' Gardens: Womanist Prose* (Harcourt Brace Jovanovitch, 1983)
Collection of essays on African American writing and politics. Still the best introduction to Walker's early fiction.

4

Asian American fiction

Helena Grice

Overview and antecedents: the evolution of Asian American fiction

Asian American literature – literature by people of Asian descent either born in, or who have emigrated to, the United States – is a rapidly growing field of ethnic American literature. This growth has occurred mainly since the watershed period of the 1960s, which saw a massive expansion in Asian immigration to the US, and an increased political self-awareness on the part of Asian Americans (inspired by the example of the radical social movements of the 1950s and 1960s – see the Introduction). Yet, Asian American literature has a history which extends back to the mid-nineteenth century, and any survey of Asian American literature should pay attention to its *history*, as well as to the contemporary flourishing of Asian American literature, therefore I want to start this chapter by offering a survey of this history.

As Carole Boyce Davies has also noted in relation to black women's writing, 'Asian American literature' is not a 'fixed, geographical, ethnically or nationally bound category of writing' (Carole Boyce Davies, *Black Women, Writing, and Identity: Migrations of the Subject*, Routledge, 1994, p. 4). Instead, it is a term which is used to refer to texts written by North American writers of Asian descent, gathering together writers of diverse national origins, including Chinese, Japanese, Koreans, Filipinos, South Asians

(Indians, Pakistanis, etc.) and Pacific Islanders, amongst others. One justification for using this term, as King-kok Cheung reminds us, is that Asians in the United States and Canada 'have had parallel experiences', in terms of the conditions of social acceptance they encountered in Canada and America (King-kok Cheung, *Articulate Silences: Hisaye Yamamoto, Maxine Hong Kingston, Joy Kogawa*, Cornell University Press, 1993, p. xv). However, some dissent has recently been voiced regarding the merit and academic (if not institutional) usage of such a term. Increasingly, academics working on Asian American literature choose either to discuss a particular group (Korean Americans, for example), or, more often, stress that use of the term 'Asian American', and its spatial equivalent, 'Asian America', is a limited conceptual term, an imagined geocultural space and a narrow discursive category.

The term 'Asian American' therefore not only covers an enormous variety of ethnic groups, religions, and languages, it also arguably obscures the differences *within* these constituent groups. For example, so-called 'Chinese Americans' may trace their ancestry to mainland China, Taiwan, Hong Kong (which was, of course, until recently a British colony), or Singapore. Depending upon their ancestral region, they may speak Cantonese, Mandarin, or one of any number of local dialects. In addition, class differences and levels of economic security may also be obscured: there is a great deal of difference between an educated and financially secure immigrant from Hong Kong and a refugee from Vietnam. These differences become relevant in the study of Asian American literature, as particular writers often refer to, or pun upon, particular languages, religions, or other cultural practices. Maxine Hong Kingston, for example, discussed later in this chapter, makes several jokes about and puns upon Cantonese words.

Chinese American literature

Asians began emigrating to the United States in large numbers in 1849, when Chinese men began to arrive in the United States, in order to escape the 'intense conflicts in China caused by the British Opium Wars ... the turmoil of peasant rebellions ... and the bloody strife between the *Punti* (Local People) and the *Hakkas* (Guest

People) over possession of the fertile delta lands' (Ronald Takaki, *A Different Mirror: A History of Multicultural Identity*, Little, Brown, 1993, p. 192). This early immigration was mainly to California, where Chinese immigrants joined the 'Forty-Niners' in the search for gold during the period of the Californian Gold Rush. This initial surge of movement resulted in the Chinese term for the United States, 'Gold Mountain', a name that is still in use today. Early Chinese immigrants encountered harsh conditions in America, including what we would now call forms of institutionalised racism. The Chinese Exclusion Acts which were in force between 1882 and 1943, for example, banned the entry of certain groups of Chinese immigrants to America (notably women), and several laws were also passed restricting Chinese Americans' ability to work in California and other states. As prospecting for gold dried up in the 1850s and Chinese immigrants were made to feel increasingly unwelcome in California, many moved into railroad construction, becoming involved in the building of the transcontinental Central Pacific Railroad, in the 1860s. Once the railroad was complete, and this mode of employment disappeared in 1869, the Chinese immigrants either moved to Californian cities, where they took low-paid service sector work as laundry men, or entered jobs in manufacturing, or in more rural areas they became involved in agriculture and construction work. These early migrants were virtually all male; not only did Chinese tradition and culture limit the migration opportunities for women, but several laws (such as the 1875 Page Law) prohibited the emigration of Chinese women to California too. Despite this, some Chinese women travelled alone to the United States, mostly in order to become prostitutes.

Owing to the difficult conditions that the Chinese immigrants encountered, many considered themselves *huaqiao* ('overseas Chinese'), who intended to return to China, and this inevitably influenced the emergence of Chinese American literature. In addition, most early immigrants were poorly educated peasants, who could neither write nor read. As a result, as Elaine Kim discusses at length in *Asian American Literature: An Introduction to the Writings and their Social Context*, early Chinese American literary production was mainly limited to a few autobiographies and oral testimonies by male writers, often Chinese (Temple University Press, 1982, pp. 23–32).

Much of this literature was heavily influenced by Chinese literary traditions, which incorporated elements reminiscent of oral culture, and was often imitative of Chinese literary forms. An example of such writing is the collection *Island*, edited by Him Mark Lai, Genny Lim and Judy Yung, which is a collection of the poems (originally written in Chinese) which were carved on the walls of the immigration station on Angel Island in San Francisco Bay, through which all new immigrants to the United States had to pass, in the period up to 1940. These poems document the despair and difficulty experienced by early Chinese immigrants and are an important surviving resource. Many of the first Chinese American narratives in English were written by students. Lee Yan Phou's *When I Was a Boy in China* (1887), has recently received extensive critical attention as a proto-Asian American autobiography, and was one of the first to be written in English. *When I a Was Boy in China* describes its author's life in China before he emigrated as a student to America, under the auspices of the Chinese Educational Mission, and it is quite self-consciously written for an American readership. Its attempts to counteract prevailing stereotypes of Asians and Asian life are evident when Lee Yan Phou notes that 'I still continually find false ideas in America concerning Chinese customs, manners, and institutions', for example (*When I Was a Boy in China*, D. Lothrop Co., 1887, p. 41). Some of the first Chinese American female writing, as Amy Ling has made clear in *Between Worlds: Women Writers of Chinese Ancestry*, was by upper-class female emigrées, including Helena Kuo, Mai-mai Sze and Lin Tai-yi, who were Chinese-born and Westernised, and who often came from diplomatic backgrounds (Pergamon, 1990, p. 14). Probably the very first Chinese American woman writer was the Eurasian writer Edith Maud Eaton, who wrote stories and magazine articles under the Chinese-sounding pseudonym of Sui Sin Far, in the early twentieth century. In a time of intense Sinophobia, Eaton's stories are sensitive and elegant portrayals of the Chinese in America. In the autobiographical essay, 'Leaves from the Mental Portfolio of an Eurasian', Eaton articulated her lifelong struggle with racism and the contradictions of ethnic identity. She published her only book of stories, *Mrs. Spring Fragrance*, in 1912; Eaton's sister Winnifred was more prolific and wrote numerous novels, under the Japanese-sounding pseudonym of Onoto Watanna. Although it may seem strange that these two sisters adopted pseudonyms in order to write, this may be explained by their sense of a need to 'mask' their true identities as Eurasians in what was undoubtedly a fiercely racist environment. At least by adopting Asian-sounding pseudonyms, the two writers were accepted on the basis of their 'exotic' Asian perspectives.

In the light of this fact, it is unsurprising that subsequent Chinese American writing continued to evince a heightened awareness of racism towards Asians. This is exemplified in Jade Snow Wong's autobiographical *Fifth Chinese Daughter* (1945), which describes Wong's experience of growing up in America as the daughter of strict and traditional Chinese parents, who demanded filial piety and an adherence to Chinese expectations of women. The narrative also charts Wong's struggle to reconcile these demands with her attempts to assimilate into American society. She never successfully resolved this dilemma. On one hand she accentuates the positive aspects of her Chinese identity: she provides mouthwatering descriptions of delicious Chinese dishes (together with instructions on how to make them), and emphasises the respectability of Chinese family life. On the other hand, her autobiography illustrates her eagerness for acceptance into white society, on American terms. It is worth noting in relation to this dilemma the conditions in which Wong wrote her narrative. Although she was encouraged to write her autobiography by a white publisher, s/he extensively edited the manuscript, cutting two-thirds of the original and instructing Wong on what to include.

Owing to the gender imbalance of early Chinese American immigration, one feature of a series of narratives written by Chinese immigrant men was their focus upon bachelor society. Louis Chu's novel *Eat a Bowl of Tea* (1961), for example, depicts the life of a group of ageing Chinese American men in Chinatown in New York, who have left their wives in China in order to search for a better existence. The men are labourers, who work in laundries and restaurants, and lead lonely, impoverished lives in cramped apartments and basements, punctuated and enlivened only by visits to prostitutes, and mah jong games. The novel focuses upon the story of the old-timer Wah Gah, and his son, Ben Loy, who is destined to live the same life as his father. Yet despite the rather depressing theme of the novel, it is a lively, often humourous and engaging account of Chinatown life. Other 'bachelor' novels include Chin Yang Lee's *The Flower Drum Song* (1957) and Lin Yutang's *Chinatown Family* (1948).

Since these publications, Chinese American writing has proliferated, with a series of well-known novels and autobiographies, published in the post-war period. These include writings by several well-travelled and upper-class female novelists. Diana Chang's novel *The Frontiers of Love* (1956), set in Shanghai during the Second World War; and the novels and autobiographies of Han Suyin, and Chuang Hua's experimental modernist novel *Crossings* (1968), are set in a variety of locations, including China, France, and England, as well as America. A notable feature of more contemporary Chinese American women's writing is an emphasis upon mother/daughter relations, which can be seen in the novels and memoirs of Maxine Hong Kingston (*The Woman Warrior* (1975), *China Men* (1977), *Tripmaster Monkey* (1989)), the novels of Amy Tan (*The Joy Luck Club* (1989), *The Kitchen God's Wife* (1991), *The Hundred Secret Senses* (1995)), and Gish Jen (*Typical American* (1991), and *Mona in the Promised Land* (1996)). These texts have been phenomenally successful, perhaps because they keyed into a popular area of attention for feminists in the latter part of the twentieth century.

Japanese American literature

The pattern of development of Chinese American cultural production is largely mirrored by early Japanese, Filipino and Korean immigration and writing. Japanese people began emigrating to the United States following the economic hardships in Japan of the 1880s, at a time when the Japanese government allowed limited Japanese emigration. Unlike the gender imbalance of Chinese migration however, Japanese women emigrated too, mainly to Hawai'i and California, where they became involved in agricultural work (often as sugar-cane labourers). This pattern of Japanese immigration had a crucial effect on the Japanese American demographic profile in the early twentieth century, as well as upon its literary production. Since women emigrated at the same time as men (largely as a result of the 1907 'Gentleman's Agreement' between

Japan and the United States, which permitted immigration for both sexes), the Japanese in the United States started families far earlier than the Chinese, so a *nisei*, or second, generation appeared quite swiftly. Elaine Kim argues that this led to substantial numbers of *nisei* writing from the 1920s and 1930s onwards, both male and female (Kim, *Asian American Literature*, p. 73). Possibly the first of these texts was Etsu Sugimoto's autobiographical novel *A Daughter of the Samurai*, published in 1925, which juxtaposes Sugimoto's American life with both real and fictional portraits of Japan. Like the work of the early Chinese immigrant writers, Sugimoto's narrative seems to be written with the aim of offering a favourable picture of Japanese life for the reader, and provides a similarly complimentary perspective on America. Elaine Kim calls her an 'ambassador of goodwill' for this reason (*Asian American Literature*, p. 24). Although Sugimoto's narrative is highly sensitive in its portrayal of Japan, it also offers veiled criticism of Japanese feudal practices, particularly concerning the treatment of women.

Another notable group of Japanese American texts is a series of autobiographies and fictions written in response to the American government's treatment of Japanese Americans during the Second World War. During this time, in response to the Japanese bombing of Pearl Harbor, the American government interned large groups of Japanese Americans in camps across the US, labelling them 'enemy aliens'. Several Japanese Americans wrote highly critical retrospective narratives detailing their internment experiences, and these include Monica Sone's autobiographical *Nisei Daughter* (1953), John Okada's novel *No-No Boy* (1957), the short stories of Toshio Mori, in *Yokohama, California* (1949), and Hisaye Yamamoto's stories, in *Seventeen Syllables and Other Stories* (1985). Like the early Chinese American writers, these texts bear testimony to their authors' desire for acceptance in America. This is especially true of Monica Sone's interesting, and commercially successful narrative, *Nisei Daughter*, one of the most accomplished autobiographical accounts of the internment experience. An awareness of both her American readership and of growing international tensions at the time dominates *Nisei Daughter*. Sone is acutely conscious of a white readership, and seeks to project an accommodating image of Japanese Americans, throughout, especially in relation to food and cultural practices. If anything, she stresses the dominance of her Americanness. For example, when she visits Japan with her family, she notes that she views it through the eyes of a foreigner, and desires a return to America: 'This America, where I was born, surrounded by people of different extractions, was still my home' (p. 108). Sone takes care to establish a harmonious view of her life in America and her identity as American in a way which conforms to ideals of assimilation. Although she retains the ethnic 'piquancy' of descriptions of the odd Japanese meal or celebration, Sone emphasises that this does not interfere with her overriding identification as a 'Yankee'. Her story follows a fairly traditional autobiographical pattern, starting with early childhood, and with lots of detail about her family life. Yet she experiences racism on a regular basis, a fact which she feels continues to highlight her 'Asianness'. Her final statement, 'the Japanese and American parts of me were now blended into one', appears to assert the reconciliation of her two identities, Japanese and American. As many critics have noted however, this final resolutionary statement seems premature and unconvincing. Sone's resolutionary ending seems to signal her *desire* for a reconciliation of her problems of identity, rather than a resolution itself. Because Sone is clearly addressing a white readership, her premature claims to the resolution of her 'hyphenated identity' may signal an attempt to plead a harmonious existence of Japanese Americans in the United States during a particularly difficult period in American race relations, during the Second World War. Sone learns that choices of identity – Japanese or American – are not always available and unlimited. Racism brings with it the shock of recognition that identity for racialised Americans may be externally imposed, for Sone as *Japanese*, however strange that identity may feel, and that an 'American' identity could remain out of reach. This learning process may be traced through a discernible loss in the narrator's confidence in herself. Early on, Sone's confidence in her ability to choose identifications shines through: 'I was a Yankee', she tells us proudly (p. 18). This contrasts sharply with her later professed need to revitalise and replenish her damaged self-image, in the wake of encounters with racism, when Sone's dampened self-confidence nearly silences her: 'I was so overcome with self-consciousness I would not bring myself to speak' (p. 131). Likewise, the style of the text, as Elaine Kim has noted, shifts from exuberance to a subdued and even stilted style in the later pages.

More recent post-war Japanese American writing includes the work of many more women: the complex, futuristic novels of Cynthia Kadohata, *The Floating World* (1989) and *In the Heart of the Valley of Love* (1992); Julie Shigekuni's novel about mothers and daughters, *A Bridge Between Us* (1995), and Gail Tsukiyama's story about Chinese girl labourers, *Women of the Silk* (1991); as well as autobiographical works by Kyoko Mori, *The Dream of Water: A Memoir* (1995), and Lydia Minatoya, *Talking to High Monks in the Snow: An Asian American Odyssey* (1993).

Korean American literature

Ronald Takaki pinpoints the beginnings of Korean immigration as 1903 (Ronald Takaki, *Strangers from a Different Shore: A History of Asian Americans*, Penguin, 1989, p. 53). Like the Japanese, many of these pioneer Korean immigrants went to Hawai'i, escaping Japanese aggression in Korea at the turn of the century. As the early Korean immigration also included women, the same early appearance of a second generation occurred as it did with the Japanese. One of the most important early Korean writers was the intellectual Younghill Kang, who arrived in the United States from Korea in 1921, and who was writing at the same time as Etsu Sugimoto. But unlike Sugimoto, Kang did not view himself as a guest in the United States, as Elaine Kim has observed (*Asian American Literature*, p. 32). Instead, he desperately desired both acceptance and to make America his home. Like Carlos Bulosan, whose work I discuss in detail later, Kang's perspective is simultaneously that of outsider-observer and immigrant. His novels, *The Grass Roof* (1931) and *East Goes West* (1937) describe both life in Korea and the experience of Korean immigrants in America in the 1920s and 1930s, from a decidedly critical viewpoint. Like his later Chinese American counterpart, Louis Chu, Kang tended to emphasise male experiences in his work.

Surprisingly, given that Korean men and women both emigrated to America early on in the twentieth century, Korean American women were slow to start publishing. Elaine Kim discusses the work that Younghill Kang produced between 1931 and 1937 at some length, but she mentions no female writers (Kim, pp. 32-43). Korean American female writing really came of age in the 1980s and 1990s, when Margaret K. Pai published the autobiographical *The Dreams of Two Yi-min* (1989), which recounts the life of her family in Hawai'i, and Mary Paik Lee published her story of immigration to California, *Quiet Odyssey* (1990). Both of these autobiographical accounts retrospectively deal with the experience of their subjects as immigrants at the turn of the century through to the 1920s, although they were only written in the latter part of the century.

A notable exception to this lack of writing by Korean women is Kim Ronyoung's novel, *Clay Walls* (1987), published just two years before her death in 1989 at the age of sixty-three. Like *The Dreams of Two Yi-min* and *Quiet Odyssey*, *Clay Walls* tells the story of early Korean immigrants who arrived in Los Angeles in the 1920s. But unlike Pai and Lee, Kim Ronyoung's interest lies specifically in the lives that Korean immigrant women led in America. As such, the narrative stresses the story of the central female character, Haesu, and that of her daughter Faye, comparing and contrasting the experiences of first- and second-generation women, including the employment opportunities available to them, and their experiences of racism.

Most Korean American writers grapple in different ways with the effects of the Japanese colonisation of Korea. Korean American writing is distinctive in that it has a history of political activism, both in its depiction of Korean and Korean American activists and through the political propaganda purposes of the writing itself (which is to protest colonial intervention in Korean internal affairs), elements which can be found in Mary Paik Lee's *Quiet Odyssey*, Margaret K. Pai's *The Dreams of Two Yi-Min* and Ronyoung Kim's *Clay Walls*. All of these texts depict to varying degrees Korean American resistance to Japanese colonial rule, protest against the racist treatment of Korean Americans by the American state, as well as imparting a strong nationalist spirit. But it is the writer Theresa Hak Kyung Cha who explores these political issues most extensively in a more recent text which is becoming increasingly well-known, the experimental *Dictee* (1982). Theresa Hak Kyung Cha was born in Korea in 1951, and emigrated with her family to the United States in 1962, where she lived first in Hawai'i and then in San Francisco. After graduating in film and performance theory from the University of California, she embarked upon a career as a film maker and artist, and her work won several prestigious awards. Cha first published *Dictee* in 1982, the same year of her premature death, and the critical acclaim accorded to the text has thus largely occurred posthumously. *Dictee* weaves together a variety of narrative modes, including poetry, journal entries, letters and excerpts from history books, to document both Korean life under Japanese colonial control and the immigrant experience in America. The text is punctuated by non-textual material, such as photographs, maps and calligraphy. Because of its complexity, *Dictee* is an intriguing text, which has been read variously as a post-modernist narrative, protest memoir and Korean American autobiography. South Korean American novelist Chang-Rae Lee's very successful first novel *Native Speaker* (1995), by contrast, raises no such questions of classification and can, unusually for an Asian American text, be characterised as genre fiction. It tells the story of a Korean American spy, Henry Park, who becomes entangled in the corrupt world of a Korean American councilman, John Kwang. It is Henry's task to uncover the secrets of Kwang's rise to power, and this endeavour is set against the backdrop of the alienating and turbulent cityscape of New York City. A gripping book, *Native Speaker* has marked something of a new departure for Asian American literature, moving as it does away from the more traditional preoccupations with ethnic identity and the processes of Americanisation.

One of those traditional images (we might even say stereotypical) of the Asian woman, is contested in Nora Okja Keller's novel *Comfort Woman* (1997), which tells the story of the Korean 'comfort women'. Comfort women were young girls, usually of school age, sometimes as young as twelve, who were forcibly drafted into prostitution to service the Japanese military, during its occupation of Korea, between the late 1930s and 1945. Keller's protagonists in the novel are Akiko, a refugee who has fled to the US, and her daughter by an American missionary, Beccah. Set in Hawai'i, the novel charts Akiko's struggle to come to terms with her past as a comfort woman, the story of which she gradually reveals to her daughter. In relation to the concentration upon female experiences in very recent Korean

American writing by women, it is possible to see how Theresa Hak Kyung Cha's work has influenced writers such as Nora Okja Keller. Critical attention is increasingly being paid to the stories of Korean Military 'comfort women'. Until the late 1980s, the issue had hardly been discussed. Records and documents relating to the practice have been suppressed (the Japanese government 'classified' documents relating to comfort women), and this was coupled with an intentional amnesia on the part of many of the victims (Elaine Kim and Chungmoo Choi, *Dangerous Women: Gender and Korean Nationalism*, Routledge, 1998, p. 3). It is only recently that oral testimonies, written accounts and academic research have begun to appear on the subject; apart from Keller's fictionalised account, there is now also an edited collection by several former comfort women, entitled *The True Stories of the Korean Comfort Women*.

Filipino American literature

Like Korean American writing, Filipino writing has a noticeable gender imbalance. Filipinos began migrating to the United States in large numbers between 1900 and the 1920s following the United States' annexation of the Philippines. Most of these early migrants were farm and agricultural workers, although a few were students. Filipinos also often brought their wives with them, although the large majority of men who migrated were single and unmarried women did not migrate. There are no early texts by women comparable with Carlos Bulosan's autobiographical narrative *America is in the Heart* (discussed later in this chapter), which was published in 1943; or Bienvenido N. Santos's *Scent of Apples: A Collection of Stories* (1979). It is only in the last few years that Filipino American texts by women in English have started to be widely published, the most notable example being Jessica Hagedorn's very commercially successful novel *Dogeaters* (1991), which she recently followed with another novel, *The Gangster of Love* (1996). *Dogeaters* is especially interesting because it draws extensively upon vernacular modes, particularly gossip. It tells the stories of a range of Filipino characters, from the precocious and privileged young girl Pucha, to the impoverished youth Joey, who turns to prostitution as his only means of survival. Hagedorn's many characters represent the spectrum of society in the Philippines, but she favours the stories of the disenfranchised fringes of that society. As Lisa Lowe has extensively argued, Jessica Hagedorn 'radically alters the form and function of the novel and of historical narrative through explorations of alternate means for representing the history of "the popular"' (*Immigrant Acts*, p. 112). She juxtaposes the discourses of history, such as Jean Mallat's 1846 history of the Philippines, with what Lowe calls popular genres, like radio melodramas, and vernacular forms like gossip, in order to cover a range of generic and discursive registers in the novel. Thus, *tsismis* (the word for gossip), becomes one of the central modes of 'knowing' in the text.

South Asian American literature

Indian American immigration, or South Asian immigration (the preferred term), has a slightly different history from those groups mentioned so far. A very short burst of immigration occurred from 1907 to 1917, after which immigration was halted by the United States Congress. This immigration was almost exclusively male: although these young men were mainly married, their wives stayed at home. In addition, the 1917 Immigration Law prohibited men from bringing their wives to America anyway. Initial South Asian immigration was largely a reaction to British colonial activities in India, but due to immigration restrictions this early wave of immigration was not sustained. Takaki notes that by 1940, the Asian-Indian population in the United States numbered only 2,405, sixty per cent of whom resided in California (Takaki, *Strangers from a Different Shore*, p. 314). This uneven immigration pattern helps to explain the relative absence of South Asian American writing until the 1970s and 1980s, when writers like Bharati Mukherjee (author of five novels and two collections of short stories), Meena Alexander (author of two novels, a memoir, and several poetry collections), and Chitra Banerjee Divakaruni (author of two novels) began publishing their work. Bharati Mukherjee's novels, in particular, are becoming increasingly well-known, especially her two most accomplished books, *Wife* (1975) and *Jasmine* (1989). *Wife* tells the story of Dimple Dasgupta, the daughter of middle-class Indian parents, who marries Amit Basu, an engineer, and emigrates to the United States. Dimple has high expectations of her life in America, but her experiences turn out to be very different. She encounters a world of racism and prejudice, where Amit cannot obtain the kind of work he is qualified for and Dimple herself is increasingly isolated. Dimple sees her flat as a refuge from the perilous landscape of New York beyond the front door: 'The air was never free of the sounds of sirens growing louder, or gradually fading. They were reminders of a dangerous world (even the hall was dangerous, she thought, let alone the play-ground and streets)', and she finds herself increasingly isolated (p. 120). In fact, many of Mukherjee's novels depict the new immigrant woman trapped inside her house, and alone, for fear of what lies beyond the door. The more recent novel, *Jasmine*, by contrast, is characterised by constant movement and flight, and can almost be read as a postmodern version of *Wife*. *Jasmine's* heroine, the epony-mous Jasmine Vijh, emigrates to America alone in order to escape her fate as a widow in a small Indian village. Her transformation into Jane Ripplemeyer, wife of a successful Iowa banker and mother of an adopted Vietnamese child, forms the subject of the story. But along the way, Jasmine is raped, exiled, rendered homeless and penniless, and discriminated against as an immigrant, and this reflects Mukherjee's perennial preoccupation with the fractured lives of female immigrants in America. Yet, unlike Dimple Dasgupta, Jas-mine's story is resolutely one of success: she 'makes it' in the US.

The groups whose history I have described – Chinese, Japanese, Filipinos, Koreans and South Asians – together form the earliest Asian presence in the United States. Hence it is no coincidence that these groups (and especially Chinese and Japanese Americans), have the most developed and more prolific literary traditions in America. Newer and later immigration groups include Laotians, Vietnamese and Cambodians, many of whom have emigrated since the 1965 Immigration Law, which abolished immigration quotas. A large proportion of these new immigrants were seeking temporary sanc-tuary from civil war and famine. The end of the Vietnam War, in particular, resulted in many refugees seeking asylum in the US. Takaki observes that many Vietnamese, for example, view them-selves as sojourners, and thus do not see their stay in the United States as permanent, a fact that has affected the literary production of these groups (Takaki, *Strangers from a Different Shore*, p. 455).

Since the 1965 law was passed, there has also been a new wave of immigration from China, the Philippines, Korea and from South Asian countries, notably from Pakistan. These bursts of immigration have invigorated the literary production of their respective ethnic groups, producing a new generation of writers. In fact, the abolition of immigrant quotas since 1965 has dramatically altered the demographic profile of Asian America. Whereas previous to this, American-born Asians outnumbered foreign-born Asians, currently the opposite is true, with sixty per cent of the population of Asian America now foreign-born. At present, Asians comprise one-third of legally admitted immigrants to the US, and Asian Americans constitute three per cent of the total US population (some eight million people). Of these, approximately one-quarter are Chinese American, nineteen per cent Filipino, and roughly ten per cent each of Japanese, Korean, Vietnamese and South Asian Americans.

Periods of intense Asian American literary production, then, map quite exactly on to the history of Asian reception in the United States, and on to the relationship between the United States and various Asian countries at particular moments. For example, the relatively powerful position that Japan's Meiji government enjoyed on the world stage at the end of the nineteenth century, facilitated Japanese immigration and also affected the reception Japanese received in America. The Chinese, in contrast, experienced a far more hostile reception from the United States government due to China's relatively weak position at that same time. Thus, Japanese American literary production flourished quite early, but, during the Second World War, when Japanese Americans were interned by the United States government, very little work was published by them in what was an anti-Japanese climate. Later, Japanese Americans retrospectively wrote about this time, in a newly conciliatory climate after the War. The close relationship between cultural acceptance and literary production is perhaps most starkly illustrated by the rapid development and proliferation of Asian American writing after the 1965 Immigration Law, a time which also witnessed the new social movements which sought to combat discrimination of different kinds in the United States. In particular, the education curriculum innovations that emerged out of the new social movements paved the way for more self-conscious reflections upon issues of identity and ethnicity, like those in the texts that I will discuss later in this chapter. In fact, the advent of Asian American Studies programmes in the 1960s was a catalyst for the self-conscious advancement of Asian American interests. Unlike the writing of other politicised groups of the 1960s, however, Asian American Studies programmes have been concerned to stress the *Americanness* of Asian America, often at the expense of the respective Asian heritage. (There is a clear difference here from other social movement writing of the period, which asserted cultural, racial or gender *difference*.) This emphasis upon America and Americanisation can be detected in the proliferation of literary and autobiographical texts which have emerged since 1965, which largely focus upon the problems of assimilation and encounters with racism, and are usually set in the United States (even when, as in Maxine Hong Kingston's *The Woman Warrior*, the Asian country is 'visited' in the mind of its protagonists).

Amy Ling has recently argued that the United States is increasingly becoming more 'pro-ethnic', notably through the critical attention being paid to so-called minority literatures (Amy Ling, '"Emerging Canons" of Asian American Literature and Art', in *Asian Americans: Comparative and Global Perspectives*, edited by Shirley Hune *et al.*, Washington State University Press, 1991, p. 191). Ling cites the recent publication of the Heath and Norton American literature anthologies, with their extensive inclusions of non-Anglo writers, as an apposite example. She goes on to note: 'we may say with great excitement and anticipation that we are now on the brink of an Asian American literary and artistic renaissance' (Ling, '"Emerging Canons"', p. 192). The reason for this renaissance, Ling suggests, is 'the matrix of political, social, economic, historical, and cultural forces today. The time is ripe, and the majority seems at this moment more and more ready to listen to the *other* and to its own formulations of the *other* as reflected in texts produced by these others' (Ling, '"Emerging Canons"', p. 194). This can be seen in the recent proliferation and commercial success of much Asian American writing.

Asian American fiction and recent literary theory

The field of Asian American studies grew out of an ethnically-con-scious move to coin the term 'Asian American' as a *political* category; and the field has remained committed to the politics which led to its genesis. As I have noted, 'Asian American' was partly a useful cate-gory because in the late 1960s it facilitated the development of a new academic field and institutional identity, with the inception of Asian American Studies programmes in American universities on the West coast. The term has remained in use as a conceptual category since its inaugural moment.

Asian American literary studies has begun to flourish in the last twenty-five years, with increasing academic interest in Asian Amer-ican writers within the academy. As early as 1972, Kai-yu Hsu and Helen Palubinskas published the anthology, *Asian-American Authors*. 1982 saw the publication of the first book-length study of Asian American literature by Elaine Kim, entitled *Asian American Literature: An Introduction to the Writings and their Social Context*, a groundbreaking book which excavated a long-standing tradition of writing by Asian American authors. King-kok Cheung and Stan Yogi's *Asian American Literature: An Annotated Bibliography* appeared in 1988. Amy Ling's *Between Worlds: Women Writers of Chinese Ancestry* (1990) (the first book specifically on Chinese Amer-ican women writers), Stephen Sumida's *And the View from the Shore: Literary Traditions of Hawai'i* (1991) (which specifically focused upon the oral/textual storytelling traditions in Hawai'i), Amy Ling and Shirley Goek-lin Lim's edited collection of essays, *Reading the Literatures of Asian America* (1992), and Sau-ling Wong's *Reading Asian American Literature: From Necessity to Extravagance* (1993), all appeared in quick succession. Something of a revolution has particularly occurred in the 1990s. Before this decade, although Asian American literature was rapidly gaining crit-ical and commercial attention inside the United States, it was largely unknown abroad, with the exception of the successful novels of Maxine Hong Kingston and Amy Tan. The theoretical material per-taining to the body of Asian American literature amounted to three texts (which were historical/sociological surveys of the context or the content of Asian American literature). Since the early 1990s new theoretical treatments have appeared almost monthly, each one with a more specific focus, such as Asian American representations of race and ethnicity on the contemporary stage, Asian American writing and nationalism, Asian American literature and citizenship, the use of silence by Asian American women writers, Asian American poetry, and images of women by Asian American women writers (for details of these books, see the annotated secondary bibliography). Specific authors such as Maxine Hong Kingston and Hisaye Yamamoto have had whole texts devoted to them. There are texts dealing with the politics of Asian American publishing, Asian American popular cultural representation, Asian American ceremonies, and literary representations of early Asian America in preparation. Many of these new works are edited collections, which display both the range and variety of work currently being produced in this field and the proliferation of scholars interested in Asian American writing. Anthologies of American, women's or ethnic literatures now also routinely include texts by Asian American writers.

Much of this theoretical work has benefited from and responded to the expansion of literary and cultural theory in recent decades. Early Asian American literary criticism tended to have a historical or sociological basis, partly in order to illuminate the social conditions of literary production by a group of then largely unknown immigrant writers. This criticism includes Elaine Kim's *Asian American Literature: An Introduction to the Writings and their Social Context* (1982) and Amy Ling's *Between Worlds: Women Writers of Chinese Ancestry* (1990). Although these texts undertook important cultural work in drawing attention to a new corpus of writing, much of this work has been (perhaps unfairly) subsequently criticised as un(der)theoretical, a criticism which has periodically been levelled at the field by both its participants and observers, until very recently. A later phase of critical work highlighted recurrent themes or tropes within Asian American literature: Sau-ling Wong's work on the tropes of necessity and extravagance in *Reading Asian American Literature: From Necessity to Extravagance* (1993) and King-kok Cheung's analysis of the function of silence in *Articulate Silences: Hisaye Yamamoto, Maxine Hong Kingston, Joy Kogawa* (1993), are examples of this. Wong's *Reading Asian American Literature* approaches the study of a series of key Asian American texts through four recurrent motifs – food/eating, the figure of the Doppelgänger, mobility, and play, which in turn are unified by the tropes of 'necessity' and 'extravagance', two rhetorical figures from Maxine Hong Kingston's novel *The Woman Warrior*. In this wide-ranging analysis, she makes use of feminist, ethnic and cultural literary theory. Cheung's *Articulate Silences* also draws upon feminist and ethnic literary theory, to discuss the modalities of speech and silence in the work of three contemporary Asian American women writers. Even more recent studies, including Lisa Lowe's *Immigrant Acts: On Asian American Cultural Politics* (1996), Jinqi Ling's *Narrating Nationalisms: Ideology and Form in Asian American Literature* (1998) and David Leiwei Li's *Imagining the Nation: Asian American Literature and Cultural Consent* (1998), owe a clear debt to contemporary post-colonial, post-modernist and historicist literary theories. Lowe's *Immigrant Acts* argues that the histories of citizenship and gender (in relation to the enfranchisement of white women), and the histories of citizenship and race (in relation to the enfranchisement of non-white males), are interconnected, insofar as the legally defined racial position of Asian Americans has always also been a gendered formation. Lowe then reads a series of texts through their counter-cultural potential to disrupt this formation, including Korean American writer Theresa Hak Kyung Cha's multigeneric text *Dictee*. Jinqi Ling's *Narrating Nationalisms* reads five texts from the period 1957–80: John Okada's *No-No Boy*, Louis Chu's *Eat a Bowl of Tea*, Frank Chin's *The Chickencoop Chinaman* and *The Year of the Dragon*, and Maxine Hong Kingston's *The Woman Warrior*, through the lenses of post-structuralist and post-modernist literary theory. Ling is particularly concerned to counteract the tendency in Asian American criticism, as he sees it, to privilege content over form, and to prioritise contemporary writing over older texts. David Leiwei Li's *Imagining the Nation* is in some ways quite similar to both Lisa Lowe's and Jinqi Ling's books, in its focus upon Asian American citizenship, the notion of 'nation', and Asian American cultural critique. Li's analysis concentrates upon the post-1970s period, and especially upon the well-documented war of words which took place between Maxine Hong Kingston and Frank Chin upon the publication of *The Woman Warrior* in 1976; and between advocates of an Asian American feminism, and those intent on establishing an Asian American cultural nationalist agenda (for a summary of this important debate, see the case study on Maxine Hong Kingston later in this chapter).

As I have noted, increasingly, Asian American cultural criticism is moving away from its traditional focus upon the historical and sociological background of texts and writers, perhaps because it is no longer quite so necessary to illuminate the social conditions of literary production of a group of writers who are increasingly well – or at least better – known. Similarly, as many commentators have observed, denationalisation is a growing trend in Asian American studies, with Asian American cultural studies moving away from a cultural nationalist agenda, shifting instead towards an increasingly globalised, diasporic perspective. Asian American feminist critic Sau-ling Wong's 'Denationalization Reconsidered', for example, refers to three noticeable recent phenomena in Asian American studies: the easing of cultural nationalist concerns, academic cross-pollination between Asian American and Asian studies (what Wong calls the 'growing permeability between Asian and Asian American' (p. 5)), and the shift towards a globalised perspective. Texts such as the already mentioned David Leiwei Li's *Imagining the Nation* (1998), Lisa Lowe's *Immigrant Acts* (1996) and Jinqi Ling's *Narrating Nationalisms* (1997), in their focus upon Asian American citizenship, the idea of 'nation', and Asian American cultural critique, provide both evidence of, as well as commentary upon this shift. These analyses also concentrate upon the post-1970s period, for example by tracking Asian American literature through a series of crucial moments in the development of Asian American cultural critique, from 'emergence' in the 1970s, through to the late-1990s' focus upon issues of ethnic and cultural difference and diaspora. These authors discuss a series of key post-war Asian American texts, including the life writings of Maxine Hong Kingston, the novels and non-fiction writings of Bharati Mukherjee, Louis Chu's *Eat a Bowl of Tea*, John Okada's *No-No Boy*, Gish Jen's *Typical American*, Fae Myenne Ng's *Bone*, David Wong Louie's *Pangs of Love* and David Henry Hwang's *M. Butterfly*, amongst others. In so doing, they provide innovative readings of a refreshing choice of texts, with an unusually high proportion of texts by Asian American men, and with a good mix of canonical and lesser-known texts and writers.

These books have added interesting new voices and perspectives to the Asian American critical debate.

The most recent book to deal with transnational perspectives on Asian American literature is Rachel C. Lee's highly innovative study, *The Americas of Asian American Literature: Gendered Fictions of Nation and Transnation* (1999), which takes a similar approach to the texts discussed above, but brings gender more resolutely back into the analysis. Her project, she states, is to examine how 'political power and contests over political power occur within and beside gendered and sexual processes usually thought separate from and of lesser importance than the state and the global economy' (p. 140). Although some of the texts mentioned above do also attempt to do this, Lee provides a far more sustained study. The book's central proposition is that gender and sexuality remain instrumental to the ways in which Asian American writers conceive of and write about 'America' (p. 3). Lee uses a deliberately plural and shifting conception of 'America' and the 'Americas' (for example, she includes the Philippines in her analysis). She notes the importance of examining 'gender, not detached from, but in relation to what America the nation, America the imperialist invader, and America the capitalist developer means' in relation to a set of post-war American novels (p. 140). Lee uses an interesting choice of texts to effect this analysis: two of them are by Filipino American writers, one from the 1940s (Carlos Bulosan, discussed later in this chapter), and one from the 1990s (Jessica Hagedorn). Both authors focus extensively upon the Philippines as well as (or in the case of Hagedorn, rather than) upon America, and this is one way in which Lee extends her study beyond the boundaries of the United States to include American protectorates as well. She also discusses a contemporary Chinese American writer, Gish Jen, and a contemporary Japanese American writer, Karen Tei Yamashita. Yamashita is a particularly interesting choice, as her 1990 novel, *Through the Arc of the Rain Forest*, is actually set in *Matacão*, an imaginary site in Brazil's Amazon Basin. In considering this text, Lee's analysis also moves beyond Asian American cultural criticism to consider more thoroughly a globalised perspective on American influence. Lee suggests that Yamashita's more extensive focus upon globalisation than that which is to be found in many other Asian American texts, requires a rethinking of traditional definitions of Asian American literature, which often place too great an emphasis upon US nationalist politics, or extend to consider only Asia-Pacific Rim or Asian-influenced locations, such as Australia. A displacement thus occurs from the 'east-west dichotomy' in order to tackle globalisation through a focus upon the fictional site in South America, *Matacão* (p. 107). As Lee shows, each of these texts reveal different perspectives on the Asian American relationship to the nation state. Each also probes various configurations of masculinity, femininity and sexuality. Bulosan's 1946 autobiography *America is in the Heart* presents the US as a place of racial disharmony and violence, a dimension many critics have commented upon (and which I discuss later in this chapter). However, Lee also argues that Bulosan's narrative is unconsciously haunted by images and moments of eroticism, which are often linked to the representation of America as a brutal environment, and explores the manner in which the allure of eroticism becomes almost as perilous for Filipino immigrants as the threat of racist attacks. In her discussion of Gish Jen's novels, *Typical American* and *Mona in the Promised Land*, Lee suggests that the immigration narrative is also inflected with issues of gender, such as female desire and friendship between women. The final two texts discussed by Lee, Jessica Hagedorn's *Dogeaters* and Karen Tei Yamashita's *Through the Arc of the Rain Forest*, both present America in a more attenuated manner as a Western 'civilising' cultural and political influence (upon the cityscape of Manila and the territory of the Amazon basin respectively), rather than as a pivotal preoccupation and setting. Central to Lee's analysis of *Dogeaters* is the manner in which American cinema inscribes a particular version of femininity in Filipino society in the novel, which simultaneously constrains the female characters and also enables an extensive exploration of the politics of gender representation. Lee's reading of *Through the Arc of the Rain Forest* argues that the various stories which comprise the narrative depict crises within the gendered formations of households, families and communities, which are pressured by both ethnic and gender concerns.

Another important, and perhaps groundbreaking, recent critical study is Sheng-mei Ma's 1999 book, *Immigrant Subjectivities in Asian American and Asian Diaspora Literatures*. Like the texts discussed so far, Ma's analysis focuses upon the contemporary period, and all of the texts (and films) he discusses are post-war. The book opens with an interrogation of representations of immigrants in Asian American and Asian immigrant literatures. Ma includes discussions of the work of Maxine Hong Kingston (particularly *Tripmaster Monkey* and *China Men*), Frank Chin (*The Chickencoop Chinaman* and *The Year of the Dragon*), Hualing Nieh (*Mulberry and Peach*), Bharati Mukherjee (*Wife*), and Amy Tan (especially *The Joy Luck Club*), and the films of Ang Lee (*Eat Drink Man Woman*, *Pushing Hands*, *Wedding Banquet*). The book has three sections. In the first, Ma suggests that immigrant subjectivities in many texts (specifically in the work of Hualing Nieh, Pai Hsien-yung, Bharati Mukherjee and Kazuo Ishiguro) are often subsumed in the project of claiming an (Asian) American identity, so the result is an 'immigrant schizophrenic' (p. 1). He discusses at length Maxine Hong Kingston's and Amy Tan's use of the ethnographic myths of Fa Mu Lan and the Kitchen God. He goes on in part two to suggest that the desire to claim America manifests itself as an eroticisation of white bodies in the work of several male immigrant and minority writers (Frank Chin, Bienvenidos Santos, Carlos Bulosan, John Okada and Louis Chu), which Ma views as a version of 'orientalism' (in other words, the construction of the 'orient' as 'other'). In this sense, Ma's analysis has similarities with the work of Rachel Lee. The similarity is also evident in this section in Ma's use of Western feminist theories of subjectivity, gender and post-coloniality. Ma's final section, like Lee's analysis of Yamashita's work, moves beyond the boundaries of America, to consider Taiwanese immigrant literatures, and particularly *Hsiang-t'u wen-hsueh* ('home-soil' or nativist literature) and overseas student literature of the 1970s, including Hualing Nieh's *Mulberry and Peach*, Chang Hsi-kuo's *Rage of Yesteryear* and Yu Li-hua's *Again the Palm Trees!* In this last section, too, Ma considers the films of the Taiwanese immigrant film maker, Ang Lee, which Ma reads as the latest phase of *Liu-hseuh-shen wen-hseuh* (overseas student literature). Ma suggests that Lee's films are conceived globally in relation to immigrant dilemmas and cultures (for example, the films are set in various locations including Taipei, New York's Chinatown, and California). Ma's use of film in his study reflects another recent trend in Asian American criticism. In the light of increasing uses of cultural studies approaches, many critics analyse not just literature, but film, photography, and other non-textual media too. Like Rachel Lee's analysis, Ma's book maps out a terrain largely uncharted by Asian American critics. But perhaps more than Lee, Ma offers an entirely new way of approaching Asian American texts, reading as he does canonical Asian American writers alongside Asian diaspora literatures through the unifying perspective of immigrant (self) representation. But both critics' trans-Pacific and trans-hemispheric conception of the 'Americas' of Asian American and Asian diaspora literatures, provide an exciting new direction in Asian American studies.

In line with the increase of academic interest in Asian America, the last three decades have witnessed the appearance of a range of journals dedicated to the study of ethnic American cultures generally, and Asian American cultures in particular. The first and longest-standing of these is the interdisciplinary journal *Amerasia*, based at the University of California, Los Angeles and founded in 1971. *Melus,* the journal for the Society for the Study of the Multi-Ethnic Literature of the United States, was founded in 1974. Established more recently are the University of California, Berkeley journal, *Hitting Critical Mass: A Journal of Asian American Cultural Criticism* (established in 1993), and the very new Johns Hopkins University Press journal, *Journal of Asian American Studies* (*JAAS*).

The literary production of Asian America has continued to grow apace, with a recent explosion of publishing activity by Asian American writers. The majority of Asian American texts which have appeared since 1993 are by Asian American women. This body of texts is emerging as the literary vanguard of the Asian American movement and of Asian American literature. Asian American women's texts uniquely navigate the tricky waters of identity and cultural identification in ways which often question prevalent theories of identity formation. However, the treatment of Asian American women's writing as a distinct corpus remains a relatively new critical development. The only studies dealing specifically with the writings of Asian American women as a group are Esther Ghymn's *Images of Asian American Women by Asian American Women Writers* (1995), and Phillipa Kafka's *(Un)Doing the Missionary Position: Gender Asymmetry in Contemporary Asian American Women's Writing* (1997).

Asian American writing and experiential realities have suffered from being marginalised in both canonical critical discourses and wider cultural locations. The recognition of this, and the self-identification as marginalised, throws Asian American textual negotiations of identity together in what Sau-ling Wong has termed 'a textual coalition' (Sau-ling Wong, *Reading Asian American Literature: From Necessity to Extravagance*, Princeton University Press, 1993, p. 9). Part of the uniqueness of these texts is their disruption of generic distinctions, especially those between modes of life writing and also of a writer/theorist binary. The next section discusses three important works of Asian American literature. Although all three are prose fictions, all to varying degrees are also autobiographical, and the critical attention each has attracted has been partly due to the generic experimentation of the writer in question. The three texts are also representative of different phases of Asian American writing. Carlos Bulosan's *America is in the Heart* is an example of early literature which sought to address Asian reception in the United States, and accompanying issues such as assimilation, racism and citizenship. Maxine Hong Kingston's *The Woman Warrior* is perhaps the most well-known of the 'mother-daughter' texts which received critical acclaim and achieved phenomenal success in the 1970s, 1980s and early 1990s. As well as being representative of the growing corpus of Asian Canadian literature, Joy Kogawa's semi-autobiographical novel *Obasan* is typical of Asian American fictionalised life writing which focuses upon issues of identity and ethnicity, often from a female perspective.

Case studies: three important works of Asian American fiction

Carlos Bulosan, America is in the Heart (1943)

Received with great acclaim when it was first published, this is the partly fictionalised autobiography of a well-known Filipino poet, who emigrated to the United States as a young man in 1930. Bulosan was born in 1913 in Binalonan in the central Philippines, into a poor peasant family. *America is in the Heart* describes his impoverished childhood, his struggle to save enough money for passage to the

United States, and his subsequent life in the United States as an itinerant labourer and union activist. Carlos Bulosan is one of the best-known Filipino writers in the United States, and he wrote poetry, short stories and essays about Filipino American life between the 1930s and the 1950s. In *Asian American Literature: An Introduction to the Writings and their Social Context* (1982), Elaine Kim mentions his entry into *Who's Who* from 1932 onwards, and also notes that Bulosan's literary fame accelerated during and after the period of the Second World War, when he was at his most pro-lific, producing several well-known works, such as *Letter from Amer-ica* (1942), *The Voice of Bataan* (1944), *Laughter of My Father* (1944) and *The Dark People* (1944) (Kim, pp. 43–57). Nevertheless, Bulosan is undoubtedly best-known for *America is in the Heart*, which has received extensive critical attention since its publication, and has been translated into several languages. Bulosan's literary reputation has been uneven though: in the period just before his death in 1956, his popularity had declined, and was not entirely resurrected until the republication of *America is in the Heart* in 1973, and the publica-tion of E. San Juan Jr.'s extensive study of Bulosan, *Carlos Bulosan and the Imagination of the Class Struggle* (1972).

The narrative opens in 1918 with a description of the young Carlos's older brother Leon returning from the war in Europe. This introduces a preoccupation to which Bulosan returns repeatedly: that of American cultural imperialism in the Philippines, which had increased steadily since the peace treaty which ended the Spanish-American war. Bulosan identifies a 'radical social change' underway in the archipelago – a schism between those agitating for national independence, and those who welcomed the opportunities that the US involvement in the Philippines brought (Carlos Bulosan, *Amer-ica is in the Heart*, 1943, University of Washington Press, 1973, p. 5). Even for the five-year-old Carlos, the image of his older brother Leon returning from a 'strange war in Europe' to 'follow … the plow again' rouses a 'righteous anger' (p. 4; p. 5).

Bulosan paints a picture of extreme economic hardship and suf-fering for his family: 'At this time we had four hectares of land, which were barely sufficient to keep our family from starving. We had crop rotation as an insurance against starvation, and the gen-erosity of the soil was miraculous' (p. 5). The first few chapters of

America is in the Heart describe his early life as an apprentice farmer working in the fields alongside his father. Although his family was large (he had four brothers and one sister), only Carlos and Amado are left to work with his father. His other relatives are employed elsewhere: Macario as an apprentice teacher, Luciano is completing his military service in the Philippine Scouts (a native detachment of the US army), Leon farms in another village and Carlos's mother is a trader in a nearby town. The Bulosan family's life is harsh: they are victims of unsympathetic absentee landlords, failing crops and unscrupulous money lenders, and endure perpetual poverty. In addition, the family suffers a series of personal tragedies, including the death of Carlos's sister Irene; an accident which leaves Carlos with broken arms and legs, and the loss of the family land. These misfortunes culminate in the three remaining brothers leaving the family home in search of a better future. Yet these early chapters describe the rural 'Pinoy' (Filipino) life in lyrical language and with a certain nostalgia. Bulosan's style when writing about the Philippines is eloquent, vivid and engaging – Elaine Kim describes it as possessing a 'pictorial clarity' – and in sharp contrast to the often laboured and faltering style of the later chapters (p. 56).

Once he has left the family home in Binalonan, Carlos travels to the mountain city of Baguio, where he is taken under the wing of an American librarian, Miss Mary Strandon, who encourages him in his quest to travel to America. But when he returns to his home village two years later, he finds his father ill and his mother exhausted. After a brief period working as a fisherman in the nearby town of Lingayen, Carlos returns home once more, to say goodbye to his family before embarking for America.

Part Two of the narrative sees Carlos arrive in Seattle, where he finds lodging in a Filipino hotel, and then work in the fish canneries of Alaska, a familiar route taken by Filipino immigrants to America. It is at this stage of his story that Carlos first comes into contact with the Filipino labour movement, which later becomes the driving force of his life. Carlos embarks upon an existence as an itinerant labourer, travelling between the fish canneries of Alaska and the fruit farms of California, finding work where it was seasonally available, and eking out a meagre existence on the paltry hourly wages that he earns. He is increasingly appalled at the conditions in which the

Pinoy have to live in America, forced into a ghettoised existence by a hostile and racist society:

> I almost died within myself. I died many deaths in these surroundings, where man was indistinguishable from beast. It was only when I had died a hundred times that I acquired a certain degree of immunity to sickening scenes ... that I began to look at life with ... cold cynicism. Yet I knew that our decadence was imposed by a society alien to our character and inclination, alien to our heritage and history. It took me a long time then, to erase the outward scars of these years, but the deep, invisible scars inside me are not wholly healed and forgotten. (p. 135)

Carlos continues to live and work as a labourer until he receives word of his father's death in the Philippines. This marks a turning point in his ability and willingness to continue to work hard and endure the harsh conditions of his existence. Increasing hardship and racist victimisation have also eroded Carlos's ability to accept his fate:

> My distrust of white men grew, and drove me blindly into the midst of my own people; together we hid cynically behind our mounting fears, hating the broad white universe at our door. ... Was it possible that, coming to America with certain illusions of equality, I had slowly succumbed to the hypnotic effects of racial fear? ... My father's death was the turning point of my life. I had tried to keep my faith in America, but now I could no longer. (pp. 153–4)

Carlos tries different ways to escape his poverty in America: he turns periodically to crime, and also to gambling, but always returns to the labouring life he knows best. During this time, he starts to write about the life of the Pinoy in America for a local newspaper. Here he comes into contact with a group of socialist labour activists, who help him to crystallise his vision of a better life for Filipino Americans. One tells him: 'This is a war between labor and capital. To our people, however, it is something else. It is an assertion of our rights to be human beings again, Carl' (p. 186). Another, Felix Razon, succinctly articulates what Carlos had been feeling but had not yet put into words:

> It is but fair to say that America is not a land of one race or one class of men. We are all Americans that have toiled and suffered and known

oppression and defeat, from the first Indian that offered peace in
Manhattan to the last Filipino pea workers. America is not bound by
geographical latitudes. America is not merely a land or an institution.
America is in the hearts of men that died for freedom; it is also in the
eyes of men that are building a new world. America is a prophecy of a
new society of men: of a system that knows no sorrow or strife or suffering. America is a warning to those who would try to falsify the
ideals of freemen. (p. 189)

This articulation closes Part Two. Part Three documents Carlos's
transformation into a radicalised and politically conscious union
activist for the Filipino Workers' Association, and a writer for *The
New Tide* newspaper. It is during this time that Carlos, together with
his fellow activists José and Millar, are captured by white racists. José
is tarred and feathered, and almost lynched, before Carlos escapes.
This episode becomes the catalyst for Carlos's involvement in the
United Cannery, Agricultural, Packing and Allied Workers of
America Union (UCAPAWA). His life seems to be entering a new
stage and he is full of optimism, but then he discovers that he has
contracted tuberculosis, and that it is in its advanced stages. Inca-
pacitated, with rapidly deteriorating health, Bulosan spends many
hours reading socialist texts and histories, including the work of
Friedrich Engels and Mikhail Sholokhov, and the literary works of
Franz Kafka, Federico Garcia Lorca, Maxim Gorki, Anton
Chekhov and Ernst Toller, amongst others. At the end of this section of the narrative, Bulosan is told that he has five years to live.

   The short final section, Part Four, witnesses Bulosan achieving a
degree of literary success. Early in this part of the narrative he
describes reading Korean American writer Younghill Kang's autobiography, *The Grass Roof*, and he ponders Kang's literary success
in comparison with his own:

   Why could I not succeed as Younghill Kang had? He had come from
   a family of scholars and had gone to an American university – but was
   he not an Oriental like myself? Was there an Oriental without education who had become a writer in America? If there was one, maybe I
   could do it too! (p. 265)

This spurs him on to write his own story: 'I sat at the bare table in
the kitchen and began piecing together the mosaic of our lives in

America. Full of loneliness and love, I began to write' (p. 289). Writing for Bulosan becomes his means of fighting for a better life in America: 'The time had come, I felt, for me to utilize my experiences in written form. I had something to live for now, and to fight the world with; and I was no longer afraid of the past. I felt that I would not run away from myself again' (p. 306). Writing also becomes the means by which Bulosan finds a sense of belonging. The closing lines of his narrative read:

> It came to me that no man – no one at all – could destroy my faith in America again. It was something that had grown out of my defeats and my successes, something shaped by my struggles for a place in this vast land, digging my hands into the rich soil here and there, catching a freight to the north and to the south, seeking free meals in dingy gambling houses, reading a book that opened up worlds of heroic thoughts. It was something that grew out of the sacrifices and loneliness of my friends, of my brothers in America and my family in the Philippines – something that grew out of our desire to know America, to become part of her great tradition, and to contribute something toward her final fulfillment. I knew that no man could destroy my faith in America that had sprung from all our hopes and aspirations, *ever*. (pp. 326–7)

Bulosan has also said that he wanted to give a voice to Filipinos in America:

> What impelled me to write? The answer is – my grand dream of equality among men and freedom for all. To give literary voice to the voiceless one hundred thousand Filipinos in the United States, Hawaii, and Alaska. Above all and ultimately, to translate the desires and aspirations of the whole Filipino people in the Philippines and abroad in terms relevant to contemporary history. (Stanley J. Kunitz, *Twentieth Century Authors*, H. W. Wilson Co., 1955, p. 26, quoted in Kim, p. 44)

Bulosan died thirteen years after the publication of *America is in the Heart*, without ever becoming an American citizen. However, *America is in the Heart* serves to document the hardship and racism endured by Bulosan and others like him in the early to mid-twentieth century, and as such is an important source. The critical responses to Bulosan's work have varied widely. Elaine Kim views the text as an example of 'that inclusive and characteristically Asian American genre of autobiography or personal history dedicated to the task of promoting cultural goodwill and understanding' (Kim, *Asian American Literature*, p. 47). Many critics have seen the text as a 'personalized social document', or as a form of protest memoir (Kim, p. 48). Sau-ling Wong has read it as 'Asian America's first major mobility narrative', arguing that the particular form of enforced mobility engendered by a life as a migrant and as an itinerant labourer creates a sense of directionlessness, homelessness and doubt in the narrator, as well as a problematic sense of textual disjuncture (*Reading Asian American Literature*, p. 130). She writes:

> Carlos is continually walking, running, hopping freight trains, taking buses, hitching rides, shuttling back and forth. He is forever making on-the-spot decisions to go somewhere but repeatedly diverted from his destinations, propelled by a host of reasons ranging from the rational to the fortuitous: availability of work (or rumors thereof); racial and/or union-busting violence (or threats thereof) in the form of Filipino-hunting; vigilante executions (in one case tar-and-feathering and near-castration); harassment by police and railway detectives; nasty encounters with rapists, perverts, gamblers, prostitutes, petty criminals, drunks, wife-beaters, and other assorted riff-raff; loneliness in a strange place; chance meetings with acquaintances; happening to miss his brother at home; junky cars breaking down on the road. (*Reading Asian American Literature*, p.134)

Wong ultimately explains the book's enduring popularity and time-honoured position in the Asian American canon by suggesting that it is a

> prototypical Asian American text, situated clearly in a larger American tradition but also prefiguring certain recurrent Asian American concerns. As an extended mobility narrative, *America is in the Heart* at once calls upon and subverts mainstream myths, its very artistic imperfections highlighting the acute contradictions at the heart of American cultural clichés. (p. 136)

Lisa Lowe has rather cautiously read *America is in the Heart* as an Asian American *Bildungsroman* (a novel about early life and development), but observes that the degree of 'unsynthetic constitution

of the immigrant subject' troubles the closure and reconciliation
that is a characteristic of this form (*Immigrant Acts: On Asian American Cultural Politics*, Duke University Press, 1996, p. 45). She suggests that responding to the social and historical indeterminacies of
the text produces a reading more attentive to its oppositional potential, both in providing a critique of its own canonisation and in
rejecting the unitary demands of the *Bildungsroman* form. The most
extensive critical analysis of Bulosan's work has been undertaken by
the Marxist critic, E. (Epifanio) San Juan Jr., whose work I mentioned earlier. His book-length study *Carlos Bulosan and the Imagination of the Class Struggle*, stands out as an extensive analysis of
Bulosan's life and writing (Orion, 1975). San Juan reads Bulosan's
literary and social achievements through the lens of his life as a
sharecropper, through his expatriation and developing social con-
science, in order to present Bulosan as a pioneer Filipino American
radical intellectual. He writes:

> It is my conviction that Bulosan in the years to come will be justly
> recognized as the first Filipino writer in English who, in the period of
> transition from feudal-bourgeois to proletarian ideology, spear-
> headed the vanguard of the revolutionary working-class in its struggle
> against colonialism and exploitation. (*Carlos Bulosan and the Imagina-
> tion of the Class Struggle*, p. 1)

San Juan has subsequently built upon this work on Bulosan in a
series of extensive and influential journal articles. Bulosan has in his
own right been credited as an inspiration for a younger generation of
Filipino American writers, amongst them N.V.M. Gonzalez and
Bienvenido Santos, whose work has developed in similar ways.

Maxine Hong Kingston, The Woman Warrior (1977)

Maxine Hong Kingston's *The Woman Warrior* is undoubtedly the
best-known Asian American text in print. Published to wide critical
acclaim, it has spawned countless articles and books, as well as
arousing intense debates about such issues as genre and feminist
writing. Much of this critical debate has centered upon the book's
troubling generic status. Ostensibly a memoir – the subtitle is
'Memoirs of a Girlhood among Ghosts' – the book won the National

Book Critics Circle Award for non-fiction, but it blends elements of several genres (fiction, myth, auto/biography and memoir) together, in a manner which is not easily categorised. Kingston has been extensively attacked for what several critics have seen as her misuse of generic categories. The Chinese American critic Frank Chin, for example, accused Kingston of reinforcing white fantasies about Chinese Americans (Frank Chin, 'Letter to Maxine Hong Kingston', private correspondence); reviewer Benjamin Tong charged Kingston with writing a 'fashionable feminist work written with white acceptance in mind' (Ben Tong, 'Critic of Admirer Sees Dumb Racist', *San Francisco Journal*, 11 May 1977, p. 6); and the Chinese American writer Jeffery Chan berated Kingston's publisher, Knopf, for categorising *The Woman Warrior* as biography when, he argued, it was self-evidently fictional (Jeffery Paul Chan, 'The Mysterious West', *New York Review of Books*, 28 April 1977, p. 41). Kingston herself has largely stayed out of these debates, (which have become known as the 'Chinese American pen wars'), a subject to which I shall return later.

The Woman Warrior recounts the childhood experiences of a young girl, who is caught between her inherited Chinese (Cantonese) culture, and the American culture of her upbringing in Stockton, California. Kingston juxtaposes and interweaves her adolescent confusion and uncertain perspective with an ironic adult commentary upon her experiences. The text is split into five sections, each episode tracking Kingston's theme of the development of the young girl into the inspirational figure of the woman warrior. Each section relates the story of a particular woman who is formative in the narrator's life, and these maternal figures are both actual and mythical, ghostly and real presences in the young girl's life.

The narrative opens with an injunction to silence: 'You must not tell anyone', Kingston's mother warns her, before going on to recount the true story of Kingston's aunt's illegitimate pregnancy, shame, and eventual suicide (Maxine Hong Kingston, *The Woman Warrior*, Picador, 1977, p. 11). This 'no name aunt' hovers as an absent presence throughout Kingston's story, serving to reinforce the sense of an almost overwhelming burden of Chinese patriarchal culture on the women in the text. This initial section explores the debilitating effects of Chinese patriarchal culture upon females. The 'no name aunt' is a victim of the Chinese village community which ostracises her after she becomes pregnant. Finally, she drowns herself in the drinking-water. Her story is told to the young narrator by her mother as a cautionary tale: it is both a warning not to 'humiliate' her parents, by becoming pregnant herself, but also, and more crucially, it serves as an injunction against passing on this story of familial shame (p. 13). The narrator, though, makes her own use of this tale: as a 'story to grow up on', she uses her aunt's biography as an inspirational emancipatory narrative, preferring to view her aunt as less of a failure, and more as a heroine who successfully wrought vengeance upon those who spurned and controlled her, by throwing her body into the family drinking-well (p. 13). Rather than obeying her mother, she is 'telling' on her aunt, and her family, to the reader, although at the same time she recognises the perils attendant upon that telling, as she notes that her aunt 'does not always mean me well' (p. 22).

This opening section demonstrates the young girl's ability to sift through the cultural fragments that she inherits via her mother and to make use of them for her own purposes. She recognises, though, the confusions and contradictions she faces in separating out her two worlds: 'Chinese-Americans', she asks, 'when you try to understand what things in you are Chinese, how do you separate what is peculiar to childhood, to poverty, insanities, one family, your mother who marked your growing with stories, from what is Chinese? What is Chinese tradition and what is the movies?' (p. 13).

The second section, 'White Tigers', introduces the no-name woman's counterpart in the text, the mythical and legendary character of Fa Mu Lan, or the woman warrior. The narrator's mother, Brave Orchid, also tells this story. Brave Orchid's ambivalence in guiding and instructing her daughter is that on one hand, she offers her daughter emancipatory narratives of female avengers, such as the woman warrior, but on the other, she stresses the perils and pitfalls of womanhood through the narrative of the no-name woman. Kingston notes: 'When we Chinese girls listened to the adults talking-story, we learned that we failed if we grew up to be but wives or slaves. We could be heroines, swordswomen' (p. 25). The young girl's dilemma is that she must decide whether to become a woman warrior, or a no-name woman, and also to reconcile the two visions of her ancestral culture that she receives via these narratives. The narrator says of her mother: 'She said I would grow up a wife and a slave, but she taught me the song of the warrior woman' (p. 26).

The young girl resolutely chooses to become a woman warrior. Fa Mu Lan's escapades are given central significance in the narrative, and are related in a quasi-mythical manner, with Fa Mu Lan herself handling the story in the first person. This strategy accentuates the young girl's heightened identification with her heroine. The character of Fa Mu Lan is loosely based upon the Chinese 'Ballad of Mulan', as Sau-ling C. Wong has noted (Sau-ling Wong, 'Kingston's Handling of Traditional Chinese Sources', in *Approaches to Teaching Maxine Hong Kingston's "The Woman Warrior"*, edited by Shirley Geok-lin Lim, MLA, 1991, pp. 26-36; p. 28). However, as Wong goes on to point out, Fa Mu Lan has 'gained the status of a topos' in Chinese literature, and there are many versions of the story (p. 28). Kingston's own version should be read as a fantasy, as the whole 'White Tigers' section of the text is meant to operate on a mythic and non-naturalistic level. As Kingston herself has noted: 'Fa Mu Lan is a fantasy that inspires the girls' psyches and their politics. The myths transform lives and are themselves changed' (Maxine Hong Kingston, 'Personal Statement', in *Approaches to Teaching Maxine Hong Kingston's The Woman Warrior*, p. 24). Although Kingston has moulded the myth to suit her purposes, the version of the Fa Mu Lan story that we find in *The Woman Warrior* is faithful to some of the basic plot elements of the story, whilst changing others. Traditional versions, as Sau-ling Wong explains it, tend to emphasise the character's battles and hardships as a woman warrior, rather than her transformation into a warrior-figure (Wong, 'Kingston's Handling', p. 30). Kingston's story, unlike traditional versions, opens with the childhood heroine's encounter with an old couple who train her in martial arts, skills essential for her transformation into a woman warrior. Part of this training is the girl's endurance test in the land of the white tigers, which gives this section of the text its name. She must survive without food, shelter or warmth in an inhospitable climate alongside the white tigers as a rite of passage in her transformation into the figure of the woman warrior. She then leaves her mentors and teachers in the mountains and returns to her village, ready to avenge the wrongs done to her family and fellow villagers. Kingston has also added the next section of the tale, when Fa Mu Lan's parents carve a list of grievances onto her back, which it is her mission to avenge. Thus equipped, Fa Mu Lan gathers an army of village men, and, disguised as a man herself, leads her army to victory after victory, pausing only long enough to give birth to her child. Kingston's version ends, in line with traditional versions, with the woman warrior returning to live a life of filial piety with her parents-in-law.

Many of the elements of the Fa Mu Lan story added by Kingston correspond to fragments of other and equally well-known parables. In particular, the back-carving incident corresponds to the popular story of Ngak Fei, a male heroic figure who has characters carved on his back by his mother, also demanding his service in honour of his kinspeople. Similarly, many elements of Kingston's Fa Mu Lan story reflect classical Chinese narratives of warrior revenge and peasant revolution. These connections have led many commentators to lament Kingston's inability to render Chinese myths and parables faithfully in her work. As she herself has observed, many pirate translations and editions of the novel have 'corrected' the 'errors' to be found in her version of the Fa Mu Lan story. In responding to these complaints, Kingston retorted:

> Sinologists have criticised me for not knowing myths and for distort-
> ing them; pirates correct my myths, revising them to make them con-
> form to some traditional Chinese version. They don't understand that
> myths have to change, be useful or be forgotten. Like the people who
> carry them across oceans, the myths become American. The myths I
> write are new, American. That's why they often appear as cartoons and
> kung fu movies. I take the power I need from whatever myth. Thus Fa
> Mu Lan has the words cut into her back; in traditional story, it is the
> man, Ngak Fei the Patriot, whose parents cut vows on his back. I mean
> to take his power for women. (Kingston, 'Personal Statement', p. 24)

The reason that sinologists and critics such as those I mentioned at the beginning of this section have raised such objections to Kingston's work, is their assumption that Asian literary forms con- stitute the main inheritance for a writer who is often at least equally influenced by American (Western) literature. They therefore ignore the fact that diverse cultural influences may lead to the creation of hybrid texts. Proponents of these negative views of Kingston's work seem to be subscribing to a highly problematic notion of narrative and generic purity that is linked to cultural purity, the validity of which would not withstand recent theories of cultural exchange and hybridity.

The much-debated generic identity of *The Woman Warrior* and the 'pen wars' surrounding its reception also raise the question – or more accurately the problem – of readership for many ethnic writers. Much of the criticism levelled at *The Woman Warrior* by Asian American critics like Frank Chin, Ben Tong and Jeffery Chan, ensued from their belief in the responsibilities, as they saw them, of the ethnic writer to his or her ethnic community. This view was set out in the manifesto for Asian American writers, authored by Frank Chin together with Jeffery Paul Chan, Lawson Fusao Inada and Shawn H. Wong, in the introduction to their anthology of Asian American writing, *Aiiieeee!* (1974). In this piece, these authors' ideas about cultural and generic purity versus the 'contamination' to be found in texts like Kingston's, were linked to the idea of the 'ideal' Asian American writer as super-masculine: he would combat racist stereotyping of Asian Americans as emasculated Charlie Chan figures. (This combative view of writing obviously has ironic resonances in Kingston's own work on the woman warrior.) These and other critics who have condemned Kingston for her failure to render Chinese language, myths and traditions accurately, suggest that she has 'failed' to represent faithfully the socio-historical reality of the experience of Chinese Americans (as they see it) in her work. Katheryn Fong has summed up these objections, by addressing Kingston directly and suggesting that the 'problem is that non-Chinese are reading your fiction as true accounts of Chinese and Chinese American history' (Katheryn M. Fong, 'An Open Letter/Review', *Bulletin of Concerned Asian Scholars*, 9.4, pp. 67–9). All these charges rest upon an understanding of the ethnic writer's role in her community as an ambassador to white society, with a duty to her 'own' ethnic group. They also proceed from a hyperawareness of Anglo society. Kingston's wholehearted rejection of such responsibilities attests to her self-styled role as ethnic 'trickster', manipulating literary tools like the myths she rewrites as a means of avoiding precisely the kind of ethnic pigeonholing about which the *Aiiieeee!* critics and others have been so anxious. *The Woman Warrior* masquerades as a series of different kinds of writing, without ever faithfully fulfilling the readerly expectations of any one mode. In so doing, it addresses different readerships by turns. Kingston has discussed how her use of cultural reference points like the Fa Mu Lan myth allows her to interpolate, or exclude, certain groups of readers at different stages in her narrative. Genre acts as one such reference point in the text, which teasingly suggests itself as autobiography, myth, or fiction in turn. In this sense, at least, Kingston manipulates her readership.

The Fa Mu Lan story is immediately juxtaposed by Kingston with this comment on the narrator's own life: 'My American life has been such a disappointment' (p. 47). Through connecting the young girl's life to that of Fa Mu Lan at this moment, Kingston shifts the narrative perspective from a mythical mode focusing upon the woman warrior to that of her mother, Brave Orchid. It is at this point in the text that we see the Chinese American daughter struggling to reconcile the paradoxical versions of femininity and identity with which she is confronted via her mother's stories and teachings. On the one hand, she is inured to hearing Chinese sayings such as 'Feeding girls is feeding cowbirds', whilst on the other hand, she listens to her mother 'talking-story' about Fa Mu Lan (p. 48). On the one hand, she busies herself turning 'American-feminine, or no dates', whilst on the other, she 'went away to college – Berkeley in the sixties – and I studied, and I marched to save the world' (p. 49). On the one hand, she tells us that there 'is a Chinese word for the female *I* – which is "slave". Break the women with their own tongues!', while on the other, she imagines her own revenge upon racism and sexism:

> To avenge my family, I'd have to storm across China to take back our farm from the Communists; I'd have to rage across the United States to take back the laundry in New York and the one in California. ... A descendant of eighty pole fighters, I ought to be able to set out confidently, march straight down our street, get going right now. (p. 49; p. 50)

Kingston's solution, from the vantage point of adulthood, is her writing. At the end of this section, she notes:

> The swordswoman and I are are not so dissimilar. May my people understand the resemblance soon so that I can return to them. What

we have in common are the words at our backs. The idioms for *revenge* are 'report a crime' and 'report to five families'. The reporting is the vengeance – not the beheading, not the gutting, but the words. (p. 53)

Textual vengeance is precisely the vengeance that Kingston chooses to take.

'Shaman', the third section of the novel, deals with Brave Orchid's life. As a pioneering doctor and scholar in China, war medic, vanquisher of ghosts, emancipator of Chinese girl slaves, expert and adventurous cook, competent mother and tireless labourer in her laundry in America, Brave Orchid herself functions as a model of female strength and accomplishment, and as an admirable survivor in her daughter's imagination. As Kingston sharply contrasts the mythical woman warrior's victories with her own 'voice unreliable' attempts to shout down the 'stupid racists', so she distinguishes between her mother's valiant deeds and her 'slum grubby' existence as an immigrant in America (p. 50; p. 52). Crucially, Brave Orchid's life is related textually. The narrator herself pieces together her mother's history by sifting through the textual fragments she discovers: Brave Orchid's medical diploma, graduation photographs and photographs of her father. Although this material is partly supplemented by Brave Orchid's stories about her life, the narrator is left to imaginatively reconstruct the missing sections of her mother's life. In fact, all of the narrator's experiences of China, including mythical narratives, are mediated textually; even her knowledge of her relatives and ancestors in China is gleaned from letters to her parents.

The fourth section, 'At the Western Palace', continues the narrator's exploration of her mother's life, but shifts the focus to America. We are introduced to the narrator's aunt, Moon Orchid, who comes to stay with her sister. The exact antithesis of her sister in spirit, Moon Orchid is a frail and anxious woman, with little personality of her own. Once ensconced in her sister's house, she takes to trailing after her nephews and nieces, the narrator included, and verbally echoing their actions and movements. Moon Orchid's flimsy appearance is reflected in the present that she gives to Maxine: a paper cutout of Fa Mu Lan. Whereas her sister gives the young girl tangible role models to which to aspire, Moon Orchid is able only to offer fragile, thin paper effigies. This inefficacy continues when Moon Orchid fails to live up to her sister's expectations of her existence in America, and goes mad. As many commentators have observed, Moon Orchid thus reflects the 'lunacy' of her name.

Names are in fact crucial in the text. Not only does namelessness obliterate identity – hence the no-name woman – but the naming system in the text reflects the characters' functions in the narrator's life. As David Leiwei Li has explored in detail, all of the woman share the same family name, that of 'orchid' (David Leiwei Li, 'The Naming of a Chinese American "I": Cross-Cultural Sign/ifications in *The Woman Warrior*', *Criticism* 30.4, pp. 497-515). Fa Mu Lan roughly translates as 'wood orchid'; Kingston's mother is 'Brave Orchid', her aunt 'Moon Orchid', and the final woman we encounter in the fifth section, Ts'ai Yen, is 'sylvan orchid'. This naming serves to connect all the women in the text through a linguistic link which stresses the symbolic as well as actual kinship ties which exist amongst them, as well as their shared role as mother-figures for the young narrator. For Chinese-speaking readers, however, there is a further symbolic significance in this naming structure. Although 'Orchid' is a traditional female surname, and 'Moon Orchid' is a possible name, 'Brave Orchid' is not. This is because although 'orchid' carries female connotations in Chinese, 'Brave' carries male, warrior connotations, and this male/female, yin/yang clash would not be conceivable. Thus, the name Brave Orchid denies the confines of femininity, as too does the bearer of the name. The same is true of Fa Mu Lan. In contrast, 'Moon Orchid' is a traditional name, carrying significations of both femininity and lunacy, as does the narrator's aunt.

The final section, 'A Song for a Barbarian Reed Pipe', unites the previous sections, weaving together the narratives of mother and daughter. In so doing, this section extensively interrogates the problems and paradoxes of the mother–daughter nexus. This is particularly apparent in relation to a speech–silence dichotomy. Kingston has already charted the narrator's sometime hostility towards the mother tongue, as well as her attempts to try to escape it. Frequently the site of a repressive representation of women (as slaves, maggots and cowbirds amongst other derogatory labels), her move to escape Chinese as the language of repression and turn to English as the language of individualism runs parallel to her attempt to free herself from what she regards as a stifling maternal influence. Partly this desire for dissociation from the mother tongue is due to the embarrassment she feels at her parents' lack of accomplishment in English. For the narrator, her mother's poor English amplifies her humiliation at school: her own taciturnity causes her teachers to seek parental involvement, only to discover that 'my parents did not understand English' (p. 149). The daughter's hostility also results from the mother's attempts to press her language knowledge into service for the mother. Repeatedly, the daughter's humiliation is accentuated by her mother's insistence that she act as translator. As Kingston notes: 'You can't entrust your voice to the Chinese, either; they want to capture your voice for their own use. They want to fix up your tongue to speak for them. "How much less can you sell it for?" we have to say' (p. 152). But for the young girl, this maternal pressure paradoxically results in silencing or mangling her speech. Brave Orchid's instructions 'You just translate', preclude the narrator from doing so effectively, so her speech becomes warped: '"My motherseztagimmesomecandy," I said to the druggist' (p. 153; p. 154).

But gradually, the daughter moves away from regarding her mother and her language as negative. This move is engendered by a recognition on the daughter's part that the mother's language is actually more similar to her own than she had realised. The mother tongue is not actually Chinese; rather it is a mixture of Chinese and American, and this becomes the language of mother–daughter communication. A recognition of this shared lexicon, and the decision to speak – and write – completes the move towards resolution between mother and daughter, so that ending her text, Kingston is able to say, 'it translated well' (p. 186).

The young girl's inability to converse confidently in English is linked to a crisis of selfhood. She tells us: 'I could not understand "I". The Chinese "I" has seven strokes, intricacies. How could the American "I", assuredly wearing a hat like the Chinese, have only three strokes, the middle so straight?' (p. 150). The narrator's taciturnity is thus linked to her struggle to reconcile conflicting Chinese and American cultural inheritances. Her resolution is not to collapse these dualities and contradictions, but instead to accommodate them. The final story that the narrator relates is one told by her mother, that of the singing poetess, Ts'ai Yen. A real historical figure, Ts'ai Yen lived in AD 175, the daughter of a scholar. She was captured and made to live in 'barbarian' lands for twelve years. She composed the long poem, 'Eighteen Stanzas for a Barbarian Reed Pipe', based upon her time in captivity, from which the final section of Kingston's work takes its title. As with her other uses of Chinese myths, Kingston has edited and changed this one to fit her purpose. Most notably, the Ts'ai Yen story emphasises that those estranged from an ancestral country will retain a psychological link with that culture, but also, more crucially, that this separation can be harnessed for creative purposes, as Ts'ai Yen did, and as Kingston does too. The Ts'ai Yen story is narrated by both mother and daughter, Kingston tells us: 'The beginning is hers, the ending, mine' (p. 184). At this point, stories and selves mingle, so that the daughter contributes to the mother's text and vice-versa.

The Woman Warrior has received extensive critical attention. Early responses tended to focus upon Kingston's use of Chinese sources, and became very dominated by the controversies surrounding her work to which I alluded at length earlier. An overview of this may be found in Sau-ling Wong's essay, 'Kingston's Handling of Traditional Chinese Sources' (1991), which defended Kingston's work from the Aiiieeeee! critics and others. Later criticism approached the narrative from a range of different contexts. Many analyses viewed the text as coinciding with a moment in feminist studies and feminist literary production when the mother–daughter dyad became a focus of particular interest. Viewed in this way, the story emerges as an exploration of the ambivalence of the mother–daughter relationship, in which the daughter at once desires a separation from, but acknowledges a debt to, the mother figure as a source of subjectivity. In Between Worlds: Women Writers of Chinese Ancestry (1990), Amy Ling reads The Woman Warrior alongside Amy Tan's work in order to explore the 'problematic Chinese mother-American daughter relationship' (p. 130). Sheryl A. Mylan has more recently read the text as demonstrating an intercultural orientalism in her piece, 'The Mother as Other: Orientalism in Maxine Hong Kingston's The Woman Warrior' (1996). Other approaches explored the silence-speech dichotomy at work in the text. An early journal article by Linda Morante, 'From Silence to

Song: the Triumph of Maxine Hong Kingston' (1987) has been followed by several other analyses, including a recent example, King-
kok Cheung's book-length study, *Articulate Silences: Hisaye
Yamamoto, Maxine Hong Kingston, Joy Kogawa* (1993). It reads *The
Woman Warrior* alongside work by other Asian American woman
writers as manifesting a particular emphasis upon the importance of
silence as a strategic weapon against oppression. In addition, attention has been paid to Kingston's mixture of generic modes in her
life-writing, and the text has been read as emblematic of a specifically female mode of auto/biographical writing. Sidonie Smith has
explored the text from the perspective of filiality and women's autobiographical storytelling (1987); Leigh Gilmore has built upon this
work in analysing Kingston's focus upon the body in her quest for
self-representation (1994). More recent criticism has located the
text within the development of ethnic (women's) writing, and Asian
American writing in particular. One example is Mary Dearborn's
Pocahontas's Daughters: Gender and Ethnicity in American Culture
(1986). In another influential book, *All My Relatives: Community in
Ethnic American Literatures* (1993), Bonnie TuSmith identifies a language of community to be found in texts like *The Woman Warrior*.
Jeanne Rosier Smith has focused upon Kingston's use of trickster
figures in the text, as a characteristic of ethnic women's writing in
her study, *Writing Tricksters: Mythic Gambols in Ethnic American
Literatures* (1997). In her book on Asian American writing, *Reading
Asian American Literature: From Necessity to Extravagance* (1993),
Sau-ling Wong approaches the text from the perspective of what she
sees as a paradigmatic dichotomy in Asian American writing
between the tropes of necessity and extravagance.

Joy Kogawa, Obasan *(1981)*

Joy Kogawa is a Japanese Canadian writer, who was born in Vancouver, British Columbia, in 1935 to *issei* (first-generation Japanese
immigrants). *Obasan* and its sequel, *Itsuka* (1992) are Joy Kogawa's
partly autobiographical novels about the Japanese Canadian relocation experience during the Second World War and its aftermath.
Kogawa's novels are partly based upon the author's personal experience during the War, as well as documents and papers from the

period (many of the quotations are from the Public Archives of Canada and the letters of activist Muriel Kitigawa). Both novels have received extensive critical attention and acclaim in North America: *Obasan* won the Books in Canada First Novel Award in 1981, the Canadian Authors Association Book of the Year Award in 1982 and the Before Columbus Foundation American Book Award in 1982. Of the two novels, *Obasan* is undoubtedly the better-known. Whereas *Itsuka* picks up the story of the redress movement in Canada, *Obasan* deals with the relocation experience itself and its devastating effects upon the individuals who were involved.

During the Second World War, after the bombing of Pearl Harbor in December 1941, Canada declared the Pacific Coast a strategic military zone and forced between 21,000 and 23,000 Japanese Canadians to leave their homes in British Columbia and move to various ghost towns in the interior, leaving behind their possessions and often splitting families. Those who refused to comply faced incarceration in a camp in Angler, Ontario. Vacated properties belonging to the relocated Japanese Canadians were confiscated by the state and auctioned. Later, in 1944, Japanese Canadians were given the harsh choice of relocation to even more remote areas, or deportation to Japan. Kogawa (who herself experienced relocation along with her family), relates this history and its debilitating effects upon Japanese Canadians in *Obasan*, from the first-person perspective of her female narrator, Naomi Nakane.

The novel is a lyrical and moving narrative about the relocation and its aftermath. *Obasan*'s narrative structure is cyclical, oscillating between the narrative present in 1972, and through a series of flashbacks, to the period between 1941 and 1951. Although the time of the narrative present is the post-relocation life of Naomi, the continuing dominance of the past upon Naomi's present is signalled through the repeated returns to her history through her consciousness. The novel opens in 1972, when Naomi and her uncle Isamu are contemplating the night sky together in a field near the family house in Granton, where they had been moved to in 1951. Then the narrative switches to September of the same year, to the school where Naomi teaches in Cecil, Alberta, and where she is interrupted by a telephone call informing her of her uncle's death. Naomi then returns to the family home in Granton, to comfort her aunt, the eponymous Obasan, the wife of Uncle Isamu. Obasan is a taciturn woman, who communicates with her niece through half-phrases, gestures and her many silences. Yet we at once realise that Naomi and her aunt share a special bond, which does not operate through verbal forms of communication. For example, at this point, Naomi observes of Obasan: 'The language of her grief is silence. She has learned it well, its idioms, its nuances. Over the years, silence within her small body has grown large and powerful' (Joy Kogawa, *Obasan*, 1981; Anchor, 1994, p. 17). The next section sees Naomi remembering her uncle when she was a child. This sets the novel's narrative pattern of shifting between past and present via Naomi's memories. It becomes clear that Naomi's memories of both her childhood and the relocation are blurred and unclear, and that many gaps in the story remain. The task which confronts Naomi throughout the novel is to piece together her fragments of memory, with the information that she is able to glean from others, in order to learn the full story of her history. This history has seen her family scattered across Canada and Japan, the mysterious disappearance of her mother in Japan, the loss of the family home, and the death of several of her close relatives. The quest is partly frustrated by the elder relatives' reluctance to discuss the past with either the child or adult Naomi. Obasan is especially unforthcoming: 'Her answers are always oblique and the full story never emerges in a direct line' (p. 22). The comment Naomi most frequently hears is 'Kodomo no tame' or 'for the sake of the children', as the reason why her elder relatives withhold the truth of her past from her. Despite the family's reluctance to recall the past openly, it continues to affect their present lives, Naomi's included. She notes:

> we're trapped, Obasan and I, by our memories of the dead–all our dead–those who refuse to bury themselves. Like threads of old spiderwebs, still sticky and hovering, the past waits for us to submit, or depart. When I least expect it, a memory comes skittering out of the dark, spinning and netting the air, ready to snap me up and ensnare me in old and complex puzzles. Just a glimpse of a worn-out patchwork quilt and the old question comes thudding out of the night again like a giant moth. Why did my mother not return? After all these years, I find myself wondering, but with the dullness of expecting no response. (pp. 30–1)

Through passages like this, the identity crisis engendered by the Canadian government's treatment of Japanese Canadians emerges as ongoing. Naomi and Obasan illustrate the debilitating effects of relocation upon individual identity. Both women are depicted as stultified by their histories, unable to free themselves from the memories of relocation. Through Naomi's consciousness and Obasan's reliance upon pictures and other records, the stasis of their current lives in the shadow of relocation is communicated.

In sharp contrast to the rest of her family, Naomi's Aunt Emily is one family member who is eager for Naomi to confront her past. Emily is described as a 'word warrior', and works ceaselessly for the Japanese Canadian redress movement. Rather than becoming trapped or controlled by her past, Emily uses it, and various documents of the time, such as her diary, to attain a recognition of the wrongdoing as well as to claim a Canadian identity. She urges Naomi to 'Write the vision and make it plain', continuously bombarding her with documentary evidence about relocation in an effort to awaken Naomi's political consciousness (p. 38). At this early point in the narrative, Naomi however remains reluctant to confront her history:

> Dear Aunt Em is crusading still. In seven canonical words, she exhorts, cajoles, commands someone – herself? me? – to carry on the fight, to be a credit to the family, to strive onward to the goal. She's the one with the vision. She believes in the Nisei, seeing them as networks and streamers of light dotting the country. For my part, I can only see a dark field with Aunt Emily beaming her flashlight to where the rest of us crouch and hide, our eyes downcast as we seek the safety of invisibility. (p. 38)

The fragmentation of Naomi's family by the relocation process is all the more poignant because Kogawa stresses the long-standing intimacy and connection between the maternal and paternal sides of the family. The Katos and Nakanes are described as sharing a special unity: 'the Nakanes and the Katos were intimate to the point of stickiness, like mochi' (p. 24). Chapters one to thirteen are preoccupied with establishing the harmony of Naomi's family life in the period before relocation, and many sections see Naomi remembering the closeness that she shared with her mother, and the houses where the family lived during Naomi's childhood. Kogawa's chosen narrative style allows her to closely juxtapose Naomi's memories of the family home in Vancouver with the huts to which she and her family were later relocated in Slocan, British Columbia and Lethbridge, Alberta. In particular, she remembers the family home with longing: 'The house in which we live is in Marpole, a comfortable residential district of Vancouver. It is more splendid than any house I have lived in since. It does not bear remembering' (p. 60). For Naomi, 'home' signifies a past that must be buried in order to cope with the present, a nostalgic pre-time that is lost: 'these are the bits of the house I remember. If I linger in the longing, I am drawn into a whirlpool' (p. 64). The house in Vancouver assumes an even more charged significance as it was Naomi's childhood home. For Naomi, the childhood home bespeaks the maternal, as her memories of home are indelibly intertwined with her recollections of her mother, before she left the family for Japan. The construction of this association is complex, connecting Naomi's experience of the home with the nightly ritual of storytelling, predominantly enacted by her mother: 'My mother's voice is quiet and the telling is a chant. I snuggle into her arms, listening and watching the shadows of the peach tree outside my window' (p. 66). The Japanese folk story of Momotaro acts as the connective tissue, and it is always this story that the young Naomi requests at bedtime. It is a tale of exile and homecoming: Momotaro is a young boy who is born of a peach, and reared and nurtured by an old childless couple. When he reaches adulthood, he travels and conquers bandits, returning in glory to his family. Momotaro does not just symbolise the move from exile to return, it also symbolises the crucial distinction between inside and outside of the home; the house as an image contrasts with the outside world from which it is distinct. Inside, there is shelter, nurture and warmth, protection from a hostile environment. Naomi, hearing the Momotaro story, imagines her own house in this way: 'Inside the house in Vancouver there is confidence and laughter, music and mealtimes, games and storytelling. But outside, even in the backyard, there is an infinitely unpredictable, unknown and often dangerous world' (p. 69). Not only does the inside of the house provide nurture and the outside represent danger, but Naomi sees these different locations in terms of affirmed or negated subjectivity.

Naomi's selfhood is bound up with her mother and here we can see this interconnectedness working spatially too. The dialectic of (or opposition between) inside and outside is most vividly highlighted when the homestead is contrasted with a snowy landscape. Naomi is a dreamer, and, whilst listening to the Momotaro story, inhabits a fantasy dreamworld, in which she exhibits a heightened identification with Momotaro. In the Momotaro story, the dialectic of inside and outside is exaggerated through a snowy landscape: 'the time comes when Momotaro must go and silence falls like feathers of snow all over the rice-paper hut' (p. 67). In fact, Naomi's empathy with Momotaro's story is carried beyond the terms of the tale into her later experiences of inside and outside dialectics. For example, she carries this with her when she observes the house to which the family are first relocated in Slocan. But here, unlike Momotaro's and the Vancouver homes, the house does not provide protection from the surrounding environment. Rather, Naomi's description emphasises the house's inability to provide shelter and to be a distinct place from its surroundings:

> almost hidden from sight off the path, is a small grey hut with a broken porch camouflaged by shrubbery and trees. The color of the house is that of sand and earth. It seems more like a giant toadstool than a building. The mortar between the logs is crumbling and the porch roof dives down in the middle. ... From the road, the house is invisible, and the path to it is overgrown with weeds. (p. 143)

The inside/outside opposition is critical in imagining the home as a protective haven in hostile surroundings. For this family seeking refuge from racism, especially at a time of heightened anti-Japanese Canadian sentiment, the hut in Slocan offers flimsy security. The inside/outside opposition dissolves even further in the family's next relocation to Lethbridge, Alberta: 'Our hut is at the edge of a field that stretches as far as I can see and is filled with an army of spartan plants fighting in the wind' (p. 230). Here we see the outside threatening to overcome the inside. Naomi emphasises the inadequacy of this house as shelter as well as its inability to become a home: 'One room, one door, two windows', 'uninsulated unbelievable thin-as-a-cotton-dress hovel' (p. 233). Naomi's yearning for her family home and her fear of inadequate housing lead her to fear open space. As

Naomi and her family's political situation in Canada becomes increasingly tenuous, so the family's physical space shrinks, until they inhabit this draughty hut. This is coupled with Naomi's growing fear of open space and she registers her awareness of 'a strange empty landscape', which is almost devoid of shelter (p. 228). This feeling is carried with her, and she tells us in the preface, at a point chronologically at the end of the narration: 'I hate the staring into the night. The questions thinning into space. The sky swallowing the echoes' (no page number).

At the beginning of chapter thirteen, Naomi describes her mother's inexplicable disappearance from the family home. The narrative then becomes the journal of Aunt Emily, written in the form of letters to Naomi's missing mother in Japan, and which extends to two chapters. Although this fills in some of the gaps for Naomi, the central puzzle of her mother's disappearance remains. From this point on, the narrative becomes more thoroughly concerned with the family's ordeal during the series of relocations that they are forced to make. Chapters fourteen to thirty-three chart the moves from the British Columbian coast into the interior, each time to a more remote and less comfortable environment. As with the earlier sections of the novel, these events are interspersed with Naomi's more pensive and intensely personal reflections upon the family history, and the narrative continues to shift between different temporal anchors. Finally, at the end of chapter thirty-six, when the family have congregated (in the narrative present) for Uncle Isamu's funeral, it is agreed that Naomi and her brother Stephen should be told the truth of their mother's disappearance in Japan many years earlier. In the presence of the community elder, Nakayama-Sensei, and in a quasi-religious and highly charged atmosphere, the letters from Japan which unlock the secrets of the past are read. Nakayama-Sensei says to Naomi and her brother: 'your mother is speaking. Listen carefully to her voice' (p. 279). Through the letters of Naomi's Grandma Kato, Naomi and her brother learn that their mother died as a result of the Atomic holocaust in Nagasaki. The description of the bombing and its effect upon Naomi's mother and others is detailed and horrific:

> The woman was utterly disfigured. Her nose and one cheek were almost gone. Great wounds and pustules covered her entire face and

body. She was completely bald. She sat in a cloud of flies, and maggots
wriggled among her wounds. As Grandma watched her, the woman
gave her a vacant gaze, then let out a cry. It was my mother. (p. 286)

The letters state that Naomi's mother died sometime later. The two
final brief chapters following this episode depict Naomi's meditation
upon her mother's fate and her search for a way to pay homage to her
mother and her suffering:

> Silent mother, you do not speak or write. You do not reach through the
> night to enter morning, but remain in the voicelessness. From the
> extremity of much dying, the only sound that reaches me now is the
> sigh of your remembered breath, a wordless word. How shall I attend
> that speech, Mother, how shall I trace that wave? (p. 289)

In common with the rest of the novel, Naomi's attentiveness to her
mother's memory and story at this point is figured through a
speech/silence dichotomy, as the above quotation shows. Now that
Naomi has heard (rather than simply imagined) her mother's story,
she is able to find a kind of peace, and it is with this image that the
novel closes.

Kogawa's retelling of the histories of Japanese Canadian relocation and the Japanese Holocaust at Nagasaki in *Obasan* works as a
kind of cultural remembering which has as its ethical aim the gov-
ernmental granting of redress and apology for those atrocities.
Itsuka develops this endeavour more thoroughly, culminating at the
end of the text in the announcement that redress will proceed. It is
through the exorcism of a traumatic past that Japanese Canadian
female identity is negotiated in *Obasan*. The exorcism of the past
functions as a rite of passage for Naomi Nakane, involving her in a
confrontation with the ravages of both her personal and ethnic histories. These histories are ultimately seen to extensively impinge
upon Naomi's present, and memory in the text thus becomes a
defining feature of identity. *Obasan* and its sequel, *Itsuka*, also have
an interesting extra-textual relationship with their subjects. Both
document the struggle for redress and the struggle to assert a personal interpretation of the story of relocation in opposition to official versions. Both *Obasan* and *Itsuka* were actually used as evidence
in the redress hearings in Canada, held in 1988.

Critical responses to *Obasan*, perhaps unsurprisingly, have tended to focus upon the silence/speech dichotomy which is so prevalent in the text. One of the earliest of these was Gayle K. Fugita Sato's essay, '"To Attend the Sound of Stone": The Sensibility of Silence in *Obasan*', published in 1985, which argued that Naomi's and Obasan's taciturnity is not simply cultural reticence, but is instead a form of attentiveness or intuitive responsiveness. A more extensive discussion of 'attentive' silence in *Obasan*, was undertaken by the feminist critic King-kok Cheung in her study, *Articulate Silences: Hisaye Yamamoto, Maxine Hong Kingston, Joy Kogawa* (1993). Cheung argued that Anglo–American feminist criticism of women's texts has tended to valorise speech at the expense of silence, and that this Eurocentric critical perception has ignored the many modalities of silence to be found in ethnic women's texts. Reading *Obasan* alongside Kingston's *The Woman Warrior* and the Japanese American writer Hisaye Yamamoto's short stories, Cheung persuasively locates Kogawa's novel within a tradition of writing by Asian American women which collectively presents silence as 'articulate' in its many nuances.

Other critical work has read *Obasan* as a 'literature of trauma', focussing upon the novel's cycles of memory and loss. Gurleen Grewal, for example, in her essay, 'Memory and the Matrix of History: The Poetics of Loss and Recovery in Joy Kogawa's *Obasan* and Toni Morrison's *Beloved*' (1996), analyses the ways in which the novel enacts an exorcism of the past through a ceremonial performance of memory. A final group of essays have approached the text through its formal characteristics. These include Teruyo Ueki's '*Obasan*: Revelations in a Paradoxical Scheme', which suggested that the novel operates through a series of formal paradoxes; Marilyn Russell Rose's analysis of a politics/art split in the text, in 'Politics into Art: Kogawa's *Obasan* and the Rhetoric of Fiction' and Donald Goellnicht's 'Father Land and/or Mother Tongue: The Divided Female Subject in Kogawa's *Obasan* and Hong Kingston's *The Woman Warrior*', which views the novel in terms of a balance between mother tongue/culture (Japan), and father land (Canada), as represented though Naomi's oscillation between different linguistic modes and registers.

Investigating further

A useful starting point for further investigation of the range of Asian
American writing would be one of the several anthologies of writing
which have been published in the last twenty years. The earliest of
these is Kai-yu Hsu and Helen Palubinkas's *Asian American Authors*
(1972). However, more recent collections offer a wider historical
survey and broader scope, including Shawn Wong's *Asian American
Literature: A Brief Introduction and Anthology* (1996). Jessica Hagedorn's *Charlie Chan is Dead: An Anthology of Contemporary Asian
American Fiction* (1993), and Sylvia Watanabe and Carol Bruchac's
Into the Fire: Asian American Prose (1996) offer more contemporary
selections, while the Asian Women United of California edited collections, *Making Waves: An Anthology of Writing by and about Asian
American Women* (1989) and *Making More Waves: New Writing by
Asian American Women* (1997) gather together a diverse range of
writings specifically by and about Asian American women. Extend-
ing beyond the parameters of fictional writing, an interesting collection edited by Garrett Hongo, *Under Western Eyes: Personal Essays
from Asian America* (1995), contains pieces which use auto/biogra-
phy as a way of addressing a range of social and political issues
affecting Asian Americans, including assimilation, generational differences and racism. Poetry anthologies include Garrett Hongo's
The Open Boat: Poems from Asian America (1993), and Juliana
Chang's *Quiet Fire: A Historical Anthology of Asian American Poetry
1892–1970* (1996).

In addition to the fictional texts mentioned already, the 1980s and
1990s have seen the publication of several new forms of Asian American writing, including genre fiction. Examples are Japanese American Cynthia Kadohata's futuristic science fiction novel, *In the Heart
of the Valley of Love* (1992), and Korean American Willyce Kim's
mystery/adventure novels, *Dancer Dawkins and the California Kid*
(1985), and *Dead Heat* (1988).

A significant recent development is a series of critically and commercially successful texts which recount personal experiences of the
Cultural Revolution and its aftermath in China. Texts which 'write
red China', include Nien Cheng's *Life and Death in Shanghai* (1986),
Jan Wong's *Red China Blues* (1996), Anchee Min's *Red Azalea*

(1993), Adeline Yen Mah's *Falling Leaves: The True Story of an Unwanted Chinese Daughter* (1997) and Hong Ying's *Daughter of the River* (1997).

For readers interested in broadening their knowledge of the social and historical contexts of Asian American literature, in addition to Elaine Kim's *Asian American Literature: An Introduction to the Writings and their Social Context* (1982), and King-kok Cheung's edited *An Interethnic Companion to Asian American Literature* (1997), I would recommend Ronald Takaki's excellent and accessible history of Asian America, *Strangers From a Different Shore: A History of Asian Americans* (1990).

Annotated short bibliography

Primary

What follows is a very brief selection of writing representing each ethnic group within Asian American literature. I have listed only prose writing.

Chinese American literature

Chang, Diana, *The Frontiers of Love* (1956; University of Washington Press, 1994)

> Set in Japanese-occupied Shanghai in 1945, this novel explores issues of cultural identity and Western colonialism. Chang is a prolific and well-established Chinese American writer.

Chu, Louis, *Eat a Bowl of Tea* (University of Washington Press, 1989)

> Published in 1961, this Chinese American classic tells the story of a community of ageing bachelors in New York's Chinatown.

Chuang, Hua, *Crossings* (Northeastern University Press, 1986)

> A formally experimental, modernist novel about the geographical, cultural, chronological and emotional crossings undertaken by a Chinese American woman in search of her identity.

Wong, Shawn, *Homebase* (Reed Books, 1979)

> Now an Asian American classic, *Homebase* is about a Chinese American's search for and claims to an American identity.

Japanese American literature

Kadohata, Cynthia, *The Floating World* (Viking, 1989)

——, *In The Heart of The Valley of Love* (Viking, 1992)

Kadohata's accomplished first novel, *The Floating World*, addresses the experience of Japanese immigrants in America in the 1950s. *In the Heart of the Valley of Love* is a futuristic dystopic novel, set in 2052, about a Japanese American woman's struggle to make sense of a world gone mad.

Okada, John, *No-No Boy* (Washington University Press, 1980)

Okada's haunting novel is set in Seattle just after the end of the Second World War, and recounts one Japanese American's rebellion against racial hysteria and the effects of the Japanese American internment experience.

Shigekuni, Julie, *A Bridge Between Us* (Anchor, 1995)

A recent novel about the interwoven lives of four generations of Japanese American women.

Sone, Monica, *Nisei Daughter* (University of Washington Press, 1979)

An autobiographical narrative about the Japanese American internment experience.

Yamamoto, Hisaye, *Seventeen Syllables and Other Stories* (Kitchen Table: Women of Color Press, 1988)

'Seventeen Syllables' is a frequently anthologised story about an American daughter and her Japanese mother, which also addresses intercultural misunderstanding and generational conflict. The 'seventeen syllables' of the story's title refers to the Japanese poetry form of haiku, the form of which structures the story.

Korean American literature

Cha, Theresa Hak Kyung, *Dictee* (Third Woman Press, 1995)

A highly experimental mixed-media meditation upon issues of nationality, identity and gender.

Kim, Ronyoung, *Clay Walls* (University of Washington Press, 1994)

A narrative about the early Korean immigrant experience in America in the decade prior to World War II.

Filipino/a American literature

Hagedorn, Jessica, *Dogeaters* (Pantheon, 1990)
  Hagedorn's novel is set in the world of 'dogeaters' (a slang term for Filipinos), and tells the stories of a range of Filipino characters, including a pimp, a freedom fighter and a movie star.
Villanueva, Marianne, *Ginseng and other Tales from Manila* (Calyx, 1991)
  Set in the Philippines, these stories convey the extremities of urban violence and poverty in the provinces.

South Asian American literature

Divakaruni, Chitra Banerjee, *Arranged Marriage* (Black Swan, 1997)
——, *The Mistress of Spices* (Doubleday, 1997)
  Divakaruni's short stories are about the contradictions of creating a new life in America for Indian-born women. *The Mistress of Spices* develops this theme, focusing upon the story of an immigrant woman who runs a spice shop in Oakland, California.
Mukherjee, Bharati, *Jasmine* (Virago, 1990)
  A prolific novelist (author of over six novels), Mukherjee's novels are usually set in America (although sometimes in India), and always focus upon women's experiences and opportunities – or lack of them. *Jasmine* also illustrates Mukherjee's concern with the fractured lives of female exiles in America.

Secondary

Cheung, King-kok, *Articulate Silences: Hisaye Yamamoto, Maxine Hong Kingston, Joy Kogawa* (Cornell University Press, 1993)
  Cheung takes an interesting approach to these three well-known Asian American women writers, focussing upon their use of silence.
——, ed., *An Interethnic Companion to Asian American Literature* (Cambridge University Press, 1996)
  An invaluable starting point for anyone interested in Asian American literature. Each composite area is discussed by an expert in the field, with suggestions for further reading. The collection also includes more general essays on issues such as Asian American literature and theory, and immigration and diaspora.

Kim, Elaine H., *Asian American Literature: An Introduction to the Writings and their Social Context* (Temple University Press, 1982)
The seminal introduction to the field, still an excellent starting point. Contains useful contextual material on the history and culture of Asian America.

Lee, Rachel C., *The Americas of Asian American Literature: Gendered Fictions of Nation and Transnation* (Princeton University Press, 1999)
An interesting focus upon the 'Americas' as opposed to 'America', with excellent readings of a range of very contemporary literary texts, including works by Gish Jen, Jessica Hagedorn and Karen Tei Yamashita.

Li, David Leiwei, *Imagining the Nation: Asian American Literature and Cultural Consent* (Stanford University Press, 1998)
A very recent book, which re-examines cultural debates circling around the development of Asian American literature, such as the controversies surrounding Maxine Hong Kingston's work and the cultural nationalism of the *Aiiieeee!* writers, informed by contemporary post-colonial theory.

Ling, Amy, *Between Worlds: Women Writers of Chinese Ancestry* (Pergamon, 1990)
The seminal work on Chinese American women writers, which juxtaposes the narratives of American-born and Chinese immigrant women from the turn of the twentieth century up to 1990.

Ling, Jinqi, *Narrating Nationalisms: Ideology and Form in Asian American Literature* (Oxford University Press, 1998)
Another very recent text, which provocatively re-examines five canonical Asian American texts from the perspective of cultural studies, post-modernism and post-structuralism.

Lowe, Lisa, *Immigrant Acts: On Asian American Cultural Politics* (Duke University Press, 1996)
Lowe's book is a series of essays on aspects of and issues pertinent to Asian American cultural politics, including immigration, citizenship, canonicity and institutionalisation. Not for the beginner.

Wong, Sau-ling Cynthia, *Reading Asian American Literature: From Necessity to Extravagance* (Princeton University Press, 1993)
Probably the most extensive analysis of Asian American literature published thus far, both in terms of breadth and depth. Wong draws upon contemporary literary theory, feminist theory and theories of ethnicity in an elegant and comprehensive study of Asian American writing in the twentieth century.

5

Chicano/a fiction

Candida Hepworth

Overview and antecedents: the evolution of Chicano/a fiction

> I am to speak to you ... about Chicano Literature and about its iden-
> tification ... [and] since the spirit of Roshomon prevails when the
> words Chicano and identification are mentioned in the same breath, I
> find that I may be taking my life in my hands. (Rolando Hinojosa,
> 'Chicano Literature: An American Literature in Transition', in *The
> Identification and Analysis of Chicano Literature*, ed. Francisco
> Jiménez, Bilingual Press/Editorial Bilingüe, 1979, p. 37)

When Francisco Jiménez published *The Identification and Analysis
of Chicano Literature* in 1979, it was not without good reason he
selected for his lead essay a short piece, written by Luis Leal, entitled 'The Problem of Identifying Chicano Literature'. The word
'problem' occurs frequently in writing about such literature. In
Britain, for example, a basic yet very real 'problem' has been the difficulty of gaining access to the material, although this situation is
improving as on-line bookshops provide easier access to resources
previously only available in the United States. Nevertheless Chi-
cano/a literature is a field that is only 'beginning' to be studied in
Britain and the rest of Europe. Additionally, despite the fact that
work by Chicano/a writers *has* started to filter through onto the
reading lists of 'ethnic literature' courses taught in British universities, students who are new to Chicano/a writing may find its cul-

tural referents bemusing if they fail to appreciate the broader context of Chicano/a history and culture. Within the United States
there are also problems. Programmes in Chicano/a Studies tend
chiefly to appear in areas of the nation where a Chicano/a presence
is high – in the Southwest and on the West coast, for example, and
in states of the Midwest such as Illinois – a fact which suggests that,
while these schools and universities are responding to demand, elsewhere there is little non-commissioned interest in the subject.
Indeed Chicano/a scholars in the United States contend that they
must fight constantly to make their voices heard. The 'problem'
becomes more acute when they articulate their voices in Spanish.

These preliminary observations bring us closer to the more specific 'problem' identified by Leal in his brief essay: that of trying to
define who the Chicano/a actually is. And, if the very identity of the
Chicano/a is open to debate, how does one go about determining
what constitutes Chicano/a literature? More than twenty years on
from the publication of Leal's essay these questions are still being
debated. The pages which follow can therefore offer only the
briefest insight into some of the passions and complexities that have
governed the discussion. Before picking our way through their intricacies, we should establish why questions about Chicano/a identity
have attained a problematic status in the first place. To a degree,
those of us who study the subject outside of the Americas have less
of an incentive to become embroiled in the arguments. Distance
mediates the intensity of the issue. As Ralph Grajeda has remarked,
'personal and social identity is never a "problem" until it is threatened' (Ralph F. Grajeda, 'Tomás Rivera's Appropriation of the Chicano Past', in *Modern Chicano Writers: A Collection of Critical
Essays*, eds, Joseph Sommers and Tomás Ybarra-Frausto, Prentice-
Hall, Inc., 1979, p. 77). In Europe, where the physical presence of
the Chicano/a is negligible, there is no real occasion to take issue
with either those who would proclaim themselves, or the literature
which is promoted as, Chicano/a. In the United States, however,
where circumstances give rise to a different story, the implications of
a Chicano/a identity carry much greater consequence. The
Manichean division between 'self' and 'other' which so commonly
forms part of the discourse surrounding ethnic and socially 'dominant' literatures relates to the Chicano/a in as much as he or she can

be conceived as threatening to an 'American' identity which is premised on what sociologist Werner Sollors terms a kinship of '*consent*' rather than '*descent*' (Werner Sollors, *Beyond Ethnicity: Consent and Descent in American Culture*, Oxford University Press, 1986, p. 6). This '*consent*' school of thought echoes the declaration of Franklin Delano Roosevelt in 1943 that 'Americanism is not, and never was, a matter of race and ancestry' and goes some way towards explaining earlier debates as to whether Chicano/a literature may properly be regarded as 'American' (Arthur M. Schlesinger, Jr., *The Disuniting of America: Reflections on a Multicultural Society*, W.W. Norton & Company, 1992, p. 37). But if the consensus standpoint feels threatened by the advocacy of ancestral, '*descent*' relationships, it simultaneously prompts this opposite camp to adopt both a defensive and offensive stance in the promotion of their own particular ethnic identity, too. Indeed, there is much within Chicano/a literature that can attest to the group's insistence upon 'hereditary qualities, liabilities, and entitlements' (Sollors, *Beyond Ethnicity*, p. 6). Yet herein lies a further complication, for if previously we have talked of a classification based on '*descent*', even amongst those who share the same ancestry there is *dissent* as to who may properly be identified as a Chicano/a. In other words, notwithstanding the fact that one might be *externally* described as belonging to the group, the group has a say in the matter as well. Hence, where people 'who identify ethnically with a group also identify ethically with it ... [and] feel constrained to assume certain obligations', those who variously take charge of defining these 'certain obligations' may well judge others to fall short of the mark (George de Vos and Lola Romanucci-Ross, eds, 'Ethnicity: Vessel of Meaning and Emblem of Contrast', *Ethnic Identity: Cultural Continuities and Change*, Mayfield Publishing Co., 1975, p. 382). Regardless of the process of external or self-ascription, therefore, in the eyes of the group one may well find oneself – and one's literature – 'severed from ... [that] context' (Rosa Linda Fregoso, 'The Discourse of Difference: Footnoting Inequality', *Critica: A Journal of Critical Essays*, 2:2, 1990, p. 183).

The fundamental 'problem' in identifying Chicano/a literature, then, is that even among the principal candidates themselves there is no clear consensus as to who the Chicano/a is. Inclusions and exclusions of membership are made for a host of differing reasons. Bruce-Novoa, mindful that to restrict definitions would undermine the diversity of the literature, proposes 'that *Chicano* remain undefined' (Bruce-Novoa, *RetroSpace: Collected Essays on Chicano Literature, Theory and History*, Arte Público Press, 1990, p. 94). Yet when our objective here is to examine the literary production of this particular ethnic group, if only for the purposes of making a 'beginning' it is imperative to attempt identifying who Chicano/as are and what Chicano/a literature is. For a working definition at the most basic level, let us start by assuming that 'Chicanos are people residing in the United States who trace their ancestry to Mexico' (Carl R. Shirley and Paula W. Shirley, *Understanding Chicano Literature*, University of South Carolina Press, 1988, p. 4). Whilst undeniably simplistic, as further discussion shall reveal, this '*descent*'-based definition is enlightening on three counts. First, when efforts are made to explain the etymological origins of the word 'Chicano/a' there is general agreemet that it derives from the sixteenth-century corruption in pronunciation of *mexicano* to *meschicano* which then, with the dropping of the '*mes*', obviously becomes *chicano*. Second, the fact that *mexicanos* use the gender-specific language of Spanish accounts for the distinction sometimes made between Chicano (male) and Chicana (female). Typically, therefore, when the group as a whole is being discussed it is the masculine identity which is privileged, since this follows the linguistic rules of the Spanish language. And the third reason why this working definition is useful is because it makes it very clear that, not least because the very origins of the word 'Chicano/a' are so evidently rooted there, Chicano/as have a very important historical relationship with Mexico. It is to this aspect of the Chicano/a's cultural heritage that we now turn our attention.

Even a cursory examination of the significant events in Mexico's history is highly recommended as a preface to the study of Chicano/a literature and culture. Precisely because the Chicano/a identity is predicated upon notions of '*descent*', the legacy of the past, as an integral part of the present, will frequently be encoded within the text and hence also be transposed onto the reading experience. Witness, for example, the short story entitled 'Eyes of Zapata' which appears in Sandra Cisneros's *Woman Hollering Creek* (1991). The story derives its inspiration from the historical figure of Emiliano

Zapata, a celebrated participant in Mexico's Revolution in the early decades of the twentieth century. Through reading stories such as these, those of us unfamiliar with Mexican history and conflict along the international border are introduced to a new cultural dimension. In the words of D. Emily Hicks, we 'cross over into another set of referential codes' (D. Emily Hicks, *Border Writing: The Multidimensional Text*, University of Minnesota Press, 1991, p. xxvi). But depending upon our attitude as readers, how we choose to respond to this situation can vary. For example, where a multidimensional work by the culturally hybrid Chicano/a is found to be exacting, readers may react to the literature in one of two ways. These contrasting approaches have been described by Reed Way Dasenbrock as, on the one hand, that adopted by 'the so-called universalist critics' and, on the other, that which assumes the 'contextualist position' (Reed Way Dasenbrock, 'Intelligibility and Meaning fulness in Multicultural Literature in English', *PMLA (Publications of the Modern Language Association of America)*, 102:1, 1987, p. 11; p. 12).

The 'universalist' school of thought believes that the reader's experience of historical and cultural deterritorialisation should be pre-empted by the writer's having built into the text an infrastructure of familiar signification. That is to say, the Chicano/a author is expected to become what, in a different context, Willard Gingerich has referred to as a 'translating narrator' (Willard Gingerich, 'Aspects of Prose Style in Three Chicano Novels: *Pocho*, *Bless Me, Ultima* and *The Road to Tamazunchale*', in *Form and Function in Chicano English*, edited by Jacob Ornstein-Galicia, Newbury House Publishers, Inc., 1984, p. 211). Where allusions are made to people and events of the Mexican past, then, their significance would be explained within the course of the narrative and the reader's 'existing semiotic system' would not be disrupted (Hicks, *Border Writing*, p. 7). But this, suggests Fredric Jameson, is a style of reading which constitutes a hegemonic strategy of containment whereby the ethnic writer is obliged to bow down to the 'interpretive master code' (Fredric Jameson, *The Political Unconscious: Narrative as a Socially Symbolic Act*, Routledge, 1993, p. 10). Further, it is an approach towards literature which, remarks Masao Miyoshi, 'subjugates through assimilation' and is thus often rejected by exponents of a particular cultural identity (Masao Miyoshi, cited by Barbara Harlow, *Resistance Literature*, Methuen, 1987, p. 17). According to the 'contextualist position', it is 'up to the reader, not the author, to do the work' of appreciating these culturally alien referential codes (Dasenbrock, 'Intelligibility and Meaningfulness', pp. 11–12). This philosophy is echoed in the form of a remark made by 'the wri[ter]' in Rolando Hinojosa's *Dear Rafe*: 'The reader is expected to arrive at a personal conclusion and not wait for the writer to tie the noose round the ring to lead the reader by the nose' (Rolando Hinojosa, *Dear Rafe*, Arte Público Press, 1985, p. 66). The two approaches therefore assign the onus of responsibility differently – one to the writer, the other to the reader – but in both cases the building of a bridge across the cultural/historical divide is deemed necessary.

We should consider now the ways in which historians have traced the origin and evolution of Chicano/a culture. Reflecting on the manner in which Matt Meier and Feliciano Rivera have chosen to style their narrative history, helps orient us to how historians have gone about framing Chicano/a history. Originally published in 1972 under the title *The Chicanos: A History of Mexican Americans*, upon revision in 1993 this was amended to *Mexican Americans/American Mexicans: From Conquistadors to Chicanos*, an alteration which lays far greater emphasis upon the historical trajectory of this cultural group. Although the shift in focus marked by the inversion of 'Mexican Americans' to 'American Mexicans' speaks more to present circumstances than to the past and, as such, is of less immediate concern to our project here, it does, nonetheless, suggest a discernible transition in the source of influence over the course of time, a transition which is also played out when one examines generational trends in the Chicano/a's language use. The fact that Meier and Rivera reach back to the time of the conquistadors is of greater import to our current discussion. They begin their account by characterising the Indian civilisations of Mesoamerica and pay particular attention to the Aztecs, whose history extends from Aztlán (their mythical homeland in what is widely supposed to be the area now known as the American Southwest) to Tenochtitlán (heart of the Aztec empire and the site of present-day Mexico City). The opening chapter, entitled 'The Meeting of Two Worlds', explains that the earliest origins of the Chicano/a stem from the sixteenth century defeat of the Aztecs by the Spanish conquistadors – the most renowned of whom is Hernán Cortés – and the subsequent fusing of the Indian and Spanish cultures through the process of miscegenation, or *mestizaje*. It is to this earliest period that contemporary writers such as Gloria Anzaldúa allude when they invoke the names of such Indian deities as Coatlicue and Huitzilopochtli, or speak of characters like Malintzín, the Indian woman who, in her relationship with Cortés, is reputed to have betrayed her country. In addition, it is to this earliest period that the political activists of the 1960s and 1970s related when they formed the student group *El Movimiento Estudiantil Chicano de Aztlán* (MEChA) and created a manifesto entitled *El Plan Espiritual de Aztlán*.

The next significant development in the Chicano/a's history is characterised by Meier and Rivera as a period of 'Revolution and Disarray', prompted by the priest Miguel Hidalgo y Costilla's utterance in 1810 of the now infamous and oft-cited 'Grito de Dolores', calling the people to arms against their Spanish oppressors. After a decade of political turmoil, Mexico gained its independence in 1821 but soon had to contend with encroachments into its northern territory by the 'westering' Anglo-Americans. These people came in such numbers that, according to a survey conducted by Juan N. Almonte in 1834, of the 24,700 people living in the area now known as Texas, only 4,000 were Mexican while the remainder were from the United States, including 1,000-2,000 slaves (Andreas Reichstein, 'Was there a Revolution in Texas in 1835-36?', *American Studies International*, XXVII:2, 1989, p. 77). In 1836 Texas severed its links with the Mexican authorities and declared itself a Republic – a move which incensed the then president of Mexico, General Antonio López de Santa Anna, and precipitated a military challenge to what was considered the Texans' seditious revolt. Remember the Alamo? This San Antonio mission marked the scene of a Santa Anna victory in March 1836, but in a further confrontation in April that same year the Mexican president and general was less successful. The ensuing Treaty of Velasco recognised Texas independence and the following decade it was incorporated into the United States. In his novel *Becky And Her Friends*, Rolando Hinojosa records of his character Doña Mauricia Puig that she 'was born a Spanish subject in 1814; at age ten she was a Mexican citizen; by the summer of

1836, she was a Texan. Later, in 1845, an American when Texas was annexed that December 21st' (Rolando Hinojosa, *Becky And Her Friends*, Arte Público Press, 1990, p. 107).

The year 1846 saw the beginning of what Bruce-Novoa has described as 'the definitive historical event in Chicano history', for this was the year in which the Mexican-American war broke out (Bruce-Novoa, 'The Heroics of Sacrifice: *I Am Joaquín*', in *Chicano Poetry: A Response to Chaos*, University of Texas Press, 1982, p. 61). The conflict ended in February 1848 with the signing of the Treaty of Guadalupe Hidalgo. In defeat Mexico ceded her claims to approximately one million square miles of land, territory which today forms the states of California, Nevada, New Mexico and parts of Utah, Arizona and Colorado. When combined with the United States' 1854 Gadsden Purchase of over 45,000 square miles of land in southern Arizona and parts of New Mexico, almost fifty per cent of Mexico's national territory had changed hands within a matter of years. This was a momentous experience for Mexico even if American historians like David Montejano, himself a fourth-generation Texan, recognise that most people in the Southwest today have only a 'fragile historical sense' that the region's annexation was 'a major historical event' (David Montejano, *Anglos and Mexicans in the Making of Texas, 1836-1896*, University of Texas Press, 1988, p. 1). The estimated 80,000 Mexicans who were caught up in the catchment area of the Treaty of Guadalupe Hidalgo awoke one morning to find that the border had been shifted. Permitted a year in which to decide whether to stay in the United States and become the first official Mexican Americans or else 'return home', the vast majority, for whom the second option was farcical, found themselves 'living in the Other's space' (Bruce-Novoa, 'The Heroics of Sacrifice', p. 49). The huge land cession and the implementation of a new international border helps explain the titles of such Chicano/a histories as John R. Chávez's *The Lost Land: The Chicano Image of the Southwest* (1984) and accounts for a motif which is hugely popular in Chicano/a literature: that of the border as a scar. In the words of Gloria Anzaldúa, it is a '1,950 mile-long open wound / dividing a *pueblo*, a culture / running down the length of my body, / staking fence rods in my flesh' (Gloria Anzaldúa, *Borderlands/La Frontera: The New Mestiza*, Spinsters/Aunt Lute, 1987, p. 2).

In the ongoing development of Chicano/a history, as Meier and Rivera remark, the period '1848 to the end of the nineteenth century … is notable for the effects of change from Mexican to American rule' (p. 4). In the late nineteenth and early twentieth centuries growing unrest in Mexico at the economic policies of the Porfirio Díaz administration led to the outbreak of the Revolution in 1910. This conflict precipitated a massive movement of Mexicans north to the United States. The diaspora created a new group of Mexican Americans such as Ernesto Galarza, who documents his journey from Jalcocotán to Sacramento in the autobiographical *Barrio Boy* (Ernesto Galarza, *Barrio Boy*, University of Notre Dame Press, 1986). Simultaneously a dazzling array of Mexican personalities was thrown into the limelight – characters such as the aforementioned Emiliano Zapata, Francisco Madero, Victoriano Huerta and Francisco (Pancho) Villa, many of whom are mentioned in such works of Chicano/a literature as Rolando Hinojosa's *The Valley* (see the later section on case studies). As both historians and literary writers attest, Chicano/as throughout the twentieth century have been vulnerable to the vagaries of the United States economy. Expelled during the Depression of the 1930s, Mexican labourers were later courted during World War II for their desperately needed labour. With the 1960s campaign for civil rights, it is unsurprising that we should witness the proclamation of the Chicano Movement, *El Movimiento*. From Conquistadors to Chicanos, in the 1960s there was a great insistence upon the richness of their cultural heritage, for as Tomás Rivera has explained, 'the past is what we have and it is all that we have. It is from the past that we are able to perceive, create and give life to our ritual; it is from this that we derive strength, that we can recognize our existence as human beings' (Tomás Rivera, 'Chicano Literature: Fiesta of the Living', in *The Identification and Analysis of Chicano Literature*, edited by Francisco Jiménez, Bilingual Press/Editorial Bilingüe, 1979, p. 21).

The temporal boundaries of Chicano/a literature have been drawn at various places within this historical legacy. Charting the literature's evolution through five historical stages – Hispanic, the sixteenth century to 1821; Mexican, 1821 to 1848; Transition, 1848 to 1910; Interaction, 1910 to 1942; Chicano, 1943 to the present – Luis Leal has provoked no little controversy by contending that the writings of the Hispanic period represent 'an early stage of Chicano literature' (Luis Leal, 'Mexican American Literature: A Historical Perspective', in *Modern Chicano Writers: A Collection of Critical Essays*, eds Joseph Sommers and Tomás Ybarra-Frausto, Prentice-Hall, Inc., 1979, p. 22). Leal argues that the histories, journals, poems and religious plays of such explorers as Alvar Núñez Cabeza de Vaca, Gaspar Pérez de Villagrá and Fray Marcos de Niza constitute the earliest Chicano/a literature. Héctor Calderón and José David Saldívar remain unmoved by this claim and insist that the writer of such work 'is not a Chicano but a Spaniard' (*Criticism in the Borderlands: Studies in Chicano Literature, Culture, and Ideology*, edited by Héctor Calderón and José David Saldívar, Duke University Press, 1991, p. 2). Most commentators argue that while Chicano/a literature has absorbed the rich oral and popular culture of the Spanish colonial period – expressed through folktales, *corridos* (ballads) and *cuentos* (stories) – in actuality Chicano/a literature does not begin until the third of Leal's phases, namely after the signing of the Treaty of Guadalupe Hidalgo in 1848. 'It was at that historical juncture', writes Juan Rodríguez, 'that the literary expression of the Mexican people living in the conquered territory turned from what might have developed into a regional variety of Mexican literature, a Northern Mexican variety, and became – at least in principle – a literature of resistance to Anglo cultural imperialism' (Juan Rodríguez, 'Notes on the Evolution of Chicano Prose Fiction', in *Modern Chicano Writers*, pp. 67–8).

Given the working definition with which this overview began – 'Chicanos are people *residing in the United States* who trace their ancestry to Mexico' – 1848 can certainly be understood as the political boundary beginning the literary expression of the Chicano/a. Yet Rodríguez's comment suggests that the literature is identified by a further criterion: the element of 'resistance to Anglo cultural imperialism'. *Corridos* relating the details of border skirmishes were certainly a popular literary form at this time, as Américo Paredes' study '*With His Pistol in His Hand': A Border Ballad and Its Hero* (University of Texas Press, 1958) makes apparent. *The Squatter and the Don*, a novel written by María Amparo Ruiz de Burton and originally published in 1885 in San Francisco, is also fêted as the first fictional narrative written in English 'from the perspective of the conquered Mexican population that, despite being granted full rights of citizenship by the Treaty of Guadalupe Hidalgo in 1848, was, by 1860, a subordinated and marginalized national minority' (Rosaura Sánchez and Beatrice Pita, 'Introduction', in *The Squatter and the Don*, María Amparo Ruiz de Burton, Arte Público Press, 1992, p. 5). Sánchez and Pita continue: 'At a moment when the few histories narrated by Californios themselves remained in manuscript form and were even then already collecting dust in ... archives, the very act of writing and publishing this historical romance was a form of empowerment for the collectivity' (p. 5). Even where the literature of this period does not speak of resistance directly, the fact of its usually being written in Spanish in itself constitutes an act of defiance. Only very occasionally able to move in the publishing circles of the English speakers, the Mexican American's literary production during this period of 'Transition' appeared chiefly in the popular form of serialised novels and short stories in the Spanish-language newspapers of the Southwest. This fact refers us back to the linguistic 'problem' identified earlier. Aristeo Brito is now in the minority for believing that Chicano/a literature ought only to be written in Spanish 'for it is in that language that our authenticity lies', but the field known as Chicano/a literature is nonetheless limited if the reader is a monolingual English speaker (from an unpublished letter of 1977, cited by Shaw N. Gynan and Erlinda Gonzales-Berry in 'Chicano Language', *Chicano Writers, First Series*, edited by Francisco A. Lomelí and Carl R. Shirley, Gale Research Inc., 1989, p. 307). Joseph Sommers contends that '[s]pecialists in American literature should be expected to know Spanish in order to command a full understanding of their field'. He further argues that as long as Spanish-language literary sources remain unexplored, much of the work from the period of transition will remain inaccessible (Joseph Sommers, 'Critical Approaches to Chicano Literature', in *Modern Chicano Writers*, p. 39).

A general lack of critical attention has similarly rendered the literature of the 'Interaction' years difficult to access. Notwithstanding the increased use of English at this time, publication opportunities for the Mexican Americans were few and far between and so newspapers, journals and periodicals continued to serve as their major vehicles of literary expression. The constraints posed by such publishing outlets meant that writing tended towards shorter forms, like poetry and the short story, and it was not until the 1940s and the 1950s that 'the novel again appeared as a viable genre in Chicano letters' (Rodríguez, 'Notes on the Evolution of Chicano Prose Fiction', p. 71). Where Rodríguez makes reference to Josephina Niggli's *Step Down Elder Brother* (1947) and Fray Angélico Chávez's *La Conquistadora* (1954) in this category, most discussions of the contemporary Chicano/a novel indicate José Antonio Villarreal's *Pocho*, published in 1959, as its starting point. (*Pocho* is written in English, so occasionally it is proposed that Tomás Rivera's ... *y no se lo tragó la tierra* – published in 1971 in the bilingual form ... *y no se lo tragó la tierra / ... and the earth did not devour him* – be accepted as the first Chicano/a novel to have been written in Spanish). In the post-World War II decades there emerged a clear discrepancy between the antecedents of Chicano/a literature and Chicano/a literature itself. Along with this came a new determination of who and what the Chicano/a was.

With the advent of the 'Chicano/a' period, one has to be wary of assuming that 'Chicano/a' is simply synonymous with 'Mexican American'. Although certainly this assumption is commonly made and texts frequently use the terms as interchangeable, much evidence exists to suggest that, in the words of Edward Simmen, 'while it will be readily agreed that all Chicanos are Mexican-Americans, it will not be agreed that *all* Mexican-Americans are Chicanos' (Edward Simmen, *The Chicano: From Caricature to Self-Portrait*, The New American Library, 1971, pp. xii–xiii). Chicano/as are expected to possess a Mexican American bloodline, to pass, as it were, the *prueba de sangre* (test of blood) – but in Simmen's scheme, and in the minds of many like him, what distinguishes the Chicano/a from the Mexican American is a particular philosophical outlook (Bruce-Novoa, 'Canonical and Noncanonical Texts', *The Americas Review*, 14:3–4, 1986, p. 128). Remembering our earlier discussion, inevitably there is some dissent concerning the particular details, but it seems fair to say that many commentators structure their definitions of 'Mexican American' and 'Chicano/a' around a theory which is based upon 'the concept of what sociologists and political scientists have termed a "political generation"' (Mario T. García, *Mexican Americans: Leadership, Ideology and Identity, 1930-*

1960, Yale University Press, 1989, p. 3). Hence for Carlos Muñoz, Jr., while 'Mexican American' is a generic allusion to anyone of Mexican descent born or raised in the United States, 'Mexican-American' (hyphenated) specifically denotes the generation shaped by the United States' politics in the 1930s and 1940s. With Franklin Delano Roosevelt's New Deal, he argues, and with the creation of employment and education opportunities during World War II, a generation was fostered whose behaviour was shaped by a philosophical perception 'that Mexican Americans were finally about to profit from democracy and the "American way of life"' (Carlos Muñoz, Jr., *Youth, Identity, Power: The Chicano Movement*, Verso, 1989, p. 44). By the 1960s, however, this outlook had changed. In common with minority groups across the United States large numbers of Mexican Americans campaigned for political, economic and social recognition during the 1960s and 1970s, and as they did so they came to identify themselves as Chicano/as.

In the radical atmosphere of the 1960s, to describe oneself as 'Chicano/a' symbolised a new assertiveness. It represented, says Bruce-Novoa, 'an act of conscious self-creation' and the desire to 'live out' one's 'intercultural essence openly' (Bruce-Novoa, *Retro-Space*, p. 39, p. 38). Where Niggli's *Step Down Elder Brother* and Chávez's *La Conquistadora* had not fulfilled these criteria, Villereal's *Pocho* had. *Pocho* begins with the exploits of Juan Manuel Rubio, an exile of the Mexican Revolution who settles with his family in Santa Clara, California, fully intending that their residence in the United States will only be temporary even though 'deep within he knew he was one of the lost ones' (José Antonio Villarreal, *Pocho*, (1959) Doubleday, 1989, p. 31). The focus of the novel shifts from Juan to his eldest son, Richard, as the boy struggles to come to terms with the 'strange metamorphosis' that is a life hugely influenced by Mexico yet now firmly allied to the United States (p. 132). Joe Rodríguez argues that Richard must 'synthesize these unique legacies and at other moments ... choose among them' in order to realise an independent identity (Joe Rodríguez, 'The Chicano Novel and the North American Narrative of Survival', *Denver Quarterly*, 16:3, 1981, p. 66). Moreover, argues Rodríguez, in coming to understand himself as Chicano, Richard 'takes the notion of chaos and transforms it from a spectre to a creative source of being' (p. 67). This burgeoning celebration of 'Chicanismo' was an integral part of other art forms, too, many of which were frequently created specifically to reflect the social and political objectives of *El Movimiento*, or the Chicano Movement. In 1965 Luis Valdez, whose name has become almost synonymous with Chicano/a theatre and is also known in the world of film, created the Teatro Campesino in support of César Chávez's United Farm Workers Union and toured the country performing satirical and improvised *actos* (short skits) to highlight the plight of the agricultural labourers. Two years later, in 1967, Rodolfo 'Corky' Gonzales, a staunch advocate of Chicano nationalism and founder of the Denver-based civil rights organisation the Crusade for Justice, created the epic poem 'Yo Soy Joaquín/I Am Joaquín' in which the historical trajectory from Mesoamerican civilisations to the urban plight of the contemporary *barrio* is skilfully presented in such a way as to illustrate the endurance and the pride of the Chicano/a people. Poetry, indeed, was to prove an immensely prolific, popular and accessible forum for the passionate expression of social protest. Abelardo Delgado, Ricardo Sánchez, José Montoya, Tino Villanueva, Luis Omar Salinas, Sergio Elizondo, Alurista – these rank amongst the most outstanding representatives of Movement poetry. But as the authors of *Understanding Chicano Literature* have remarked, it is the novel which has tended to be 'the only literary form written by Chicanos to attract more than passing national attention from the US literary establishment' (Shirley and Shirley, *Understanding Chicano Literature*, p. 140).

In the time which has elapsed since the publication of *Pocho*, the Chicano/a novel has undergone many transformations. While early and successful publications like Tomás Rivera's *… y no se lo tragó la tierra* (1971) and Rudolfo Anaya's *Bless Me, Ultima* (1972) adopted the format of the *Bildungsroman* and echoed, in that search for self-realisation, one of the focal concerns of *El Movimiento*, significant new stylistic developments were already developing by the mid-1970s. As the climate of radical social awareness cooled, so the content of the novels moved away from sociopolitical concerns. In the words of Francisco Lomelí, 'an intense interest in experimentation effected new trends' (Francisco A. Lomelí, 'Chicana Novelists in the Process of Creating Fictive Voices', in *Beyond Stereotypes: The Critical Analysis of Chicana Literature*, edited by María Herrera-Sobek,

Bilingual Press/Editorial Bilingüe, 1985, p. 34). There is no better example of this than Ron Arias's *The Road to Tamazunchale* (1975), with its qualities of magical realism. Additionally, and perhaps even more significantly, in spite of considerable opposition from their male counterparts it was at this point that Chicana fiction became prominent on the literary scene. Although little read now, early fictions such as Berta Ornelas's *Come Down from the Mound* (1975) and Isabella Ríos's *Victuum* (1976) represented a major milestone in the evolution of Chicano/a literature. Since then Chicana writing has gone from strength to strength. Sandra Cisneros (*The House on Mango Street*, 1984; *Woman Hollering Creek*, 1991), Denise Chávez (*The Last of the Menu Girls*, 1986; *Face of an Angel*, 1995), Ana Castillo (*The Mixquiahuala Letters*, 1986; *Sapogonia*, 1990; *So Far From God*, 1994; *Loverboys*, 1996; *Peel My Love Like an Onion*, 1999), Lucha Corpi (*Delia's Song*, 1988; *Eulogy for a Brown Angel: A Mystery Novel*, 1992; *Cactus Blood*, 1995) and Helena María Viramontes (*The Moths and Other Stories*, 1985; *Under the Feet of Jesus*, 1995) are all now leading figures in the Chicano/a literary world. With the Movement more a memory than a motivation, the texts produced by Chicano/as today continually challenge 'the concepts of Chicano literature' (Bruce-Novoa, *RetroSpace*, p. 85). 'Ethnicity is no longer the ultimate aim', says Francisco Lomelí, 'but instead becomes a natural component of those who participate in the action' (Francisco Lomelí, 'Chicana Novelists in the Process of Creating Fictive Voices', pp. 34–5). Like Sonny Baca and Rafe Buenrostro, both of whom are fictional characters in the emergent field of the Chicano/a murder mystery (the creations of Rudolfo Anaya and Rolando Hinojosa respectively), we as readers must now follow the trail in order to see where the action takes us.

Chicano/a literature and recent literary theory

As *A Reader's Guide to Contemporary Literary Theory* informs us, 'if we are to be adventurous and exploratory in our reading *of* literature, we must also be adventurous in our thinking *about* literature' (Raman Selden, Peter Widdowson and Peter Brooker, *A Reader's Guide to Contemporary Literary Theory*, Prentice Hall/Harvester Wheatsheaf, 4th edition, 1997, p. 4). This, of course, is the very *raison d'être* of literary criticism. Whilst still by no means prolific, critical interest in Chicano/a literature has indeed been growing. Since the bulk of this critical output has appeared in the form of journal articles, however, it can be difficult to access if one's library does not carry the titles which specialise in ethnic cultural production. *Aztlán: A Journal of Chicano Studies, Bilingual Review/Revista Bilingüe, Confluencia: Revista Hispanica de Cultural y Literatura* and *The Americas Review* (formerly known as *Revista Chicano-Riqueña*) have each been rich sources of critical material, although their circulation has been somewhat limited. Journals which historically catered more to the establishment now feature more criticism of Chicano/a texts, though, *American Literary History* and *American Literature* among them. While full-length scholarly texts devoted to the critical analysis of Chicano/a literature are not yet abundant, with major publishing houses having been fairly slow to take an interest in the field, this situation is changing.

The literary criticism applied to Chicano/a literature today is far more appreciative of the 'complex predicament of theories and theorists' than it was in the past, insist Héctor Calderón and José David Saldívar (*Criticism in the Borderlands*, eds Calderón and Saldívar, p. 6). 'Not simply trendy theoretical positions grafted onto the Chicano', moreover, contemporary debates about post-modernist, post-colonialist theories and the like 'stake out critical realms that Chicano cultures traverse' (Rafael Pérez-Torres, *Movements In Chicano Poetry: Against Myths, Against Margins*, Cambridge University Press, 1995, p. 4). These sophisticated discourses are nonetheless indebted to their predecessors and so I shall discuss earlier critical efforts in order to give us an insight into the central preoccupations of these later, more theoretical narratives. Since Joseph Sommers is widely credited as the first person to attempt theorising critical orientations toward Chicano/a literature, the three kinds of criticism he identified – termed 'formalist, culturalist and historical–dialectical' – will form the critical skeleton with which we begin (Sommers, 'Critical Approaches to Chicano Literature', p. 31).

Sommers' purpose in distinguishing between these approaches was, in the words of Peter Widdowson and Peter Brooker, primarily to show that 'the effect of theorizing literature is to see how different theories raise different questions about it from different foci of interest' (Raman Selden, Peter Widdowson and Peter Brooker, *A Reader's Guide to Contemporary Literary Theory*, p. 4). With a personal preference for the historical-dialectical, Sommers did not perceive the formalist and culturalist approaches to be rewarding avenues for the interpretation of Chicano/a literature. The formalist approach, most prominent in academic publications at the time, was disparaged for examining the text as an autonomous, non-referential entity; for judging the literature according to the assumption that there existed some universal (for which read dominant, Anglo-American) standard of excellence in which regional and historically specific subject matter had no place; and for focusing solely on the written word, as a consequence of which it was instantly dismissive of the Chicano/as' oral and popular culture. The culturalist approach, on the other hand, was considered overly compensatory for the formalist's failings. As its name implies, the methodology was to lay particular emphasis on the cultural characteristics of the Chicano/a. And as a consequence of actively seeking to celebrate 'the notion of *cultural uniqueness*' derived from such supposedly traditional characteristic features as 'family structures, linguistic and thematic survivals, anti-gringo attitudes, pre-Hispanic symbology, notions of a mythic past, and folk beliefs ranging from *la llorona* to the Virgin of Guadalupe' (Sommers, 'Critical Approaches to Chicano Literature', p. 34), it was too quick to offer unswerving support to any literary manifestation of the like.

As numerous critics have attested, this culturalist approach to literary criticism was exceptionally popular amongst Chicano/as in the 1960s, allied as it was to the spirit of cultural nationalism. During the heady days of the Movement, the Chicano/a cause, or *la causa*, was so keenly promoted that, in retrospect, Chicano author Rudolfo Anaya believes writers rather 'hit the reader over the head with ideology' (John Crawford, 'Rudolfo Anaya', *This is About Vision: Interviews with Southwestern Writers*, edited by William Balassi, John F. Crawford and Annie O. Eysturoy, University of New Mexico Press, 1990, p. 90). If one consequence of the interest of this approach was that there was a great expectation on the part of Chicano/a writers to perform to certain criteria, as Anaya's comment in part implies, there were also repercussions for the reader. Tomás Rivera admits that Chicano/a writers displayed 'little concern

regarding acceptance by the larger/majority population' during
the 1960s and early 1970s (Tomás Rivera, 'Richard Rodríguez's
Hunger of Memory as Humanistic Antithesis', in *Tomás Rivera:
The Man and His Work, 1935-1984*, eds Vernon E. Lattin, Rolando
Hinojosa and Gary D. Keller, Bilingual Review/Press, 1988, p. 32).
In fact, culturalist criticism actually took this to the stage of assuming 'that Chicano literature can be understood only by Chicanos
and interpreted only by Chicanos' (Sommers, 'Critical Approaches
to Chicano Literature', p. 35). While Sommers himself did not
entirely dissent from this belief, he nonetheless expressed misgiv-
ings about a critical methodology so 'designed for and limited to'
a specific ethnic readership that it denied the possibility of other
literatures having 'comparable structural features (such as an oral
tradition or the bilingual mode or historical trajectories involving
confrontation with class exploitation and institutional racism)'
(p. 36).

Unlike culturalist criticism, Sommers insisted, the historical–
dialectical approach placed a particular emphasis on 'a *critical* criticism'. Sommers further advocated the practice as a form of interpretation which, unlike formalist criticism, incorporated a concern
for 'the sociology of literature', according to which the written word
was studied not in isolation but 'in relation to its cultural ambience'
(p. 38; p. 37; p. 36). Read in this more Marxist light, Chicano/a literature could be understood as an integral part of Chicano/as'
struggle for the right to their own cultural expression. Seeing this as
the least reductive of the three critical theories, Sommers called for
it to be 'practised with creativity and openness' (p. 40). But, as critics like Wilson Neate have since commented, in this practice, too,
the literary text is 'a closed work[,] whose meaning is accessible so
long as the critic situates it as a mirror, or an allegory, of the historical events in process'. Neate further argues that Sommers' 'understanding of referentiality appears to demand that literature, at least
the Chicano/a literature worthy of study, comprise a mode of representation which documents reality in an unproblematic, reflective
way' (Wilson Neate, *Tolerating Ambiguity: Ethnicity and Community
in Chicano/a Writing*, Peter Lang, 1998, p. 27, pp. 27–28).

Where formalist criticism was taken to task for its reliance upon
what we might call, after Edward Said, the 'sanctioned narratives' of

the hegemonic, critical discourse now articulates the deconstructive strategies of post-modernism and post-colonialism ideology (Edward Said, *Culture and Imperialism* (1993) Vintage, 1994, p. 380). Where culturalist criticism was treated warily for its unquestioning advocacy of the unique qualities of Chicano/a culture, more recent cultural studies have interrogated the very concepts of 'culture' and 'ethnicity', as well as 'nationality' and 'identity'. Indeed, a vast array of publications exist to challenge the coherency and validity of all these terms of reference, so that literary theory in the present decade is more aware than ever of the 'insistence on a pluralist, multidimensional, or multi-faceted concept of self' (Michael M. J. Fischer, 'Ethnicity and the Post-Modern Arts of Memory', in *Writing Culture: The Poetics and Politics of Ethnography*, edited by James Clifford and George E. Marcus, University of California Press, 1986, p. 196). Of the recent critical theory applied to Chicano/a literature, feminist criticism has been most responsible for promoting an awareness of the complexities of the subject position.

As with the feminist movement at large, the initial impetus behind the development of a Chicana feminist critical theory was the perceived need to challenge the repression of the female at the hands of the male and traditional Mexican *machismo*. Not only was there a reaction against the partriarchy implicit in such things as Mexican Catholicism but also against the institution of what Rafael Pérez-Torres has referred to as 'mythic memory ... that realm in which myths, legends, folktales resurface' (Rafael Pérez-Torres, *Movements in Chicano Poetry*, p. 15). With a popular legacy hugely influenced by the negative image of Malintzín on the one hand (representing betrayal) and a reified image of the Virgin of Guadalupe on the other (representing innocence, love and virtue), Chicanas had repeatedly been cast as one or other of these historically-laden, if erroneous, stereotypes. As María Herrera-Sobek puts it, women's characters were rigidly defined by 'the whore-virgin-mother triad' (*Beyond Stereotypes*, p. 19). Inevitably these limiting representations have come to be challenged and with the advent of Chicana literature in the mid-1970s there began to emerge a host of 'female characters who are a contradictory blend of strengths and weaknesses, struggling against lives of unfulfilled potential and restrictions imposed upon them because of their sex' (Yvonne

Yarbro-Bejarano, 'Introduction' to Helena María Viramontes' *The Moths and Other Stories*, Arte Público Press, 1985, p. 8).

If the feminists' deconstruction of the Chicano/a subject challenges the 'constructedness' of femininity, the act of consciously challenging established boundaries assumes an especial relevance for Chicana lesbians (Carmen Tafolla, *To Split a Human: Mitos, Machos y la Mujer Chicana*, Mexican American Cultural Center, 1985, p. 2). The writer/theorists Gloria Anzaldúa and Cherríe Moraga have led the way in this endeavour in their texts *Loving in the War Years: lo que nunca pasó por sus labios* (Cherríe Moraga, 1983), *This Bridge Called My Back: Writings By Radical Women of Color* (eds Cherríe Moraga and Gloria Anzaldúa, 1983) and *Borderlands/La Frontera: The New Mestiza* (Gloria Anzaldúa, 1987). These texts are literary hybrids which combine autobiography, theory, poetry and prose. One of the writers' key messages is that 'the future depends on the breaking down of paradigms', not only in relation to gender and sexuality but also in their rejection of what we might call 'closed texts' (Anzaldúa, *Borderlands/La Frontera*, p. 80). For these women, as for the post-modernists, 'fragmentation is an exhilarating, liberating phenomenon, symptomatic of our escape from the claustrophobic embrace of fixed systems of belief' (Peter Barry, *Beginning Theory: An Introduction to Literary and Cultural Theory*, Manchester University Press, 1995, p. 84).

In an interview published in 1983, playwright, poet, actor and director Luis Valdez suggested that the historical, cultural and literary narratives of the United States have indeed functioned as 'closed texts'. They derive, he suggested, from 'the white man's sense of arrogance and belief that the truth resides in Western European culture, and that whether you are talking about capitalism or communism, or about Protestantism or Catholicism, only *their* science, *their* religion, *their* politics and *their* arts are sophisticated enough to be valid' (Roberta Orona-Cordova, 'Zoot Suit and the Pachuco Phenomenon: An Interview with Luis Valdez', *Revista Chicano-Riqueña*, 11:1, 1983, p. 84). In the Chicano/a's desire for 'escape' from such attitudes of mind, there is, insists Rafael Pérez-Torres, a relationship between post-modernism and multiculturalism. As post-modernism seeks liberation from 'fixed systems of belief', so multiculturalism, at least as it is understood by Robert Hughes, asserts that people 'can learn to read the image-banks of others, that they can and should look across the frontiers of race, language, gender and age without prejudice or illusion, and learn to think against the background of a hybridized society' – just as the Chicano/a, product of a border culture and a multifaceted cultural heritage, is required to do on a daily basis (Robert Hughes, *Culture of Complaint: The Fraying of America*, Oxford University Press, 1993, p. 116). What Arthur Schlesinger Jr. effectively proved with the publication of *The Disuniting of America: Reflections on a Multicultural Society* in the early 1990s, therefore, was that 'the representation of ethnicity, as a symptom of the repressed, has been and is always threatening to the national consciousness' (Neate, *Tolerating Ambiguity*, p. 2). Operating with an assumption that his own representation of the United States holds the centre ground whilst the groups from whose voices the hegemony wishes to distract attention are 'relegate[d] to the margins of the national psyche' (Bruce-Novoa, *RetroSpace*, p. 23), Schlesinger reveals in his declaration that the 'cult of ethnicity exaggerates differences, intensifies resentments and antagonisms, drives ever deeper the awful wedges between races and nationalities' that the view of the United States he espouses is not a multicultural one at all (*The Disuniting of America*, p. 102).

The post-modern and multicultural idea of intertextuality is an important consideration when contextualising Chicano/a literature within the developing field of post-colonial literary criticism. Chicano/as, the reader is reminded, popularly conceive themselves to have been colonised twice: once through the arrival of the Spanish in the sixteenth century and then again with the appropriation of Mexican land by the United States in 1848. The fact of having been dispossessed of their land is, says John Chávez, a 'formative and continuing influence on the collective Chicano mind' (John R. Chávez, *The Lost Land: The Chicano Image of the Southwest* (1984) University of New Mexico Press, 1989, p. 1). And although it is true to say that the extensive amount of migration and immigration across the United States–Mexican border in the twentieth century has caused many now to question the relevance of the colonial paradigm – notwithstanding claims by such as Alfredo Mirandé that 'to view Chicanos as an immigrant group is to miss the essence of internal colonialism' – it is not to be denied that the colonial sensibilities of the Chicano/a have frequently found expression in their literary output (Alfredo Mirandé, *The Chicano Experience: An Alternative Perspective*, University of Notre Dame Press, 1985, p. 5). Indeed, retorts Alfred Arteaga, 'the Chicano derives *being* not only from the Spanish colonial intervention but also from Anglo-American colonialism' (Alfred Arteaga, *Chicano Poetics: Heterotexts and Hybridities*, Cambridge University Press, 1997, p. 27).

Interpreting Chicano/a literature from the perspective of post-colonial criticism brings many issues to light. It exposes, for instance, what Luis Valdez earlier described as the 'sense of arrogance' that surrounds colonial discourse. Typically, the homogenous 'other' – in this particular context, the Chicano/a – is either dismissed to a subaltern position or romanticised as strangely exotic, as when one New York editor, dismayed at the form in which the writer's project was progressing, is reputed to have told the Chicano: 'You should write your book in stories – not as a series of essays. Let's have more Grandma' (Richard Rodriguez, *Hunger of Memory: The Education of Richard Rodriguez* (1982) Bantam Books, 1988, p. 7). Given the culturalist enthusiasm of the 1960s and early 1970s, it is perhaps inevitable that the Movement promoted texts like Raymond Barrio's *The Plum Plum Pickers* in order to insist on a visibly Chicano/a identity. Barrio's novel is replete with references to and images of a history which predates the arrival of Cortés – the baby, Cati, for instance, being described as a 'wiggly fat Mayan statuette' – but it is in the character Ramiro Sánchez, a migrant labourer who 'picked from prehistory into glassbright civilization. / From precolumbian artifacts to freeways to the future. / From Aztec elegance to the latest word in slums', that the reader encounters the epitome of the oppressed warrior described by Frantz Fanon in *The Wretched of the Earth*, watching, waiting, biding his time prior to mounting a challenge to the colonialists (Raymond Barrio, *The Plum Plum Pickers* (1969) Bilingual Press/Editorial Bilingüe, 1984, p. 41, p. 131). As has since proved to be the case in relation to Barrio's novel, with the writer's bloodline revealed not actually to be that of a Chicano, such attitudes of hegemonic defiance did sometimes 'result in an unexamined nativism that values without scrutiny those things it takes to be precolonial' (Pérez-Torres, *Movements in Chi-*

cano Poetry, p. 9). Over time, however, the strategies of resistance, frequently characterised as being counterdiscursive, may be said to have become more sophisticated. Or as a subheading in *Chicano Poetics* implies, the writers have learned more 'Responsible Tricks' (Arteaga, *Chicano Poetics*, p. 50).

In this regard, Alfred Arteaga's post-colonialist presentation of Chicano/a literature identifies its ability to employ what he calls 'the trope of chiasmus', 'chiasmus, "placing crosswise," from the Greek letter X, "chi"' (Arteaga, *Chicano Poetics*, pp. 48–9). This is a strategy by which one can overcome 'the silencing of the other by articulating marginalized discourses that cross, but do not supplant, the dominant discourse' (Arteaga, *Chicano Poetics*, p. 49). What this effectively means is that Chicano/a literature, in common with that of other colonised peoples, is able to effect a manipulation of inherited forms of writing in such a way as to reinstate its own colonised voice. Perhaps the most obvious example of this occurrence lies in the employment of a linguistic strategy commonly known as code-switching or interlingualism, whereby two or more languages are used within any given speech act. This is a particularly feasible strategy for a group with the linguistic history of the Chicano/a, not least because with the imposition of the new geopolitical border between Mexico and the United States in 1848, 'Spanish, the great metropolitan language of the region, was reduced to a foreign tongue' while English became 'the triumphal crushing metaphor' (Richard Rodriguez, 'Night and Day', *Frontiers*, ed. Ronald Eyre *et al.*, BBC Books, 1990, p. 206). For many Chicano/as, the issue of language has been of crucial consideration in their post-colonial condition; the political attention given to 'English Only' propositions and bilingual education schemes in states such as Florida and California in recent years has only served to sharpen the issue. Sociolinguists caution against interpreting culture on the basis of language usage, and further, as Gloria Anzaldúa remarks, there is 'no one Chicano language just as there is no one Chicano experience' (Anzaldúa, *Border-lands/La Frontera*, p. 58). Nonetheless bilingual Chicano/a writers are acutely aware of what John Baugh terms the 'competing values' inherent in the writer's choice of language (John Baugh, 'Chicano English: The Anguish of Definition', in *Form amd Function in Chicano English*, ed. Jacob Ornstein-Galicia, Newbury House Publishers, Inc., 1984, p. 10). Language, that is to say, carries a cultural and political message and can certainly be manipulated as a counterdiscursive weapon.

Such creativity is, says D. Emily Hicks, a crucial aspect of 'border writing', a literary process performed by people who are a hybrid of different cultural vectors. Perceiving border writing as 'a mode of operation rather than ... a definition', Hicks sees that the creativity of such writing is not confined to the page (Hicks, *Border Writing*, p. xxiii). Rather, engaging with the earlier proposition of culturalist criticism that related to the relationship between literature and reader, Hicks believes that the border text may be seen to offer a 'region of encounter in between, an area of contest but also of consort between cultures' (John Mack Faragher, 'A Nation Thrown Back Upon Itself: Turner and the Frontier', *Culturefront*, 2:2, 1993, p. 75). Borderlands and Chicano/a literature: both are presented as sites of energy and transformative power, supporting 'a new *mestizaje*, as it were, fundamentally more tolerant than other cultural paradigms' (*Border Theory: The Limits of Cultural Production*, edited by Scott Michaelson and David E. Johnson, University of Minnesota Press, 1997, p. 29). Speaking of tolerance, as we begin our consideration of three significant Chicano/a novels, let us recall the exhortation of Bruce-Novoa. 'What I want', he says, 'is post-analysis, that is, for the critic, publisher, reader, anyone, to read first, without any pre-established norms, without fixed absolutes. Enter a book not to see something in particular, but open to whatever it contains. The book will reveal itself' (Bruce-Novoa, *RetroSpace*, p. 17).

Case studies: three important works of Chicano/a fiction

Rolando Hinojosa, The Valley (1983)

Rolando Hinojosa is one of the best-known and most highly respected authors in the field of contemporary Chicano/a literature. Creator of the 'ever expanding opus' known as the *Klail City Death Trip Series*, he is also one of the most prolific: to date, the *Series* has fourteen instalments. *The Valley* is the English-language equivalent of *Estampas del valle y otras obras*, the Quinto Sol award-winning

work with which Hinojosa began the *Series* back in 1972. Not only
is it a novel which affords the reader great insight into the principal
aims of the early Chicano/a literary project, it also gives expression
to many aspects of the wider Chicano/a experience. Even its existence as the English rendition of a Spanish original bears testimony
to this, although importantly *The Valley* is not simply a literal translation of *Estampas*. Published just over a decade apart, even a cursory
reading of the two books will reveal clear differences between them,
and this in spite of their having the same basic story. In a wider consideration of the *Klail City Death Trip Series* than there is room for
here, one would address the circumstances and consequences of the
author's decisions concerning Spanish/English language usage –
not least because the same kind of strategy *is* employed in the pair-
ings *Klail City y sus alrededores* (1976)/ *Klail City* (1987), *Mi Querido
Rafa* (1981)/ *Dear Rafe* (1985) and *Becky And Her Friends*
(1990)/ *Los Amigos de Becky* (1991) but *not* in relation to such as
Korean Love Songs (1978) or *Ask A Policeman* (1998), texts which
have only appeared in English. Yet whilst we cannot engage in a full
interrogation of the *Series'* relationship with the issue of language,
we should at least consider why so many critics refer to the collected
works of Hinojosa as, quite simply, 'the novel'. For example, Bruce-
Novoa describes Hinojosa as 'slowly and unconventionally creating
a novel on a grand scale' (Bruce-Novoa, 'Rolando Hinojosa', *Chicano Authors: Inquiry by Interview*, University of Texas Press, 1980,
p. 49). The *Series* constitutes a vast and unfinished jigsaw, the purpose of which is to depict a place and its people. While individual
instalments stand as separate entities, each is designed to supply the
reader with a few more of the jigsaw's pieces – a new character here,
another aspect of somebody's personality there, a little more detail
about a scene which had started to take shape in another text. The
Series at large and *The Valley* in microcosm work, thus, 'in the
manner of a mosaic' (Bruce-Novoa, 'Rolando Hinojosa', p. 49). Our
task as readers, like that of the unidentified narrator at the end of
Tomás Rivera's *… y no se lo tragó la tierra/ … and the earth did not
devour him*, is '[t]o discover and rediscover and piece things together.
This to that, that to that, all with all' (Tomás Rivera, *… y no se lo
tragó la tierra/ … and the earth did not devour him*, translated by
Evangelina Vigil-Piñón, Arte Público Press, 1990, p. 206).

A prefatory remark entitled 'On The Starting Blocks' warns us from the outset that the structure of *The Valley* is likely to be confusing; much like the hair of one Mencho Saldaña, we are told, 'the damn thing's disheveled' (Rolando Hinojosa, *The Valley*, Bilingual Press/Editorial Bilingüe, 1983, n.p.). This is a deliberate narrative strategy. For reasons soon to be made apparent, it is by design that Hinojosa's stories are 'not held together by the *peripeteia* or the plot as much as by *what* the people who populate the stories say and *how* they say it' (Rolando Hinojosa, 'The Sense of Place', *The Rolando Hinojosa Reader: Essays Historical and Critical*, edited by José David Saldívar, Arte Público Press, 1985, p. 21). Although Hinojosa is at pains to draw attention to the *what* and the *how*, he is much less concerned always to stipulate the *who*. As a collective, 'the people' of *The Valley* are of vital importance. Indeed, the novel introduces a cast of over 230 named characters, not to mention the crowd of 4,000 that is estimated to have attended the funeral in the passage entitled 'Bruno Cano: Lock, Stock, and Bbl' – 'people'll use anything for an excuse to get out of the house' (Hinojosa, *The Valley*, p. 40)! But by the same token, sometimes it is beyond our capabilities specifically to identify the voice of the narrator, just as it is well-nigh impossible to summarise neatly the various exploits of this vast array of characters. Therefore rather than undertake a step-by-step analysis of the four, seemingly discontinuous, major sections into which *The Valley* is divided, I shall instead attempt to explain *why* Hinojosa has chosen to write *The Valley* in the way that he has. For as Bruce-Novoa once said in describing the purpose of Chicano/a literature in general, '[a]rmed with meaning we can resist the chaos which threatens us' (Bruce-Novoa, *RetroSpace*, p. 96).

In the 1960s, when the literary project of the Chicano/as began in earnest, promoters of the Chicano/a cause were keenly aware of what sociologist Robert Ardrey had discovered in *The Territorial Imperative*: that everyone needs to feel themselves in possession of a 'space'. Deprived by the hegemony of their 'enabling histories and myths', the prevailing psychological need of the Chicano/as was that these 'histories and myths' be restored to them (Fischer, 'Ethnicity and the Post-Modern Arts of Memory', p. 221). It was of paramount concern, in other words, that the ethnic group retrieve its sense of belonging. Taking hold of the people's confusion –

represented through the fragmentary style of his narrative – Hinojosa sets out to create for the community a 'space' of its own. The duo text, *Estampas/The Valley*, precursor to the ongoing *Klail City Death Trip Series*, is the result of this imperative. Hinojosa creates a linguistic space, where Chicano/a cultural identity may be articulated, and a fictional space, where Chicano/as imaginatively retrieve once-lost territory. Bruce-Novoa describes this endeavour as a 'geographical rescue operation' (*RetroSpace*, p. 102). Thus we see how Hinojosa produces in *The Valley* the literary 'space' of Belken, a fictional county in the Río Grande Valley of Texas which is often compared with William Faulkner's Yoknapatawpha.

In line with this evocation of place, Hinojosa prefaces *The Valley* with a map of Belken County, a visual illustration which marks not only the location of all the principal towns in his narrative, but also their proximity to the Río Grande river and the Mexican border. This incorporation of a map into the space of the novel calls to mind a remark made by Edward Said: that one 'might call *cartographic*' the impulse of a colonised people to retrieve the 'concrete geographical identity' which has been denied them by 'the loss to an outsider of the local place' (Edward W. Said, 'Yeats and Decolonization', in *Nationalism, Colonialism, and Literature*, edited by Terry Eagleton, Fredric Jameson and Edward W. Said, University of Minnesota Press, 1990, p. 77). Said's comment also helps us understand that whilst Belken is entirely the fabrication of the author, it has knowingly been located within a real-life territory, one that, for the Chicano/a at least, is replete with historical significance. As a territory simultaneously in fiction and fact, the world of Belken represents 'the spiritual, political and economic intersection of the Anglo and Mexican worlds' (Yolanda Julia Broyles, 'Hinojosa's *Klail City y sus alrededores*: Oral Culture and Print Culture', *The Rolando Hinojosa Reader*, p. 109). As the plunging 'V' on the cover of the Bilingual Press edition is doubtless intended to suggest, historical and political circumstances thus render the Valley a site of cultural tensions. Clear, intentional and repeated reference is made to this fact in various of Hinojosa's accumulated fragments. The passage called 'Night People', for example, testifies to how there are differences in behaviour on either 'side of the tracks'. Where sundown, for the Chicano/as, is the prompt for

everyone to come outside and chat with one another, at that same
time of day 'our fellow Texans across the tracks close their shops
and head for home' (*The Valley*, p. 109). Meanwhile, in an untitled
entry that appears under the larger section heading 'Rafe Buenrostro', the differences between the cultures are experienced far
more acutely:

> Life is fairly cheap in Flora, and if you're a Texas mexicano, it's even
> cheaper than that: Van Meers shot young Ambrosio Mora on a bright,
> cloudless afternoon, and in front of no less than fifteen witnesses.
> It took the People of the State of Texas some five years to prepare the
> case against him, and when it did, the State witnesses spoke on behalf
> of Van Meers and against the victim. (*The Valley*, p. 44)

Notwithstanding Hinojosa's various efforts to convince us of the
physical existence of Belken County, references to the landscape
are conspicuously absent in the novel. In stark contrast to such
novels as Rudolfo Anaya's *Bless Me, Ultima*, which positively radi-
ates with 'the pulse of the earth', *The Valley*'s evocation of its geographical 'space' is generated not through scenic commentary but
through the medium of its characters (Rudolfo A. Anaya, *Bless
Me, Ultima*, (1972) Tonatiuh-Quinto Sol International, 1989, p. 10).
Hence the following remark by Hinojosa is of tremendous importance to an appreciation of the working of *The Valley*: 'A place
is merely a place until it is populated, and once populated, the
histories of the place and its people begin' (Rolando Hinojosa, 'A
Writer's Sense of Place', *Hungry Mind Review*, 19, 1991, p. 31).
Laying such stress upon the input of the population explains, in part
at least, why the story of *The Valley* should be given over to its
veritable chorus of voices. The onus of responsibility that is given
to the people also reveals that what Mark Royden Winchell has said
of Joan Didion is equally applicable to Hinojosa: both believe
'that place is not just a physical entity, but is also a matrix for emotional associations; it is the frame of reference within which one
begins to know oneself and the world in which one lives' (Mark
Royden Winchell, *Joan Didion*, Twayne Publishers, 1980, p. 75).
And where Joan Didion herself remarks that 'certain places seem to
exist mainly because someone has written about them ... A place
belongs forever to whoever claims it hardest, remembers it most

obsessively', she might well be speaking of Hinojosa and his relationship to Belken County (cited by Winchell, *Joan Didion*, p. 90). With the additional motivation, perhaps, of having himself grown up in the Río Grande Valley, it is an area which Hinojosa indeed claims 'hardest' for his Chicano/as.

The narrative of *The Valley* is littered with reports that, not least because of their frequency, vehemently insist on the people's lengthy residence in the area. In one of the entries in 'Lives and Miracles' the reader is informed that, as was actually the case for the paternal side of the Hinojosa family, '[t]he Buenrostros came to the Valley with the first Querétaro colonists in 1749' (Hinojosa, *The Valley*, p. 74). Elsewhere, on being (re)introduced to the group of characters known as 'The Old Revolutionaries' – don Braulio Tapia, Evaristo Garrido and don Manuel Guzmán, veterans of the Mexican Revolution all – it is explained how these men, their parents *and* their grandparents – and 'this goes back to 1765 and earlier' – were all born in this country 'which since 1848 has been called the United States of America' (Hinojosa, *The Valley*, p. 78; p. 79). The conversation recounted in the passage called 'The Squires at the Round Table' is typical. Here, three more of Belken's old-timers are plumbing the depths of their memories in order to calculate the identity of a younger member of the community:

> 'Genaro, that boy looks familiar; who is he?'
>
> 'His name's Rafe Buenrostro.'
>
> 'Buenrostro? Which Buenrostro family is that?'
>
> 'Is he Julián's boy?'
>
> 'No, his father was Jesús Buenrostro …'
>
> 'Oh, I remember him; died young, didn't he?'
>
> 'Was he the one that worked Old Man Burns' land?'
>
> 'No, you're confusing him with Julián again. Don Jesús had some lands over by El Carmen.'
>
> 'Over by where the Texas Rangers killed those ranchhands back in '15?'
>
> 'That's the place.' (*The Valley*, p. 111)

Through this and other exchanges, Hinojosa demonstrates how the roots of the people extend deeply into the land. In *The Valley* at least, there is no disputing the fact of their belonging.

Memory plays a key role in establishing the temporal space of *The Valley*. This is made clear in the very first scene of the book. In a brief passage entitled 'Braulio Tapia', written in the present tense, the reader is introduced to an unidentified first-person narrator who is standing on his porch, watching the approach of a young man named Roque Malacara. Roque, it transpires, has come to ask our narrator for his daughter Tere's hand in marriage. It is only in the process of Roque being shown into the house that we are introduced to the character whose name is highlighted in the title. 'Turning my head slightly to the right', Tere's father says, 'I catch a glimpse, or think I do, of my late father-in-law, don Braulio Tapia' (Hinojosa, *The Valley*, p. 12). Clearly what is happening here is that Tere's father is remembering the time when he, too, came to ask for permission to marry, but at another level what Hinojosa is establishing is a narrative depth in time: first through testifying to the existence of an ongoing cultural tradition, and secondly through using a moment in the present to bring to the surface an incident, and a character, from the past. This pattern of remembering recurs in the narratives that follow.

In a different format, but to similar effect, the section of *The Valley* entitled 'Rafe Buenrostro: Delineations for a first portrait with sketches and photographs (individually and severally)' is dedicated specifically to the retrieval of memories. It comprises thirty entries, all of which are untitled and some of which are especially brief. For example, one entry in its entirety reads: 'Ma's burial day. That's the third time I've been able to cry. In my life' (p. 43). The use of intensive fragmentation in *The Valley* must be understood in the (postmodern) sense of cultural richness rather than in the (modernist) sense of a dissolution of meaning. Although the section describing Rafe Buenrostro features the reflections of just one character, and whilst indubitably revealing a vast amount about that one person's private history, the significance of Rafe as an individual is almost completely subsumed here within the larger community to which he belongs. A striking indication of this comes right after the first memory he recounts. A man by the name of Chano Ortega, we are told, was 'born and raised in Klail City' but died in the 1944 invasion of France. '*What follows*', Rafe remarks, is therefore for '*them and … a select few*' (*The Valley*, p. 43). And 'what follows' is a collage of scenes that testifies to the life of the Chicano/a in all its diversity. Concerning fights in the school playground, or his fear of *el mal de ojo* (the evil eye), or the time spent serving with fellow soldiers in Korea, or sitting simply with friends in the bar, Rafe's memories, as do those we witness elsewhere, collectively encompass a large part of the Belken County community.

The Valley, one recalls, is presented in its subtitle as 'a portfolio of etchings, engravings, sketches, and silhouettes by various artists in various styles'. From time to time it is brought to our attention that we are following a narrator who is looking at pictures through remarks such as that which opens the passage 'Epigmenio Salazar'. Informed that '[t]his one owns a good-sized house', the utterance 'this one' accompanies the pointing of a finger at Epigmenio's photograph (p. 102). Where this happens, and it does frequently, Hinojosa achieves what Liam Kennedy refers to as 'narrative "archaeology"'. Kennedy uses this phrase to argue that since emotional reactions invariably accompany the recounting of a memory, history is clearly not a thing of the past (Liam Kennedy, 'Ethnic Memory and American History', *Borderlines: Studies in American Culture*, 1:2, 1993, p. 132). A corollary to this point is found in Octavio Paz's pronouncement that man is not so much '*in* history; he *is* history' and thus times past are proved to be of continuing relevance in the present (Octavio Paz, *The Labyrinth of Solitude*, translated by Lysander Kemp (1961) Penguin Books, 1990, p. 25). These observations help explain the title of a passage we encounter in the first section of *The Valley*, a passage called 'Three Years Wrapped in One Twenty-Four Hour Day'. The period of twenty-four hours refers to the day on which the funeral of don Víctor Peláez takes place; the three years in question relate to the time that Jehú Malacara spent in the care and guidance of this man; and upon Jehú's seeing don Víctor buried, they all come flooding back: three years in one twenty-four hour day. In keeping with the ancient Mexican belief that death is 'not the natural end of life but one phase of an infinite cycle', since history lives on in the present Hinojosa has evidently adopted for his story an appropriate narrative strategy (Paz, *The Labyrinth of Solitude*, p. 54). With both *The Valley* and the *Series* intended to assert the viability of Chicano/a culture, fragmentation prevents its having a beginning, a middle and an end. Had

Hinojosa chosen to focus on an individual, then a narrative trajectory towards a perceivable conclusion may well have been expected,
but it is a community to which this fiction is dedicated and as
Erlinda Gonzales-Berry has remarked, a community replenishes
itself through 'the birth–death–birth cycle' (Erlinda Gonzales-
Berry, '*Estampas del valle*: From *Costumbrismo* to Self-Reflecting
Literature', *The Bilingual Review/La Revista Bilingüe*, VII:1, 1980,
p. 33).

For all that its structure may initially appear 'disheveled', ultimately *The Valley* works because '[t]he reader arranges the fragmented *paroles* uttered by the characters and incorporates them into
a final *langue* which is Belken' (Neate, 'The Function of Belken
County in the Fiction of Rolando Hinojosa', p. 94). The jigsaw takes
shape, that is to say, because we put the pieces together in our heads.
But what is of more importance to our consideration of the final part
of Hinojosa's literary project is the fact that the words and the language *are* those of the people of Belken. In relying upon the spoken
word, and in collecting it from a chorus of voices, *The Valley* is able
to portray 'a vision of the community from the oral roots up, not
from authorial omniscience down, nor through the eyes of a supposedly "representative" character' (Broyles, 'Hinojosa's *Klail City y
sus alrededores*: Oral Culture and Print Culture', p. 128). Hinojosa's
novel thereby challenges the presentation of what Bruce-Novoa
terms 'history as content', a history in which events are narrated by
someone who is external to the action and then handed down in the
form of a 'monological given' (Bruce-Novoa, 'History as Content,
History as Act', p. 41). The section of *The Valley* entitled 'Sometimes It Just Happens That Way; That's All (A Study of Black and
White Newspaper Photographs)' stands as obvious testimony to the
potential for error in such a scenario. Pointedly, the accounts which
appear in the local newspaper, *The Klail City Enterprise-News*,
describing how Baldemar Cordero came to kill Ernesto Tamez at the
Aquí me quedo bar are full of typographical and factual errors. The
deceased's name appears variously as 'Arnesto' and 'Tanez' where it
should actually read 'Ernesto' and 'Tamez'; the court judge's name
is rendered as 'Pehelps' in place of 'Phelps'; and as far as the newspaper is concerned, the fatal affray was simply the result of an argument 'over the affections of one of the "hostesses"' (*The Valley*,

p. 56; p. 70). The attention of this 'mainstream' publication to detail is, quite clearly, inadequate. More, the news it reports is misleading. Yet had the reader not been privy to the first- and second-hand accounts of the participants themselves, these newspaper clippings would be all that stands to record not only the event but also the (now much maligned) character of Baldemar Cordero. As Bruce-Novoa notes, it is 'an ironic *mestizaje*' that in order to preserve its voice, the oral tradition must reconcile itself to transcription on the page (Bruce-Novoa, 'The Heroics of Sacrifice', p. 64). But the enduring significance of *The Valley* is that, finally, it 'signifies a taking possession of one's own story' (Bruce-Novoa, 'History as Content, History as Act', p. 32).

Rudolfo Anaya, Bless Me, Ultima *(1972)*
Martin Padget

Rudolfo Anaya's debut novel opens with a lyrical description of the first-person narrator's attachment to the land during his childhood:

> Ultima came to stay with us the summer I was almost seven. When she came the beauty of the llano unfolded before my eyes, and the gurgling waters of the river sang to the hum of the turning earth. The magical time of childhood stood still, and the pulse of the living earth pressed its mystery into my living blood. She took my hand, and the silent, magic powers she possessed made beauty from the raw, sun-baked llano, the green river valley, and the blue bowl which was the white sun's home. My bare feet felt the throbbing earth and my body trembled with excitement. Time stood still, and it shared with me all that had been, and all that was to come. (*Bless Me, Ultima*, TQS Publications, 1972, p. 1)

The narrator, Antonio Juan Márez y Luna, is looking back on the pivotal point in his life when Ultima, an aged *curandera* (healer), came to live with his family in the small town of Guadalupe in central New Mexico. Although the narrator is clearly an adult, Anaya fills the novel's pages with the consciousness of a child undergoing a series of life-transforming experiences. Antonio is at a pivotal point of his young life, an innocent child on the cusp of experience. The start of his school education looms and he is only months away from his first confession and communion. Attending school takes him away from the home and his mother, while his religious education brings him into formal knowledge of sin. The passage above conveys the boy's attachment to the land and the ways of life it sustains. The *llano* – the Spanish name for the rolling plains of eastern New Mexico – stretches eastward towards Texas and is the land of his father, a *vaquero* (cowboy) in the years before Antonio was born. The river and the 'turning earth' refer to the other side of Antonio's heritage, his mother's farming family who for generations have lived in the village of El Puerto which lies a mere ten miles away from Guadalupe. It soon becomes apparent that Antonio feels deeply divided over the necessity of choosing to follow the livelihood of either his father's or his mother's people. As I shall explain, these alternatives are not really diametrically opposed to one another and indeed share common ground. In actuality, by the opening of the novel in the early 1940s both ways of life have been compromised already by forces of modernisation that undermine local subsistence agriculture and the older form of ranching on the llano. That Antonio's brothers have been called away to fight in World War II and that local people comment on the explosion of the first atomic bomb at Trinity Site in southern New Mexico suggest the ways in which destructive external events impact upon a small community in a relatively isolated area of the United States. In light of these perceived threats, the narrator stresses the direct and unalienated relationship between his younger self and the environment that sustained him through the image of the trembling child who is naturally responsive to the throbbing earth and lives in an eternal present without being conscious of time passing.

No doubt much of the appeal of *Bless Me, Ultima* is due to Anaya's representation of the child moving from innocence to experience. Arguably he writes nostalgically about not only childhood but also Hispano life in general in New Mexico. The magical qualities that permeate Antonio's consciousness after Ultima's arrival are not explained away by the adult narrator; indeed throughout the novel there is no clear border between 'rational' and 'irrational' forces, and the characters live in a world that is filled with the magical forces of an environment where people largely live in harmony with nature. Significantly, though, the novel opens neither with school attendance nor churchgoing, but with the killing of Lupito and the arrival of Ultima, who soon becomes Antonio's mentor. The two events complement one another insofar as Lupito's death symbolises the way that external forces threaten Guadalupe livelihoods and Ultima's curing abilities represent the means for combating such forces.

In the ensuing discussion I shall examine three conflicts within the novel: Antonio's internal strife over which side of his family heritage he should choose for his livelihood; the opposition between Roman Catholicism and pantheism as competing belief systems through which the cosmic forces at work in the world are explained; and the Manichean struggle between powers of good and evil that is represented in the conflict between Ultima and Tenorio. On re-reading *Bless Me, Ultima*, it becomes clear that although written in a deceptively simple style, the novel is rich in ambiguity and is subject to multiple interpretations. Most obviously, we should stress the way that the novel addresses universal issues such as childhood consciousness and the passage from innocence to experience, questions of spirituality and religious faith, and the role of the creative imagination in both discerning and conveying 'value' in life. Turning to the form of *Bless Me, Ultima*, we see that Anaya draws on the Anglo-American tradition of the novel, principally the *Bildungsroman* (or coming-of-age story), only to combine realist narrative with oral storytelling from the Spanish-speaking community and magical realist elements that are characteristic of much Latin American fiction. The hybrid form of the novel is complemented by its content. Antonio himself is a hybrid figure in whom contending religious beliefs and lifeways are eventually reconciled and synthesised. Not only are Catholic and pantheistic elements yoked together in his character but his schooling in the English language and Anglo-American cultural mores will become an essential part of the process whereby he truly emerges as a man of learning who can interpret and speak on behalf of his native community.

From the outset of the novel, Antonio feels divided between the two alternatives that appear to lie before him. Either he follows in the tradition of the Lunas by becoming a farmer or priest, or he avoids remaining tied to one place in an ascetic existence by embracing the freedom and wandering ways of the Márez clan. This dual heritage is illustrated early in the novel when Antonio dreams of his own birth. The newly born infant resembles the Christ child as Antonio's maternal uncles give thanks for his virgin birth. The Lunas wish Antonio to be a farmer; accordingly, they rub earth from the river valley onto the baby's forehead and place freshly harvested fruits and vegetables about his bed. Their ceremonious dignity, patience and quietness contrasts with the boisterous behaviour of the Márez uncles who, in a frenzy of activity, destroy the Lunas's gifts and replace them with their own: saddle, horse blankets, whiskey, rope, bridles, chapas and an old guitar. They also rub the earth from the baby's forehead 'because man was not to be tied to the earth but free from it' (p. 5). Further conflict between the sets of uncles is prevented by the old woman who has delivered the child. Whereas the Lunas wish to bury the afterbirth and cord in their fields and the Márez men want the winds of the llano to scatter the burned remains, it is the midwife, later identified as Ultima, who states that she alone knows the child's destiny.

In actuality there is little mystery to Antonio's fate, for less than a quarter of the way through the novel Ultima states 'sadly' that he will become a man of learning (p. 52). Nevertheless Anaya carefully characterises the differences between the Luna and Márez families. Antonio's mother boasts of her family carrying a charter from the Mexican government to settle the valley in which the village of El Puerto de las Luna is located. Her father and brothers regard the moon as a 'goddess' under whose influence they plant and harvest and, indeed, live the whole of their lives until death (p. 85). Antonio describes the late summer harvest as a romantic idyll:

> It was a world where people were happy, working, helping each other. The ripeness of the harvest piled around the mud houses and lent life and color to the songs of the women. Green chile was roasted and dried, and red chile was tied into colorful ristras. Apples piled high, some lent their aroma to the air from where they dried in the sun on the lean-to roofs and others as they bubbled into jellies and jams. At night we sat around the fireplace and ate baked apples spiced with sugar and cinammon and listened to the cuentos, the old stories of the people. (p. 47)

This patriarchal way of life clearly has great appeal for Antonio, both the young boy participating in the agricultural cycle and the adult looking back. It is, of course, a compelling image of family and community life structured about an idyllic harmony between the people and the land. The abundance of the harvest is matched by the people's sense of achievement in life. But Antonio also possesses his father's genes and, as the adult narrator explains, 'it is the Márez blood in us that touches us with the urge to wander. Like the restless, seeking sea' (p. 61).

In one of the novel's many dream sequences, Antonio's brothers explain to him that the Márez men historically were conquistadors, 'men whose freedom was unbounded' (p. 23). Colonisers of *Nuevo Mejico* on the northern frontier of New Spain, the Márez men are linked with the expansion of the Spanish colonial empire. Located in the settlement of Las Pasturas on the plains, these men became *cabelleros*, expert horsemen 'in a wild and desolate land which they took from the Indians' (p. 51). But then a process of modernisation steadily undermined their pastoral way of life. Antonio's father, Gabriel, recollects the old days: 'The llano was still virgin, there was grass as high as the stirrups of a grown horse, there was rain – and then the *tejano* came and built his fences, the railroad came, the roads – it was like a bad wave of the ocean covering all that was good' (p. 51). Gabriel's bitterness is compounded by the fact that he works with a road-building crew that, through paving the land, helps facilitate a modern commercial economy based on free enterprise, capitalist investment and an efficient system of communications. Rather than continue characterising the socio–economic factors that have caused far-reaching changes in Hispano life on the llano and in the valleys, Anaya stresses the idealist aspects of Antonio's heritage. Thus late in the novel Antonio reflects on what he discovered through the examples of his mother, father and Ultima:

> I had learned to love the magical beauty of the wide, free earth. From my mother I had learned that a man is of the earth, that his clay feet are part of the ground that nourishes him, and that it is this inextricable mixture that gives man his measure of safety and security. ... But from my father and Ultima I had learned that the greater immortality is in the freedom of man, and that freedom is best nourished by the noble expanse of land and air and pure, white sky. (pp. 219–20)

This statement suggests that Antonio moves beyond the vocations envisioned by his parents. We should add that he does remain true to the fullness of his heritage by becoming a storyteller. Thus he rejects the role of priest but does not become estranged from the Catholic Church; chooses not to become a farmer and yet values the *cuentos* told by his maternal uncles; and recognises that although a certain epoch and way of life passes with Ultima's death, he can preserve her wisdom and powers of healing through the medium of writing.

Although *Bless Me, Ultima* begins with an idyllic image of childhood, Antonio's isolation from the world of experience is soon undermined. Lupito, a Guadalupe resident who has returned home deeply traumatised after fighting the Japanese in World War II, kills the local sheriff and takes refuge by the river which runs beneath the bridge that separates Antonio's home from the village. When townsmen call on Antonio's father, the boy follows them outside. Hiding in the undergrowth near to the river, Antonio watches as Lupito is shot by the men. Fatally wounded, Lupito asks the terrified boy for his blessing. In the aftermath of this event, Antonio wonders about the fate of the dead man's soul and worries that the men, including his father, who stalked Lupito now have 'the terrible burden of dark mortal sin on their souls' and are destined for hell (p. 26).

Antonio's introduction to violent deeds makes him hungry for knowledge about God, yet God remains a cipher to him. Having witnessed Lupito's death and heard his mother claim 'what a sin it is for a boy grow into a man', Antonio's growing sense that he and his young friends have been 'born steeped in sin' makes him long to take communion so that he can be 'free of the punishment of hell' (p. 28; p. 42; p. 43). But his excitement at the prospect of his first confession and first communion at Easter contrasts with the aching disappointment he feels after he has taken Christ into his own body and the question as to why evil is abroad in the world remains unanswered. Despite this setback, Antonio continues to believe in the power of God and the forgiveness of la Virgen de Guadalupe, the figure after whom the town is named. Indeed he mimics the role of priest when his friends practise confession shortly before Easter only to find that they turn on him when he absolves Florence of the sin of blasphemy. Late in the novel, Antonio realises that Catholi-

cism does have the capacity to change to fit the needs of his generation. This insight is complemented by his father's explanation that
God does not provide understanding, and instead understanding
comes through experience. Thus Antonio learns that Ultima's
magic is her fundamental sympathy for others, an understanding 'so
complete that she can touch their souls and cure them' (p. 237).

In order to arrive at this balanced perspective about the value of
experience, enlightenment and spiritual faith, Antonio must learn
not only the ways of the *curandera* but also the pantheistic belief
system represented in the figure of the golden carp. Whereas Ultima
introduces Antonio to the '*presence*' of the river – a symbol of the
fundamental energy flowing through all creation – his friends
Samuel and Cico prepare him for viewing the golden carp. Samuel
recounts the story, told to his father by a local Indian, of how the
golden carp is the god who saved the people from being destroyed by
his fellow gods when, during a period of prolonged drought, the
people broke their taboo against eating carp. Later Antonio watches
the golden carp swim upstream and feels transformed by what he
has seen: 'I felt my body trembling as I saw the golden form disappear. I knew I had witnessed a miraculous thing, the appearance of a
pagan god. ... And I thought, the power of God failed where
Ultima's worked; and then a sudden illumination of beauty and
understanding flashed through my mind. This is what I had
expected God to do at my first holy communion!' (p. 105). Immediately after gaining this flash of insight, though, Antonio watches a
'monstrous' black bass break the surface of the river, its 'evil mouth'
hanging 'open and red'. The timeless struggle between the golden
carp and the black bass is echoed in the conflict between Ultima and
Tenorio.

Ultima is a *curandera*, 'a woman who knew the herbs and reme-
dies of the ancients, a miracle-worker who could heal the sick' (p. 4),
who comes to live with Antonio's family in her old age. Also known
as *la Grande*, Ultima hails from Las Pasturas where *el hombre
volador*, a great healer, passed on his powers to her. Although she
does not, in turn, confer her healing abilities on Antonio, she does
teach him 'to listen to the mystery of the groaning earth and to feel
complete in the fulfillment of its time' (p. 14). Just as the black bass
follows in the wake of the golden carp, so evil in the shape of Teno-

rio Trementina and his three daughters comes into Antonio's family after Ultima's arrival in Guadalupe. Her fateful decision to cure Lucas Luna of a debilitating illness inflicted on him by the Trementina sisters sets in motion a series of events that lead to her death. She exorcises evil from Lucas's body and then reverses the curse of the *bruja* (witches) by making clay dolls that resemble the sisters and sticking pins in them. Thereafter Antonio, who has participated in his uncle's cure, becomes a target of Tenorio's revenge. As Ultima's actions suggest, to combat evil she must set in motion destructive forces and for this she is both prized and feared by the community, some people accusing her of being a *bruja* herself. Raymund Paredes' observation that in Mexican folklore the owl is usually 'the *nagual* (companion) of witches' only adds to the air of ambiguity surrounding Ultima's character ('The Evolution of Chicano Literature', *Three American Literatures*, MLA, 1982, p. 68).

In the last part of this discussion, I want to draw attention to two important issues, namely the way that *Bless Me, Ultima* features images of apocalypse, and the way in which the assumptions about gender that underlie Anaya's representation of male and female characters have been challenged by critics and Chicana authors such as Sandra Cisneros. Whereas Raymund Paredes praised the novel in 1982 as 'a deeply moving work of genuine excellence', Ramón Saldívar was far more cautious in his assessment eight years later, faulting the novel for turning away from history and creating an idealist resolution of conflict (Paredes, p. 68). While Paredes had little to say about Anaya's representation of gender, Saldívar emphasised the way the novel features women who possess 'either one of only two possible roles: women are either saintly or evil' (*Chicano Narrative: The Dialectics of Difference*, University of Wisconsin Press, 1990, p. 122). As we have seen in the discussions of Chicano/a literature and recent literary theory, there was a sea change during the 1970s and 1980s when writers and critics called into question the patriarchal assumptions at work in much of the literature produced by Chicano writers. In light of feminist interpretations of Chicano/a literature and critiques such as Saldívar's which stress the need for Chicano/a writers to resist 'the existing material apparatus of American society' it is hardly surprising that the critical standing of *Bless Me, Ultima* has been called into question (Saldívar, p. 213).

About two-thirds of the way through the novel, and after watching Tenorio kill Narciso, Antonio becomes fevered with pneumonia and dreams vividly. The dream, which features Antonio's own death and his bones being laid before the doors of Purgatory, is full of anxieties about sin, retribution and justice. Despite the images of triumphant evil, the dream ends with the golden carp swallowing 'everything there was, good and evil' and rising into the night sky to become a new star (p. 168). As with the Book of Revelation in the Bible, for all the horrors that Antonio imagines there is eventual transcendence and renewal. We should note that in referring to both Catholic and non-Christian traditions Anaya stresses that each contains warnings about apocalyptic consequences if people continue to sin. But why does the novel feature such imagery? To a certain extent Antonio's dream is an apt reflection of the young boy's preoccupation with the supernatural powers of the Trementina sisters and his struggle to reconcile Catholicism and pantheistic religion. It is also the imaginative means for providing an idealistic resolution to a situation in which traditional Hispano livelihoods appear imperilled by material forces that cannot be contained by the people themselves. Ramón Saldívar argues that Anaya uses the diabolism connected to the Trementina sisters to stand in for 'the pain and havoc caused by the very real effects of the dissolution of the principles of reciprocity and organicity represented by the decline of the former life of the pueblos [villages] and the growth of wage labor under capitalist conditions'. He adds: 'This symbolic substitution allows Antonio through Ultima to personify and overcome what might otherwise remain awesomely unconquerable' (*Chicano Narrative*, p. 121). Saldívar proceeds to criticise Anaya for turning away from history and creating what he regards as a conservative resolution to the novel: one that raises to mythological status the patriarchal structure of family and community alike.

In the next case study we shall see how Sandra Cisneros writes about the Chicano/a family from a woman-centred perspective. Although the rural setting of *Bless Me, Ultima* in an area of the United States that used to be part of the Spanish colonial empire and later the independent republic of Mexico is very different from the urban setting of *The House on Mango Street* in a northern city to which Chicano/as have migrated during the twentieth century, in both locations patriarchal conditions prevail. However, whereas in Anaya's novel the Virgin of Guadalupe is revered by Antonio, who dreams that the Virgin Mary will appear before him as she did to the poor Mexican Juan Diego, the feminine principles of innocence and chastity she symbolises are called into question in the writing of Cisneros and other Chicana writers, such as Gloria Anzaldúa and Cherríe Moraga. On looking back at *Bless Me, Ultima* through the lens of subsequent Chicana writing, we see how female characters, with the obvious exception of Ultima, lack complexity and are not central to the novel. The converse of Antonio's reverence for la Virgen de Guadalupe is his fear of the women at Rosie's, the brothel he passes on his way to school. Women, then, are presented in largely polarised terms: on the one hand there is the sanctified image of la Virgen and the self-sacrificing example of Antonio's mother, while on the other hand there are the prostitutes at Rosie's brothel and the malignant evil of the Trementina sisters, who are said to be 'too ugly to make men happy' (p. 91). Anaya also refers to the archetype of *la llorona*, the figure of the weeping woman who haunts the river valley mourning the children she killed. Finally there is the character of Ultima. She is an ambiguous figure, for insofar as she is neither a wife and a mother nor sexualised and a whore, she escapes the dominant images of womanhood in the novel. As we have seen, the *curandera*'s special powers make her both esteemed and feared by the community. Clearly Ultima's ability to cure helps to preserve the patriarchal structure of both family and community in *Bless Me, Ultima*.

Sandra Cisneros, The House on Mango Street *(1984)*
Helena Grice

As Candida Hepworth notes in her overview of Chicano/a literature, it not was until the 1970s that Chicana prose work appeared on the Chicano/a literary scene. This moment saw the emergence of what Ramón Saldívar has called 'critiques of ... patriarchy in both its Anglo and Chicana forms', which includes the work of Isabella Ríos, Cherríe Moraga, and Sandra Cisneros (p. 181). Winner of the 1985 Before Columbus American Book Award, Sandra Cisneros' first novel is actually a series of forty-four interconnected vignettes or stories. It describes from an adolescent, almost childlike, female perspective life in the Latino barrio of Chicago, a life often characterised by poverty and disappointment. This urban location in the Midwest is very different from the rural and small town settings of *The Valley* and *Bless Me, Ultima* in Texas and New Mexico, respectively, but it is important to note too that many works of Chicano/a fiction are set in other city locations, such as Los Angeles and Albuquerque.

The House on Mango Street is a coming-of-age narrative, which centres upon the life of Esperanza Cordero, who relates her story in the first person. It is widely taught on both high school and college courses. Bonnie TuSmith notes that it is 'the most widely known Chicana novel', and it has also achieved something of an iconic status in Chicana letters as well (Bonnie TuSmith, *All My Relatives: Community in Contemporary Ethnic American Literatures*, University of Michigan Press, 1994, p. 157). Perhaps as a result of its popularity on high school curricula, the text has sometimes been pigeonholed as an adolescent narrative, a view which is strengthened by the deceptively simple narrative structure and the prevailing adolescent viewpoint. However, this belies the sophistication of the vignette structure which enables the construction of an elaborate series of oppositional tropes and preoccupations, which surface repeatedly in the different stories.

In the fourth section, entitled 'My Name', near the beginning of the narrative, Esperanza tells us:

> In English my name means hope. In Spanish it means too many letters. It means sadness, it means waiting. It is like the number nine. A muddy color. It is the Mexican records my father plays on Sunday mornings when he is shaving, songs like sobbing.
>
> It was my great-grandmother's name and now it is mine. She was a horse woman too, born like me in the Chinese year of the horse – which is supposed to be bad luck if you're born female – but I think this is a Chinese lie because the Chinese, like the Mexicans, don't like their women strong. ... I am always Esperanza.
>
> I would like to baptize myself under a new name, a name more like the real me, the one nobody sees. Esperanza as Lisandra or Maritza or Zeze the X. Yes. Something like Zeze the X will do. (pp. 10–11)

In this section, Cisneros introduces one of the most important recurrent tropes of the text: that of the importance of naming as an expression of identity. Like her name, Esperanza is caught between two cultures: Chicano/a and American; two languages: Spanish and American English; two versions of femininity: strong or sad; and two versions of selfhood: one full of hope and replete with possibility, and one of resignation. The central choice between hope and sadness faces all of the women in the text, and this is one of the oppositions which occurs time and again. Throughout the different stories, Esperanza encounters different versions of femininity and womanhood. As Bonnie TuSmith notes, 'female sexuality is a major liability in the Chicago barrio' (*All My Relatives*, p. 160). To be a woman in Esperanza's world is a precarious occupation. Women are depicted locked into their houses by possessive husbands, abused, raped and molested. Cisneros herself has written of femininity in the text: 'I was writing about it in the most real sense that I knew, as a person walking those neighbourhoods with a vagina' (Sandra Cisneros, 'Solitary Fate', p. 69). Many of the women in the stories have fallen foul of their sexuality. For example, Esperanza's friend Sally flirts with the local boys to avoid her abusive father, becomes pregnant, marries, and then spends her days gazing at the walls in her husband's house. Esperanza observes: 'She says she is in love, but I think she did it to escape' (p. 101). In another episode, 'A Smart Cookie', Esperanza relates her mother's story: 'I could've been somebody, you know? my mother says and sighs. She has lived in this city her whole life. She can speak two languages. She can sing an opera. She knows how to fix a T.V. But she doesn't know which subway train to take to get downtown' (p. 90). Esperanza's acute awareness of the restrictions and limitations of her mother's life (she cannot even go downtown alone), despite her obvious talents, strengthens her own resolve to escape the confinement of life on Mango Street: 'One day I will pack my bags of books and paper. One day I will say goodbye to Mango. I am too strong for her to keep me here forever. One day I will go away' (p. 110).

In common with other Chicana writers, Cisneros' exploration of different versions of femininity in the novel also provides a commentary upon and critique of wider historical Chicano myths and stereotypes of womanhood. Specifically, a dichotomy is constructed in the text between a '*virgen*' (virgin) and a '*puta*' (whore) – two archetypes which derive from two mythological figures in Chicano/a culture, la Malinche, and la Virgen de Guadalupe. La Malinche, also known as Doña Marina or Malintzín, was an aristocratic Aztec woman who was reputed to have betrayed her people by helping to ensure Hernán Cortés' conquest of the Aztec Empire at the beginning of the sixteenth century, and she also slept with him. A son resulted from this union, thus producing a 'mestizo' (mixed-race) child and subsequently a whole new hybrid race. Thus negatively iconised as a Chicana 'Eve', a *mujer mala* ('bad woman'), la Malinche burdens Chicana culture with a problematic legacy, as both Gloria Anzaldúa and Norma Alarcón have noted. (Alarcón describes la Malinche as 'a male myth' in her essay, 'Chicana's Feminist Literature', in *This Bridge Called My Back*, eds Cherríe Moraga and Gloria Anzaldúa, Kitchen Table: Women of Color Press, 1981, p. 184.) Equally problematic to Chicanas is the image and iconography of la Virgen de Guadalupe (the Virgin of Gaudalupe). Gloria Anzaldúa argues that '*La Virgen de Guadalupe* is the single most potent religious, political and cultural image of the Chicano/*mexicano*' (*Borderlands/La Frontera*, p. 30). Anzaldúa further argues she is problematic for Chicanas because she 'has been used by the Church to mete out institutionalized oppression' and 'to make us docile and enduring' (p. 30). In fact, for Anzaldúa, la Malinche, la Virgen de Guadalupe and la Llorona (the weeping woman), together work as a symbolic triptych: '*La gente Chicana tiene tres madres*. All three are mediators: *Guadalupe*, the virgin mother who has not abandoned us, *la chingada* (*Malinche*), the raped mother whom we have abandoned, and *la Llorona*, the mother who seeks her lost children and is a combination of the other two' (p. 30). Similarly, Norma Alarcón notes: 'Insofar as feminine symbolic figures are concerned, much of the Mexican/Chicano oral tradition as well as the intellectual are dominated by la Malinche/la Llorona and the Virgin of Guadalupe. …The Mexican/Chicano cultural tradition has tended to polarize the lives of women through these national [and nationalistic] symbols' ('Chicana's Feminist Literature', p. 189).

Cisneros manipulates these models of femininity for her own purposes. If female sexuality is often figured as a burden in the text, then it sometimes also offers a possible means of manipulating and even controlling patriarchal conditions. When Esperanza and her friends notice the rounding of their hips, they practise wiggling them because, as Esperanza knowledgeably tells her friends, 'You gotta be able to know what to do with hips when you get them' (p. 50). Unlike some of the women in the stories, Esperanza realises the power of her sexuality and the importance of learning to control it. The 'la Malinche' figure in the narrative is Esperanza's friend Sally, whose father says of her that to be 'this beautiful is trouble' (p. 81). Sally's sexual behaviour with the local boys is described by Esperanza as a betrayal in la Malinche-fashion: 'Sally had her own game' (p. 96). But unlike la Malinche, Cisneros implicitly suggests that Sally's actions were a response to her father's abuse of her, and her mother's neglect, thus figuring Sally's promiscuous behaviour as contingent upon circumstances beyond her control and thereby symbolically disrupting the *virgen/puta* dichotomy. Similarly, the 'Guadalupe' figure in the narrative is 'Aunt Lupe', Esperanza's sick aunt, who, while wasting away on her death bed, offers Esperanza encouragement and support by listening to and commenting upon the young girl's poems. Like la Virgen, she is long-suffering and self-sacrificing, but as with la Malinche, Cisneros connects Aunt Lupe's suffering with the harsh life of the barrio family, 'the kids who wanted to be kids instead of washing dishes and ironing their papa's shirts, and the husband who wanted a wife again' (p. 61).

The *virgen/puta* dichotomy is not the only symbolic opposition in the novel. Of equal significance is the emphasis placed upon the difference between a house and a home. The witch-woman in the text says to Esperanza: 'I see a home in the heart ... A new house, a house made of heart' (p. 64). If Esperanza's name symbolises 'hope', then her overriding hope is for a home. 'Home' is not just a dwellingplace, but also carries nuances of belonging, nurturance and origins. 'Home', as Kathleen Kirby puts it, is 'a walled site of belonging' (*Indifferent Boundaries: Spatial Concepts of Human Subjectivity*, Guildford Press, 1996, p. 21). More than a three-dimensional structure, it is a 'densely signifying marker in ideology' (Kirby, p. 21). 'Home' carries a heavy ideological weight. The yearning to belong is often linked to a desire for home ownership. As Marilyn Chandler makes clear in *Dwelling in the Text: Houses In American Fiction* (Uni-

versity of California Press, 1991), social and psychological stability
is partly engendered through economic security and thus the goal of
home ownership, one aspect of the American dream, is a preoccupation in much ethnic fiction. Chandler explores the predominance of
houses as a cultural preoccupation in America: 'Our literature reit-
erates with remarkable consistency the centrality of the house in
American cultural life and imagination' (p. 1). Chandler argues that,
stemming from its position as a post-colonial country itself, America's cultural production has focused upon the necessity of carving
out and claiming territory: 'In a country whose history has been
focused for so long on the question of settlement and "development", the issue of how to stake out territory, clear it, cultivate it,
and build on it has been of major economic, political and psychological consequence' (p. 1). Thus, part of the process of ethnic
American self-definition has always been the definition of its space.
And dominant nation-making ideologies have apprised the goal of
home ownership: 'The American dream still expresses itself in the
hope of owning a freestanding single-family dwelling, which to
many remains the most significant measure of ... cultural enfranchisement' (p. 1). For many ethnic writers in a state of 'unbelong-
ing', the objective of home ownership especially signifies the move
towards belonging to, as well as owning a corner in the world. This
is something that Esperanza recognises early on. The narrative
opens thus:

> We didn't always live on Mango Street. ... The house on Mango
> Street is ours, and we don't have to pay rent to anybody, or share the
> yard with the people downstairs, or be careful not to make too much
> noise, and there isn't a landlord banging on the ceiling with a broom.
> But even so, it's not the house we thought we'd get. (p. 3)

Esperanza's assessment of their living quarters is carefully calcu-
lated and couched in precise economic terms. She recognises that
economic stability leads to freedom: owning your own house means
not having to answer to a landlord. Yet by the same logic, she is also
aware that the house on Mango Street does not represent the fullest
of possibilities:

> I knew then I had to have a house. A real house. One I could point to.
> But this isn't it. The house on Mango Street isn't it. For the time

being, Mama says. Temporary, says Papa. But I know how those things
go. (p. 5)

If the idea of a home represents freedom for Esperanza, then she is
equally aware that the house can be a confining space for women.
The house, as the realm of patriarchal control, can become a more
hazardous place for women than the barrio outside: women are often
depicted as locked in (like the woman Rafaela), abused (like Esperanza's friend Sally), or confined by domesticity (like Esperanza's
mother). Learning this too, Esperanza's dream home becomes a
female-only space. In the penultimate section, 'A House of My
Own', Esperanza declares:

> Not a flat. Not an apartment in back. Not a man's house. A house all
> my own. With my porch and my pillow, my pretty purple petunias.
> My books and my stories. My two shoes waiting beside the bed.
> Nobody to shake a stick at. Nobody's garbage to pick up after.
> Only a house quiet as snow, a space for myself to go, clean as paper
> before the poem. (p. 108)

This is Esperanza's version of Virginia Woolf's room of her own; a
space devoid of female dependency, abuse, shame and noise. Sandra
Cisneros dedicated *The House on Mango Street* 'A Las Mujeres/To
the Women'. Her text not only gives Esperanza Cordero a home, it
also carves a space for Chicana women in the house of fiction. Many
commentators have observed the dominance of male writing in Chicano letters until relatively recently. Cisneros has said: 'the house in
essence becomes you. You are the house' ('Solitary Fate', p. 73).
Besides the echo of this quotation in the text, when the character
Alicia tells Esperanza 'Like it or not you are Mango Street' (p. 107),
Cisneros recognises in this statement the importance for Chicana
writers of constructing a narrative tradition of their own, one which
challenges masculinist Chicano assumptions and traditions. In this
regard, *The House on Mango Street* is indebted to feminist ideologies
of the 1970s and early 1980s, when women (including ethnic
women) writers were busy constructing what Elaine Showalter
called 'a literature of their own'. Certainly, Cisneros has been instrumental, along with fellow feminist Chicana writers Ana Castillo,
Cherríe Moraga, Isabella Ríos, Gloria Anzaldúa, and Helena María
Viramontes, in constructing a Chicana female literary tradition.

The House on Mango Street was originally published by the small regional press, Arte Público, based in Houston. Since then Cisneros' work has been taken up and republished by larger publishing houses: *The House on Mango Street* by Vintage, a subsidiary of Random House, and her collection of short stories, *Woman Hollering Creek* (1991), by Bloomsbury. This has increased her readership and also the body of critical work on *The House on Mango Street* in particular. She is increasingly viewed as a central figure in Chicana literature. In her essay, 'Sandra Cisneros's *The House on Mango Street*: Community-oriented Introspection and the Demystification of Patriarchal Violence' (*Breaking Boundaries: Latina Writings and Critical Readings*, edited by Asunción Horno-Delgado *et al.*, University of Massachusetts Press, 1989), Ellen McCracken notes the book's popularity and importance, and it is included in most survey studies of contemporary Chicano writing. Most critical responses to the book have focused on either the book's feminist politics, or upon the symbolic structures of the novel, notably the trope of house/home. A useful overview of and reaction to the criticism of the text, as well as some interesting commentary on Cisneros' work can be found in an interview with Cisneros by Pilar E. Rodríguez Aranda, 'On the Solitary Fate of Being Mexican, Female, Wicked and Thirty-Three: An Interview with Writer Sandra Cisneros' (*Americas Review* 18, no.1, Spring 1990, pp. 64–79).

Investigating further

References for further reading have been scattered throughout the body of this text already, and, as they often relate to key work by eminent scholars in the Chicano/a literary field, readers are urged to follow them up as and where appropriate. Meanwhile, for those who wish to paddle a while longer before taking to the high seas, try dipping into what *The Heath Anthology of American Literature* has to offer (3rd edition, Volume 2, 1998). Catering for Chicano/a literature far more extensively than *The Norton Anthology*, its 'Issues and Visions in Post-Civil War America' section includes a good introduction to the *corrido* and in addition there is an encouraging number of excerpts from Chicano/a fiction and poetry in the 'New Communities' and 'Postmodernity and Difference' sections as well.

Alternatively, a range of short story collections is now available, allowing the reader to sample the work of a variety of writers. Gary Soto's *Pieces of the Heart: New Chicano Fiction* (1993) is one charming example of such an anthology (complete with a glossary for the sprinkling of Spanish that appears in some of the stories) and Charles Tatum also edits a series of volumes that bring together contemporary fiction by established and emerging Chicano/a literary talent. Entitled *New Chicana/Chicano Writing*, there are presently three parts to this series, published by the University of Arizona Press, and they appeared in 1992 and 1993. Another Arizona Press publication, *Infinite Divisions: An Anthology of Chicana Literature* (1993), edited by Tey Diana Rebolledo, *et al.*, is one of a growing number of texts which focus specifically on Chicana writing in a range of genres. Particularly informative about the preoccupations of Mexican American women writers predating the contemporary period, it permits me now to make a few suggestions about further reading in Chicano/a history.

As may be imagined, any text relating to the history of Mexico will make a useful addition to one's knowledge and understanding of Chicano/a culture. Henry Bamford Parkes's *A History of Mexico* (1938), for example, is very detailed but offers clearly defined chapters on key periods, making it a useful reference book if one is seeking to learn of particular historical characters. *Aztlán: Essays on the Chicano Homeland* (1989), edited by Rudolfo Anaya and Francisco Lomelí, is also informative in explaining the enduring significance of the legendary homeland of the Aztecs, whilst Rodolfo Acuña's *Occupied America: A History of Chicanos* (1981) is packed with details about events that have taken place from 1848 onwards. A reading of books such as Juan Gómez-Quiñones's *Chicano Politics: Reality and Promise, 1940–1990* (1990) and Ignacio M. García's *Chicanismo: The Forging of a Militant Ethos among Mexican Americans* (1997) will expand on Carlos Muñoz's discussion of the political aspects of the Chicano Movement, whilst Roberto de Anda brings us right up to date with his edited collection, *Chicanas and Chicanos in Contemporary Society* (1996). David R. Maciel (in conjunction with María Herrera-Sobek) has recently edited *Culture Across Borders: Mexican Immigration and Popular Culture* (1998) whose chapters on 'The Celluloid Immigrant: The Narrative Films of Mexican Immigration' and 'Jokelore, Cultural Differences, and Linguistic Dexterity' should prove of particular interest to students. Chicano/a film, incidentally, is becoming a real growth area and attracts increasing attention from scholars. Rosa Linda Fregoso's *The Bronze Screen: Chicana and Chicano Film Culture* (1993), for instance, uses a variety of critical approaches to analyse such recent films as *Born in East LA, La Bamba, American Me* and *Zoot Suit*. The issue of linguistic dexterity, for those intrigued by the language issue in Chicano/a literature and culture, can be explored in the study of Rosaura Sánchez's *Chicano Discourse: Socio-Historic Perspectives* (1994), say, or Ernst Rudin's *Tender Accents of Sound: Spanish in the Chicano Novel in English* (1996). On which note, we move now to a short list of some primary sources.

Annotated short bibliography

Primary texts*

* Details given are those of the original publication, but all are available in modern editions.

Acosta, Oscar Zeta, *The Revolt of the Cockroach People* (Straight Arrow Books, 1973)
    This book stands as a powerful, sometimes shocking, record of the people and events in the heyday of Chicano/a political nationalism.

Arias, Ron, *The Road to Tamazunchale* (West Coast Poetry Review, 1975)
    Critically acclaimed as Arias's fictional masterpiece and the work of 'magical realism' which broke the convention of social realism, a marvellous story in which the dying Fausto Tejada escapes the realities of a Los Angeles *barrio* for an imaginative world far way.

Castillo, Ana, *The Mixquiahuala Letters* (Bilingual Press/Editorial Bilingüe, 1986)
    Winner of the American Book Award, Castillo's first novel is an epistolary *tour de force*. The letters written by Tere to Alicia constitute a fascinating interrogation of the limitations inherent in cultural notions of female sexuality.

Chávez, Denise, *Face of an Angel* (Warner Books, 1995)
    Regarded as the first proper novel by Chávez, this is a prize-winning account of the trials and tribulations of waitress Soveida Dosamantes as

she writes her Book of Service. Chávez also incorporates the trinity of grandmother, mother and daughter here and reflects on the relationships they have not only with their men but also with each other.

Cisneros, Sandra, *Woman Hollering Creek and Other Stories* (Random House, 1991)

Another phenomenal collection of stories, possessing much greater range and maturity than *The House on Mango Street*. 'Bien Pretty' is superb.

Islas, Arturo, *The Rain God: A Desert Tale* (Alexandrian Press, 1984)

A novel depicting the lives of three generations of the Angel family. A poignant portrayal of the family's being caught up within cultural, sexual, economic and racial prejudices.

Morales, Alejandro, *Caras viejas y vino nuevo* (Joaquín Mortiz, 1975)

Not really an example of his best work (which came later), this has nonetheless become a Chicano/a classic. Uses two teenage boys to provide a perspective on the crises of life in the urban barrio. Available now for the first time in a bilingual format – *Barrio on the Edge: Caras Viejas Y Vino Nuevo* (Bilingual Review Press, 1997) – with the translation by Francisco A. Lomelí.

Rivera, Tomás, *... y ne se lo tragó la tierra/ ... and the earth did not devour him* (Quinto Sol, 1971)

Winner of the first Quinto Sol prize for literature, this stands as a classic of Chicano/a literature. Celebrated for its innovative structure and its terse linguistic style, the story creatively documents the lives, hardships and aspirations of Mexican American migrant workers in the 1940s and 1950s.

Rodriguez, Richard, *Hunger of Memory: The Education of Richard Rodriguez* (Godine, 1982)

An interesting autobiography which has proved intensely controversial in Chicano/a circles on account of the author's allegedly assimilationist views regarding such matters as consent over descent, affirmative action and bilingual education.

Villanueva, Alma Luz, *The Ultraviolet Sky* (Bilingual Press/Editorial Bilingüe, 1988)

——, *Naked Ladies* (Bilingual Press/Editorial Bilingüe, 1994)

This poet's first and second novels both engage with an examination of the turbulent relationships that obtain between men and women, not only within the Chicano/a culture but interethnically as well.

Villaseñor, Victor, *Rain of Gold* (Arte Público Press, 1991)

An epic autobiographical account of the experience of three generations of the Villaseñor family. Following their move from Mexico to California in the wake of the Mexican Revolution, it is frequently styled the Chicano/a equivalent of Alex Haley's *Roots*.

Viramontes, Helena María, *Under the Feet of Jesus* (Dutton, 1995)

Following her collection *The Moths and Other Stories*, this is Viramontes' first novel and one which is held in high regard. Tells the story of Estrella's efforts to overcome the hardships of a migrant worker's existence.

Secondary texts

Calderón, Héctor and Saldívar, José David, eds, *Criticism in the Borderlands: Studies in Chicano Literature, Culture, and Ideology* (Duke University Press, 1991)

An oft-cited and valuable collection of essays which address a range of issues, authors and texts. Its style can sometimes be daunting to a theoretical novice, however.

Corpi, Lucha, *Máscaras* (Third Woman Press, 1997)

Compilation of interesting and informative essays in which Chicana and Latina writers discuss a host of topics – historical, linguistic, educational and cultural – that have impacted upon their lives as writers and women of colour in the United States.

Eysturoy, Annie O., *Daughters of Self-Creation: The Contemporary Chicana Novel* (University of New Mexico Press, 1996)

With a focus on Chicana coming-of-age novels, where the adolescent protagonist is searching for her self-identity and her place in the world, Eysturoy's contention is that growing up Chicana involves the negotiation not only of gender issues but also those of race and class.

Gish, Robert Franklin, *Beyond Bounds: Cross-Cultural Essays on Anglo-American, Indian, and Chicano Literature* (University of New Mexico Press, 1996)

In considering Chicano/a cultural production alongside that of other groups, a particularly useful book not only for examining attitudes towards the Chicano/as but also for placing Chicano/a literature in a broader context. Interesting and accessible.

González-T., César A., ed., *Rudolfo Anaya: Focus on Criticism* (Lalo Press, 1990)

A compilation of essays about specific works and Anaya's early fiction in general, this also contains a selection of interviews with the author himself as well as a selected bibliography. The occasional essay can be a little heavy-going.

Herrera-Sobek, María and Viramontes, Helena María, eds, *Chicana Creativity and Criticism: New Frontiers in American Literature* (University of New Mexico Press, 1996)

A new edition of the 1988 text, itself a useful collection of essays about Chicana literature, this is an impressive anthology of prose, poetry, visual art and literary criticism by and about Chicanas.

Lattin, Vernon E., *Contemporary Chicano Fiction: A Critical Survey* (Bilingual Press/Editorial Bilingüe, 1986)

The first collection to be dedicated exclusively to critical articles about the Chicano/a novel, covers all the major authors of the late 1960s and 1970s. Generally very accessible, be aware that some of the essays are written in Spanish.

Lee, Joyce Glover, *Rolando Hinojosa and the American Dream* (University of North Texas Press, 1997)

An examination of both the strong sense of place in Hinojosa's work and his treatment of the relationships that exist between Anglo and Mexican cultures.

Madsen, Deborah L, *Understanding Chicana Literature* (University of South Carolina Press, forthcoming)

Focusing on the work of six contemporary Chicana writers in particular, an accessible and informative critical overview of Chicana literature since the 1970s.

Martínez, Julio A. and Lomelí, Francisco A., eds, *Chicano Literature* (Greenwood Publishing Group, 1985)

An invaluable library resource. Contains basic biographical and critical information about major Chicano/a writers of the time, as well as essays on other key features of Chicano/a culture.

McKenna, Teresa, *Migrant Song: Politics and Process in Contemporary Chicano Literature* (University of Texas Press, 1997)

Written with the student in mind, this is both a survey and a more specific consideration of how (social) politics has impacted upon Chicano/a expression, both in oral and written forms. Includes a consideration of Hinojosa as a political writer.

Olivares, Julián, *International Studies in Honor of Tomás Rivera* (originally published, *Revista Chicano-Riqueña*, Vol. 13:3–4, 1985) (Arte Público Press, 1986)

One of several collections dedicated to the life and work of Tomás Rivera, containing pieces both by and about him.

Padilla, Genaro, *My History, Not Yours: The Formation of Mexican-American Autobiography* (University of Wisconsin Press, 1994)

Instructive consideration of how the autobiography genre has developed and functioned as a popular form of Chicano/a resistance discourse since 1848.

Quintana, Alvina E., *Home Girls: Chicana Literary Voices* (Temple University Press, 1996)

Seeking to interpret Chicana literature from an interdisciplinary perspective, this study is constructed as a series of accessible chapters which draw upon anthropological, historical, feminist and literary sources to examine both why and how some of the major Chicana authors write.

Rebolledo, Tey Diana, *Women Singing in the Snow: A Cultural Analysis of Chicana Literature* (University of Arizona Press, 1995)

First major attempt to analyse the evolution of Chicana literature since 1848 (both poetry and prose). Hugely informative in its discussion of myths, theories and major texts, Rebolledo's book deserves its wide critical acclaim.

Saldívar, Ramón, *Chicano Narrative: The Dialectics of Difference* (University of Wisconsin Press, 1990)

Highly influential critical study, intention of which is to promote the understanding of Chicano/a literature not only as a response to the social and historical experiences of its authors but also within the wider context of what constitutes 'America'. Looks in detail at various genres and certain works by key Chicano/a authors.

Index

Afrocentrism 92–4, 96
Aiiieeee! 169, 174
Alarcón, Norma 233
Alexander, Meena 145
Alexie, Sherman 18, 20
  Business of Fancydancing, The
    49
  First Indian on the Moon 49
  I Would Steal horses 49
  Indian Killer 50
  Lone Ranger and Tonto Fistfight
    in Heaven, The 50, 59
  Old Shirts and New Skins 49
  Reservation Blues 34, 49–59
Allen, Paula Gunn 20
allotment, policy of 16, 41–2
Almonte, Juan N. 195
Alurista 202
Amerasia 156
'Americanness' 9
Anaya, Rudolfo 205
  Bless Me, Ultima 202, 216,
    221–30, 231
Angelou, M. 83
Anzaldúa, Gloria 195, 196, 230,
  233, 236

Borderlands/La Frontera 7, 208,
  211
This Bridge Called My Back
  208
Apes, William: *Son of the Forest,*
  A 19
Aranda, Pilar E. Rodríguez 237
Ardrey, Robert: *Territorial*
  Imperative, The 214
Arias, Ron: *Road to Tamazunchale,*
  The 203
Arteaga, Alfred 210, 211
Ashante, Molefi Kete 93
assimilation, policy of 17, 41–2, 43
Awkward, Michael: *Inspiriting*
  Influences 113

Baca, Sonny 203
Baker, Houston 85, 87, 94
  Blues, Ideology, and Afro-
    American Literature 88
  'Generational Shifts and the
    Recent Criticism of Afro-
    American Literature' 87–8
  Modernism and the Harlem
    Renaissance 88

Baldwin, James 70, 78, 79, 80
   Another Country 79
   'Everybody's Protest Novel' 79
   Fire Next Time, The 79
   Giovanni's Room 79
'Ballad of Mulan' 167
Baraka, Amiri: 'Black Art' 81
Barrio, Raymond: *Plum Plum
   Pickers, The* 210
Baugh, John 211
Bell, Bernard: *Afro-American Novel
   and its Tradition, The* 101
Bering Strait theory of migration
   13–14
Bibb, Henry 100
Black Aesthetic 88
Black American Literature Forum 87
Black Arts movement 78, 79, 80–2,
   85, 87
Black Nationalists 17
blues 53, 70, 88
border writing 212
Brito, Aristeo 199
Brooker, Peter 204
Brooks, Gwendolyn 78, 79
   Annie Allen 78
Brown, William Wells 100, 101,
   106
   *Clotel, or, The President's
   Daughter* 71–2
Bruce-Novoa 192, 196, 201, 212,
   213, 214, 215, 220, 221
Buenrostro, Rafe 203
Bulosan, Carlos 141, 153, 155
   America is in the Heart 7, 144,
   154, 157–64
   Dark People, The 158
   Laughter of My Father 158
   Letter from America 158
   Voice of Bataan, The 158
Bureau of Indian Affairs 17
Bush, President William 86

Butler, Judith: *Gender Trouble* 97

Cabeza de Vaca, Alvar Núñez 198
Cade, Toni
   Black Woman, The 82
   Gorilla, My Love 82
   *I Know Why the Caged Bird
   Sings* 82
Calderón, Héctor 198, 204
*Call and Response: The Riverside
   Anthology of the African
   American Literary Tradition*
   64, 125
Callahan, Bob 5
Carby, Hazel 73, 95
   Reconstructing Womanhood 95
Castillo, Ana 236
   Loverboys 203
   Mixquiahuala Letters, The 203
   Peel My Love Like an Onion
   203
   Sapogonia 203
   So far From God 203
Cha, Theresa Hak Kyung 144
   Dictee 142–3, 151
Chan, Jeffery Paul 165, 169
Chandler, Marilyn 234–5
Chang, Diana: *Frontiers of Love,
   The* 138
Chávez, Denise 202
   Face of an Angel 203
   Last of the Menu Girls, The 203
Chávez, Fray Angélico:
   Conquistadora, La 200, 201
Chávez, John R. 209
   *Lost Land, The: The Chicano
   Image of the Southwest* 196
Chesnutt, Charles W. 70
   'Goophered Grapevine, The' 71
Cheung, King-kok 134, 149, 150
   Articulate Silences 151, 175, 183
Chew, Lee 3

Chicano Movement (*El
     Movimiento*) 197, 202
Child, Lydia Maria 68
Chin, Frank 155, 165, 169
     Chickencoop Chinaman, The 151,
          155
     Year of the Dragon, The 151, 155
Chin Yang Lee: *Flower Drum Song*
     138
Chinese American fiction 134–8
Chinese Exclusion Acts 135
Christian, Barbara 107, 108
     'Fixing Methodologies' 92
     'Race for Theory, The' 91–2
Chu, Louie 141, 155
     Eat a Bowl of Tea 137–8, 151,
          152
Chuang, Hua: *Crossings* 138
Churchill, Ward 24
Cisneros, Sandra 228, 229, 230
     'Eyes of Zapata' 192
     House on Mango Street, The 1,
          203, 229, 230–7
     Woman Hollering Creek 192, 203,
          237
Civil Rights movement 70, 79, 80,
     81, 86
Cleaver, Eldridge: *Soul on Ice* 79
Collier, John 16
Collins, Patricia Hill 109
Color Purple, The (film) 107
Columbus, Christopher 12
consent school of thought 191
Conzer, Kathleen Neils 4
Cook-Lynn, Elizabeth 24
Corpi, Lucha
     Cactus Blood 203
     Delia's Song 203
     Eulogy for a Brown Angel 203
     Mystery Novel, A 203
Cortés, Hernán 195, 233
Costilla, Miguel Hidalgo y 195

Crisis, The 74
Crusade for Justice 202
cultural studies 94, 95–6, 205–6
Custer, George Armstrong 56

Dasenbrock, Reed Way 193
Davies, Carole Boyce 133
Dearborn, Mary: *Pocahontas's
          Daughters* 175
Delany, Martin 69, 70
Delgado, Abelardo 202
Deloria, Vine, Jr. 14, 53, 57
descent school of thought 191, 192
Didion, Joan 216–17
disease 39
Divakaruni, Chitra Banerjee 145
doctrine of discovery 14–15
Donovan, Kathleen 35
Dorris, Michael 21
Douglass, Frederick 69, 100, 106
     *Narrative of Frederick Douglass,
          an American Slave, Written by
          Himself, The* 67–8, 97, 105
     'What to the Slave is the Fourth
          of July?' 68
Dove, Rita 84
Du Bois, W. E. B. 73, 75, 76, 77, 85
     'Criteria for Negro Art' 74
     Souls of Black Folk, The 74
duCille, Ann 98
Dunbar, Paul Laurence 65, 71, 100
     'We Wear the Mask' 71
     'When Malindy Sings' 71

Eat Drink Man Woman (film) 155
Eaton, Edith Maud (Sui Sin Far)
     136
     'Leaves from the Mental
          Portfolio of an Eurasian' 136
     Mrs. Spring Fragrance 136
Eaton, Winnifred (Onoto Watanna)
     136–7

El Movimento Estydiantil Chicano de Aztlán (MEChA) 195
El Plan Espiritual de Aztlán 195
Eliot, T. S. 100, 106
Elizondo, Sergio 202
Ellison, Ralph 52, 65, 78, 80
    Invisible Man 79, 99, 117
Equiano, O. 68
    Interesting Narrative of the Life of Olaudah Equiano, or Gustavus vassa, the African, Written by Himself 66–7
Erdrich, Louise 13, 18, 20
    Love Medicine 58–9
    Tracks 1, 16, 34, 37–49
ethnic groups, definition 2
ethnicity, definition 3–4
ethnocentric paternalism 16
Evers, Larry 34

Fanon, Frantz: *Wretched of the Earth, The* 210
Faulkner, William 215
Fauset, Jessie Redmon 75, 77
Female Subjects in Black and White: Race, Psychoanalysis, Feminism 97–8
feminism 86–7, 207
Filipino American fiction 144–5
Fire III 77
Fisher, Dexter 87
Fitzgerald, F. Scott: *Great Gatsby, The* 123
Fixico, Donald L. 17
Fong, Katheryn 169

Galarza, Ernesto: *Barrio Boy* 197
Garrison, William Lloyd 67
Garvey, Marcus 79
Gates, Henry Louis, Jr. 87, 94
    Figures in Black 88
    Signifying Monkey, The: A Theory of African-American Literary Criticism 88–9, 105
    "What's Love Got to Do with It?" Critical Theory, Integrity and the Black Idiom' 90–1
General Allotment Act (Dawes Act) (1887) 16, 41
Ghymn, Esther: *Images of Asian American Women by Asian American Women Writers* 156
Gilmore, Leigh 175
Gilroy, Paul 95
    Black Atlantic, The 96
Gingerich, Willard 193
Giovanni, Nikki 81
Gish Jen
    Mona in the Promised Land 138
    Typical American 138
Goellnicht, Donald: 'Father Land and/or Mother Tongue' 183
Gonzales, Rodolfo 'Corky': 'Yo Soy Joaquín/I Am Joaquín' 202
Gonzales-Berry, Erlinda 220
Gonzalez, N. V. M. 164
Gorra, Michael 52
Grajeda, Ralph 190
Gray, Thomas: *Confessions of Nat Turner, The* 70
Gregory, Dick 57
Grewal, Gurleen: 'Memory and the matrix of history' 183
Grice, Helena 7
Griffin, Farah Jasmine 111, 121, 123
'Grito de Dolores' 195

Haely, Alex: *Autobiography of Malcolm X, The* 80
Hagedorn, Jessica 144–5, 153
    Dogeaters 144, 154
    Gangster of Love, The 144
Hall, Stuart 95, 96

Han Suyin 138
Hansberry, Lorraine 79
  Raisin in the Sun, A 78
Harlem Renaissance 65, 70, 74, 75–6, 80, 81, 88, 111, 122, 123, 124
Harper, Frances Ellen Watkins 76
  Iola Leroy, or, Shadows Uplifted 72–3
Harris, Joel Chandler 71
Hepworth, Candida 9, 230
Herrera-Sobek, María 207
Hicks, D. Emily 193, 212
Hinojosa, Rolando
  Ask A Policeman 213
  Becky And Her Friends 195–6, 213
  Dear Rafe 194, 213
  Klail City 213
  Klail City Death Trip Series 212–13, 215
  Klail City y sus alrededores 213
  Korean Love Songs 213
  Los Amigos de Becky 213
  Mi Querido Rafa 213
  Valley, The 197, 212–21, 231
His-kuo, Chang: *Rage of Yesteryear* 155
Hitting Critical Mass: A Journal of Asian American Cultural Criticism 155
Hogan, Linda 21
hooks, bell 96–7
  Ain't I a Woman: Black Women and Feminism 96
  Outlaw Culture: Resisting Representations 96, 97
Hopkins, Pauline 73, 76
  Contending Forces 73
Hsiang-t'u wen-hsueh 155
Hsien-yung, Pai 155
Huerta, Victoriano 197

Hughes, Langston 65, 70, 76–7, 80, 122
  'Harlem' 111
  'Negro Artist and the Racial Mountain, The' 76
  'Weary Blues, The' 76
Hughes, Robert 208
Hull, Gloria 82
humour, North American Indian 53
Hurston, Zora Neale 71, 77, 95, 99, 123
  Their Eyes Were Watching God 70, 77, 115
Hutcheon, Linda 43
Hwang, David Henry: *M. Butterfly* 152

Immigration Law (1917) 145
Inada, Lawson Fusao 169
'Indian' (Native Americans), European concept of 12
Indian Reorganization Act (1934) 16, 42
Ishiguro, Kazuo 155
Island 136

Jacobs, Harriet (Linda Brent) 106
  Incidents in the Life of a Slave Girl 68–9
Jameson, Fredric 193
Japanese American fiction 138–41
Jarvis, Brian 122
Jen, Gish 153
  Mona in the Promised Land 154
  Typical American 152, 154
Jim, Rex Lee 14
Jiménez, Francisco: *Identification and Analysis of Chicano Literature, The* 189
Johnson, Basil 14, 42

Johnson, Charles
    Middle Passage, The 84
    Oxherding Tale, The 84
Johnson v. McIntosh 15
Jones, Gayle 70
    Corregidora 83
Jordan, June 84
Joyce, Joyce Ann 91
    'Black Canon, The:
        Reconstructing Black
        American Literary Criticism'
        89–90
    New Literary History 89

Kadohata, Cynthia
    Floating World, The 141
    In the Heart of the Valley of Love
        141, 184
Kafka, Phillipa: *(Un)Doing the
    Missionary Position* 155
Kai-yu Hsu 149
Kang, Younghill 141–2
    East Goes West 141
    Grass Roof, The 141, 161
Keller, Nora Okja 143–4
    Comfort Woman 143
Kennedy, Liam 219
Kim, Elaine 135, 139, 140–2, 149,
    150, 159, 162
    Asian American Literature 158
Kim, Willyce
    *Dancer Dawkins and the
        California Kid* 184
    Dead Heat 184
King, Martin Luther 68
King, Thomas 21
Kingston, Maxine Hong 134, 149,
    150, 152, 155
    China Men 138, 155
    Tripmaster Monkey 138, 155
    Woman Warrior, The 138, 148,
        151, 157, 164–75, 183

Kirby, Kathleen 234
Kitigawa, Muriel 176
Kogawa, Joy
    Itsuka 175, 176, 182
    Obasan 157, 175–83
Korean American fiction 141–4
Kristeva, Julia 94
Kroeber, Karl 36, 37
Krupat, Arnold 23–4
Kuhn, Thomas S. 85
Kuo, Helena 136

Lacan, Jacques 94
Larsen, Nella 77, 95
    Passing 97
Leal, Luis 190, 197–8
    'Problem Identifying Chicano
        Literature, The' 189
Lee, Ang 155
Lee, Chang-Rae: *Native Speaker*
    143
Lee, Mary Paik: *Quiet Odyssey*
    142
Lee, Rachel C. 154, 155, 156
    *Americas of Asian American
        Literature, The* 153
Lee Yan Phou: *When I Was a Boy
    in China* 136
Li, David Leiwei 151, 172
    Imagining the Nation 151, 152
*Life of Josiah Henson, Formerly a
    Slave, The* 106
Li-Hua, Yu: *Again the Palm Trees!*
    155
Lim, Shirley Goek-lin 149
Lin Tai-yi 136
Lin Yutang: *Chinatown Family* 138
Lincoln, President Abraham 100
Lincoln, Kenneth 34, 36
Ling, Amy 148, 149, 150
    *Between Worlds: Women Writers
        of Chinese Ancestry* 136, 174

Ling, Jinqi 151
  Narrating Nationalisms 151,
    152
linguistic mixture 8
Lipsitz, George 65
Liu-shueh-shen wen-shueh 155
Locke, Alain 74, 75, 76, 85, 122,
    123, 124
  'New Negro, The' 74–5
Lomelí, Francisco A. 202, 203
Lorde, Audre 84
  Zami 83
Louie, David Wong: *Pangs of Love*
    152
Lowe, Lisa 145, 151, 163
  Immigrant Acts 152

Ma, Sheng-mei 155–6
  *Immigrant Subjectivities in Asian
    American and Asian Diaspora
    Literatures* 154–5
Madero, Francisco 197
Madhubuti, Haki 81
Mai-mai Sze 136
Malintzín (la Malinche) 195, 233
Marshall, Paule: *Praisesong for the
    Widow* 83
Martin, Reginald 101
Mason, Mrs Rufus 75
Massachusetts Anti-Slavery
    Society 67
materialism 94
Mathews, John Joseph 20, 22
Matus, Jill 121, 122, 123
McCracken, Ellen 237
McDowell, Deborah E. 85, 91, 92,
    97, 111
McGee, Patrick 106, 107
McKay, Claude 75
  'If We Must Die' 76
McMillan, Terry: *Waiting to
    Exhale* 84

McNickle, D'Arcy 20, 22
  Surrounded, The 20
mediation 23, 36–7
Meier, Matt 194, 195, 197
Melus 156
Mercer, Kobena 95
  Welcome to the Jungle 96
Merriam Report (1928) 16
Minatoya, Lydia: *Talking to High
    Monks in the Snow: An Asian
    American Odyssey* 141
Mirandé, Alfredo 209–10
miscegenation 4, 195
Miyoshi, Masao 193–4
Momaday, N. Scott 13, 17, 20,
    21–2
  House Made of Dawn 6, 17, 18,
    22, 23, 25–37, 50, 58
Montejano, David 196
Montoya, José 202
Moraga, Cherríe 230, 236
  Loving in the War Years 208
  This Bridge Called My Back 208
Morante, Linda: 'From Silence to
    Song: the Triumph of Maxine
    Hong Kingston' 174–5
Mori, Kyoko: *Dream of Water, The:
    A Memoir* 141
Mori, Toshio: *Yokohama,
    California* 139
Morrison, Toni 9, 65, 70, 82–3, 95,
    98–9, 115
  Beloved 1, 82, 84, 92, 112, 122
  Bluest Eye, The 82, 113
  Jazz 82, 99, 116–25
  Playing in the Dark 83
  Song of Solomon 82
  Sula 82, 87, 97
  'Unspeakable Things Unspoken'
    98, 118–19
Mosley, Walter 70, 84
  Blue Light 84

Devil in a Blue Dress 84
R.L.'s Dream 84
Mourning Dove (Humishima) 20,
    22
Mukherjee, Bharati 145, 152,
    155
    Jasmine 145, 146
    Wife 145–6, 155
multiculturalism 104, 208–9
Muñoz, Carlos, Jr. 201
Munton, Alan 118
Mylan, Sheryl A.: 'Mother as
    Other, The: Orientalism in
    Maxine Hong Kingston's *The
    Woman
    Warrior*' 174

Nag Hammadi, The 119
Navajo Night Chant 18
Naylor, Gloria
    Bailey's Cafe 83
    Linden Hills 83, 108
    Mama Day 83, 112, 115
    Women of Brewster Place, The 83,
    99, 107–15
Neal, Larry: 'Black Arts
    Movement, The' 81
Neate, Wilson 206
New Deal 201
Ng, Fae Myenne: *Bone* 152
Nieh, Hualing: *Mulberry and Peach*
    155
Niggli, Josephina: *Step Down Elder
    Brother* 200, 201
Nightway Chant 25
Nixon, President 86
Niza, Fray Marcos de 198
*Norton Anthology of African
    American Literature, The* 64,
    123, 125, 237
Nugent, Richard Bruce 77
    'Smoke, Lilies and Jade' 77

Occom, Samson: *Sermon Preached
    at the Execution of Moses Paul,
    an Indian* 19
Okada, John 155
    No-No Boy 139, 151, 152
Omi, Michael 5
oral tradition 8–9, 17–20, 22,
    59
    African American fiction
    64–6
    Native American 14
Ornelas, Berta: *Come Down from
    the Mound* 203
Ortiz, Simon 17, 18, 19
    Going for the Rain 10, 11
    'Significance of a Veteran's Day,
    The' 10–11
    Woven Stone 58
Oskison, John Milton 20, 22
Other, the, paradigm of 98, 99
Owens, Louis 19, 21, 22, 27, 33,
    34, 40, 45
    Other Destinies 22

Padget, Martin 8
Page Law (1875) 135
Pai, Margaret K.: *Dreams of Two
    Yi-min, The* 142
Palubinskas, Helen 149
Paredes, Américo: *With a Pistol in
    His Hand: A Border Ballad
    and its Hero* 198
Paredes, Raymund 228
Paz, Octavio 219
Peach, Linden 123
Pérez de Villagrá, Gaspar 198
Pérez-Torres, Rafael 207, 208
Peterson, Nancy 42–3
Petry, Ann 95, 99
    Street, The 78
Pita, Beatrice 199
Poe, Edgar Allan 100, 105

Pokagon, Simon: *O-gî-mäw-kwe Mit-i-gwä-kî: Queen of the Woods* 20
Post, Amy 68
post-colonial theory 94, 97, 98
post-modernism 208–9
post-structuralism 87, 88, 91, 96
Pound, Ezra 100, 106
Power, Susan 21
Prucha, Francis Paul 15, 16
Pryse, Marjorie 95
psychoanalysis 94, 96, 98
Pucha, Francis Paul 41
Pushing Hands 155

queer theory 94, 96, 97

racial formation, concept of 5
Radin, Paul 39
Razon, Felix 160
Reagan, President Ronald 86
Reed, Ishmael 2, 65, 70, 72, 84
    Flight to Canada 99, 100–7, 116
    Mumbo Jumbo 105
    'Neo-HooDoo Manifesto' 104
    Reckless Eyeballing 107, 111
Rice, Alan 117
Rich, Adrienne 115
Ridge, John Rollin: *Life and Adventures of Joaquín Murieta, the Celebrated California Bandit, The* 20
Riding In, James 50
Ríos, Isabella 230, 23
    Victuum 203
Rivera, Feliciano 194, 195, 197
Rivera, Tomás 197, 200, 205–6
    ...y no se lo tragó la tierra 202, 213
Rodrigues, Eusebio L. 119
Rodríguez, Joe 201

Rodríguez, Juan 198
    'Notes on the Evolution of Chicano Prose Fiction' 200
Ronyoung, Kim: *Clay Walls* 142
Roosevelt, President Franklin Delano 191, 201
Rose, Marilyn Russell: 'Politics into Art: Kogawa's *Obasan* and the Rhetoric of Fiction' 183
Ruiz de Burton, María Amparo: *Squatter and the Don, The* 198
Ruoff, A. LaVonne Brown 18, 19
Ruppert, James 36–7
    Mediation and Contemporary Native American Literature 23

Ša, Zitkala 20, 22
Said, Edward 206–7, 215
Saldívar, José David 204
Saldívar, Ramón 228, 229, 230
Salinas, Luis Omar 202
Salívar, José David 198
San Juan, Epifanio, Jr.: *Carlos Bulosan and the Imagination of the Class Struggle* 158, 164
Sánchez, Ricardo 202
Sánchez, Rosaura 199
Sanchez, Sonia 81
Santa Anna, General Antonio López de 195
Santos, Bienvenido N. 155, 164
    Scent of Apples: A Collection of Stories 144
Sato, Gayle K. Fugita: '"To Attend the Sound of Stone": the Sensibility of Silence in *Obasan*' 183
Schlesinger, Arthur, Jr.: *Disuniting of America, The* 209
Selinger, Bernard 35–6, 37

Shigekuni, Julie: *Bridge Between Us, A* 141
Showalter, Elaine 236
signification 88–9
Silko, Leslie Marmon 13, 17, 20, 21
  Ceremony 58, 59
  Storyteller 60
Simmen, Edward 200
slave narratives 7, 66, 67–9, 97, 105
Smith, Barbara 94, 95, 97
  'Toward a Black Feminist Criticism' 86
  'Truth That Never Hurts, The' 114
Smith, Jeanne Rosier: *Writing Tricksters* 175
Smith, Sidonie 175
Smoke Signals (film) 50
Sollors, Werner 4, 191
  Beyond Ethnicity 3
  Invention of Ethnicity, The 3
Sommers, Joseph 199, 204, 206
Sone, Monica: *Nisei Daughter* 139–40
South Asian American fiction 145–8
Spielberg, Steven 107
Spillers, Hortense 103
  Conjuring: Black Women, Fiction, and Literary Tradition 94–5
  'Mama's Baby, Pap's Maybe: an American Grammar Book' 94
Stepto, Robert 87
Stewart, Maria 69
Stowe, Harriet Beecher: *Uncle Tom's Cabin* 100, 106
Sugimoto, Etsu 141
  Daughter of the Samurai, A 139
Sui Sin Far *see* Eaton, Edith Maud

Sumida, Stephen 149
survivance 24

Takaki, Ronald 141, 145, 146
Tan, Amy 149, 155
  Hundred Secret Senses, The 138
  Joy Luck Club, The 138, 155
  Kitchen God's Wife, The 138
Teatro Campesino 202
Terry, Lucy: 'Bars Fight' 65–6
Thornton, Russell 13
Thurman, Wallace 77
Tong, Benjamin 165, 159
Toomer, Jean: *Cane* 76, 115
Treaty of Guadalupe Hidalgo 196, 198, 199
Treaty of Velasco 195
True Stories of the Korean Comfort Women, The 144
Truth, Sojourner: 'Aren't I a woman?' 70
Ts'ai Yen: 'Eighteen Stanzas for a Barbarian Reed Pipe' 174
Tsukiyama, Gail: *Women of the Silk* 141
Turner, Nat 70, 100, 101
TuSmith, Bonnie 231, 232
  All My Relatives 175

Ueki, Teruyo: '*Obasan*: Revelations in a Paradoxical Scheme' 183
Understanding Christian Literature 202
United Farm Workers Union 202
universalist school of thought 193
Utter, Jack 13, 15

Valdez, Luis 202, 208, 210
Vechten, Carl van 75
VenderZee, James 122
Villa, Francisco (Pancho) 97
Villanueva, Tino 202

Villarreal, José Antonio: *Pocho* 200,
    201, 202
Viramontes, Helena Maria 236
    Moths and Other Stories, The
        203
    Under the Feet of Jesus 203
Virgen de Guadalupe, la 233
Vizenor, Gerald 13, 14, 17, 20, 21,
    24

Walker, A'Lelia 75
Walker, Alice 70, 95, 97, 107, 111,
    115, 123
    Color Purple, The 77, 83
    'Everyday use' 114
    In Search of Our Mothers'
        Gardens 84
    Meridian 83
    Possessing the Secret of Joy 83
    Third Life of Grange Copeland,
        The 83
Walker, Dale 58
Walker, David: *Appeal in Four*
    Articles 69–70
Wallace, Michele 96
Walsh, Richard 101, 102, 104,
    105
Washington, Booker T. 73, 79
    Up from Slavery 74
Waters, Anna Lee 21
Watanna, Onoto (Winnifred Eaton)
    136–7
Weber, Max 2–3, 4
Wedding Banquet 155
Welch, James 13, 17, 20, 21
    Fools Crow 59
    Winter in the Blood 58
West, Dorothy 95
Wheatley, John 66
Wheatley, Phillis 67, 68, 100, 106
    'On Being Brought from Africa
        to America' 66

    Poems on Various Subjects,
        Religious and Moral 66
Widdowson, Peter 204
Wideman, John Edgar
    Brothers and Keepers 84
    Homewood Trilogy, The 84
    Philadelphia Fire 84
Williams, Sherley Ann: *Dessa Rose*
        84
Willis, Susan 96
Wilson, Harriet E.: *Our Nig* 71, 72
Winant, Howard 5
Winchell, Mark Royden 216
Woman Warrior, The 1, 6
Women's Liberation 82
Wong, Jade Snow: *Fifth Chinese*
        Daughter 137
Wong, Sau-ling C. 149, 150, 157,
    163, 167
    'Denationalization
        Reconsidered' 152
    'Kingston's Handling of
        Traditional Chinese Sources'
        174
    Reading Asian American
        Literature: From Necessity to
        Extravagance 175
Wong, Shawn H. 169
Wright, Richard 77, 80, 85, 99, 115
    'Blueprint for Negro Writing'
        77
    Native Son 78, 79, 110, 111

Yamamoto, Hisaye 150, 183
    Seventeen Syllables and Other
        Stories 139
Yamashita, Karen Tei 155
    Through the Arc of the Rain
        Forest 153, 154
Yogi, Stan 149

Zapata, Emiliano 192–3, 197

Printed in the United States
144897LV00001B/2/A